# MAKING MORAL DECISIONS

# MAKING MORAL DECISIONS

## AN EXISTENTIAL ANALYSIS

*by*

## LOUIS O. KATTSOFF

*Boston College*

THE HAGUE / MARTINUS NIJHOFF / 1965

# TABLE OF CONTENTS

# CHAPTER I

# MORALS AND ETHICS

## Life and Moral Problems

All of us do many strange things during the course of a working day. Most of what we do is done mechanically without thinking. We arise at a certain hour, wash, dress, eat breakfast, and go about our daily tasks. We greet our friends, hate our enemies, are cordial to some, hostile to others, lie upon occasion, and do many things of which we might approve or disapprove if we stopped to think about them. In fact, one of the strangest things we do is to approve and disapprove all sorts of things and often without stopping to think. We are accustomed, or have been taught, to voice approval when good deeds are performed, and disapproval when bad ones are done. If, for example, we read in our newspapers, of a mother who at the sacrifice of her life saved her child from a burning building, we approve. If we read that a man had killed his wife because she burned his toast every morning, we disapprove.

In ordinary circumstances these approbations and disapprobations are so usual and so automatic, we do not appreciate exactly what has been done. The degree to which we are accustomed to approve and disapprove is measured by the extent to which we take these for granted. When our attention is called to the many puzzling features of moral situations, we may even deny that these concern us.

## Moral Decisions

Everyone ever confronted with a request for help, or ever tempted to cheat or be dishonest has been confronted with a moral problem. He may have responded automatically — without thinking. If he did, his decision was not a moral one, but it was a decision on a moral problem. There are many situations in which the reaction is automatic but, nevertheless, a decision. Most people would reply automatically to the question "How much are two and two?" The immediate reply is the sign of a learned habitual reaction. Without a great many automatic but correct reactions, life would be quite burdensome. This is well and good, as long as the reaction is the correct one. In arithmetic, the automatic solution is not an arithmetic one, yet it is a solution to an arithmetic problem. Even in arithmetic automatic responses are insufficient. If a person did not know the principles of arithmetic, he could not multiply 276 by 392, except by sheer good luck, which is most unlikely.

Similar distinctions hold in moral problems. If one is faced with a moral problem, he may respond habitually. In that case, the response, as we shall see, is not a moral one. A person who when tempted to cheat on an examination because he does not know how to do a certain problem automatically turns his back to the paper of his neighbor, has not made a moral decision. No decision not to cheat is involved, only an automatic response. The response is the correct one in the sense that this is what a moral person would do. Is the person moral? Obviously the reply depends, in this case, on how the word "moral" is defined. If to be moral is merely to behave in a certain way, then the person could possibly be said to be moral. If to be moral means to act on the basis of a decision, then he might not be given this designation.

Contrast the action of a robot so constructed that whenever someone dropped a wallet he picked up the wallet and returned it to its owner with a person who always did the same thing as a matter of principle. In most cases, I suppose, no one would want to say that the robot was moral, but most people would insist that the person was. The fact that the person did exactly what the robot did and there was no *outward* difference between his behavior and the robot's action would not lead most people to identify the two kinds of action. As long as one knew the robot for what it was, he would insist its action was neither moral nor immoral. Something like this would probably be said:

"The action of the robot was purely mechanical."

If it were urged that the action of the person was mechanical too, especially if it is an automatic response, a vigorous denial would most likely be made. Whether or not behavior is mechanical is not in itself a moral problem but on the surface appears to be a factual question. Whether or not the words "automatic" and "mechanical" are logically equivalent is a matter for discussion. Though both these problems need not detain us here, they have important bearing on ethical theory since they throw light on the possibility of making meaningful decisions.

## Statements About Moral Decisions

The denial that the robot's action is moral rests on an assumption which might be expressed generally as follows: "No mechanical act is a moral one." Notice, however, that this statement is obviously very different from "Returning a lost wallet to its owner is right" or "You ought to return the lost wallet to its owner."

The statement "No mechanical act is a moral one" is not itself a *moral* statement. It does not, like the other two statements, tell what ought to be done or that an act of a certain kind is right, but it says something about moral acts. This distinction will perhaps be more easily understood if we use an analogy. Consider the law of gravitation. It is usually expressed as follows: "Every particle attracts every other particle with a force directly proportional to the product of their masses and inversely proportional to the square of the distance between them." This is a statement *in* physics, i.e., a physical statement, which is obtained by examining actual moving physical bodies and then generalizing from what is observed. (This is not exactly dorrect, but will do for our present purposes.) Now suppose someone were to say, "The soul is not the sort of thing to which the law of gravitation applies." Here we have a statement *about* the law of gravitation, which is not a statement in physics. Similarly one might say: "If the law of gravitation holds everywhere, then the world is completely determined." This, too, is not a statement in physics, but one about the sort of world in which physical laws of this sort are possible. Or finally, to say that "the law of gravitation is an empirical assertion" is also *about* the law and not part of it.

## Morals and Ethics

But enough of analogies! The distinction is this: Morals, as a body of statements, tell what is or is not to be done. To speak of the morals of a person, is to refer to the way he lives — what acts he considers to be right and what wrong. It is possible to talk about what people do and try to find a body of true statements about behavior of the sort under consideration. This is *ethics*. Although sometimes ordinary usage does identify "ethics" with "morals," in this book they will be kept distinct. *Ethics, in other words, is the critical study of morals.* It is more like science than like practice. Ethics seeks a body of truths — not a set of precepts or commandments — and these truths are about precepts and commandments. Ethics is sometimes called *moral philosophy.*

## Objectives of Ethical Reflection

A bit more needs to be said about morals. First, however, some explanation of the reason for belaboring what appears to be a rather obvious distinction is in order. To begin with, we want to be clear about the end results of studying ethics. Ethics will not in itself make the student more or less moral. In other words, it does not follow that the study of ethics will give anyone a rule of thumb which he may apply mechanically and thereby solve all his problems. It is most likely the case that people who study ethics are no more nor less apt to cheat, lie, steal, kill, or engage in seduction than those who do not. The trained dietician does not necessarily eat properly. "To know about" is not yet "to use." Ethics, however, since it is about morals, should provide a more sophisticated insight into the nature of morality and in this way could enable the student, if he so desires, to make more adequate moral decisions. In brief, ethics is not concerned directly with making people better, but with understanding moral behavior. Ethics seeks a body of truth about morals. The chief business of the student of ethics is to reflect upon moral situations in order to answer certain questions about them.

The following example will help clarify some of the characteristics of a moral problem. A young doctor, newly wed and full of enthusiasm, went to a small town to set up his medical practice. Soon after he arrived he discovered that there was another doctor in town. This second doctor, let us call him A, had resided there for many years and was very powerful in local affairs. It did not take the newcomer (Dr. B) long to become aware that Dr. A was an abortionist. Dr. B acquired sufficient evidence to be able to prove that Dr. A performed these illegal operations. In his enthusiasm, Dr. B felt he should denounce Dr. A and compel him to cease. It became apparent, however, that should Dr. B bring legal action against Dr. A, life in this town would become extremely difficult. Dr. B was opposed not only by Dr. A but by the leading "pillars" of the town, who threatened Dr. B with unpleasant consequences should he expose Dr. A.

Dr. B was confronted with a moral problem. He had to decide what to do; i.e., what was the right thing to do under these circumstances. This, so far as Dr. B was concerned, was not an ethical problem, because the question was whether or not he should denounce what in his opinion was an immoral act. Notice that neither was the problem a medical one. So far as Dr. B knew, all the abortions performed by Dr. A may have been medically perfect operations. Dr. A was apparently a competent physician. The issue was a moral one. Dr. B was asserting: "Abortion is immoral" and *therefore* "Abortion should not be performed." This is a judgment about an act which asserts what ought or ought not to be done. It is important to realize that for Dr. B abortion ought not to be done even if no one did ever perform one. This aspect of universal and unconditional applicability is an earmark of a moral judgment. We shall have occasion to discuss this universal form of moral judgments later.

A word of warning is in order. There is a tendency to equate all moral problems with sex and drama. But moral problems are much more inclusive. For example, suppose a student confides to his friend that he has cheated on the last examination. The friend is at once confronted with a moral problem. Should he reveal what he has been told? If he does, his act can be looked upon in two ways. First, as the act of reporting someone who cheats, i.e., as an act of "squealing". Second, it may be interpreted as the act of betraying a confidence, which probably most people believe ought rarely to be done. If one believes both that cheaters ought to be reported, and that confidences ought not to be betrayed, then he is in a real dilemma. Some course of action must be chosen and the act chosen must be one which is believed to be the right thing to do. More, most people will probably feel that everyone ought to act as he or she decides to do. At any rate, a real moral problem is involved.

*Moral and Non-moral Decisions*

At this point it is easy to gather the impression that whenever one needs to act he is in a moral situation. But not all problems are moral problems as the next example indicates. A physician might be confronted with the following type of situation. He is called in to attend a very sick child. After careful examination and even after consultation with other doctors, he decides that the child suffers from one of two diseases, $x$ or $y$. For each disease there is a specific drug but if he administers the drug for one disease and the child happens to have the other disease, the child will die. Here is an extremely difficult and even tragic situation. But no moral problem is involved, only a medical one.

We can leave the doctor to decide what the correct procedure should be in such a situation. Our concern is to recognize that although the doctor is faced with a choice and must decide what is the right thing to do to effect a cure, his decision is based not on moral principles but on medical ones. Therefore, the doctor's problem is not a moral one at all, even though other aspects of the situation may give rise to one. So, for example, if the doctor indifferently allows the child to die, he may be said to be immoral. But it is not necessary to complicate matters unduly.

Loosely speaking, the doctor in this case must discover what is the "right" thing to do to cure the disease. The word "right," in this context, clearly means "correct" rather than "moral."

Notice the following two expressions:

1. It is right to be honest.
2. It is right to step on the starter if you want to start the motor.

The distinction between the two uses of "right" is fairly obvious. In (1) if the word "right" is replaced by "moral" or even by "your duty," another sentence is obtained that makes sense. If the word "right" is replaced by "correct," the meaning is somewhat altered. So "It is correct to be honest" has a different connotation from "It is your duty to be honest" or (1). Certainly, it may be correct to thank one's hostess, yet not be the right thing to do if a lie is involved.

In (2) if "right" is replaced by "correct" or "appropriate," the result makes sense, whereas if it is replaced by "moral" or "your duty," the new sentence would sound quite strange. To say: "It is moral to step on the starter if you want to start the motor," is to say something nonsensical.

There are innumerable cases where the word "right" has no moral connotation at all. In fact, it would be better if it were never used in a context such as is assumed in (2). To use "right" wherever a cause-effect relation is involved, as in (2), is particularly unfitting.

## Moral Situations and Ethical Reflections

I have tried to indicate some of the differences between a moral and a nonmoral situation. In most cases, the one is easily differentiated from the other, but sometimes there is difficulty in deciding with which we are concerned. For example, are the deliberations of a temporarily or permanently insane person who is trying to decide whether or not he will kill his neighbor moral deliberations? Since so much of the analysis of a moral situation depends upon an examination of cases, it is quite obvious that we need to be sure we have selected cases of the type of thing we are studying. It may very well be that there are no cases at all of moral situations in the ordinary sense, as, for example, most strict determinists would hold. Even so we would need some criterion to select those cases which one is tempted to call moral.

The setting for ethical reflection is completely different from that of moral decision-making. To engage in ethical reflection does not entail doing anything more than thinking about morals. It is this fact that determines many of the distinctions between morals and ethics. An analogy may help tie together the various differences we have indicated. Consider the contrast between a doctor and, say, a biochemist. The doctor is confronted with practical situations. Given such and such symptoms and such and such medical principles, how should he treat his patient? This is the doctor's problem. However, the doctor may have a patient showing symptoms for which the doctor has no principle; what does he do? He may refer the matter to the biochemist who will ask such questions as, "What do these symptoms mean?" or "What causes these symptoms?" and so on. The biochemist does not treat patients; he is interested in questions about the disease. The biochemist, in other words, seeks a theory about the disease which will explain what the physician ought to do when confronted with a patient who has the ailment. The ethicist is to the moralist much what the biochemist is to the physician.

Ethical reflection may be induced by moral situations, but does not usually arise in them. In the midst of a situation demanding a decision to act in one way or another, one is not likely to stop to reflect on the meaning of "ought" or to consider why he should worry about being moral, or raise any other ethical questions. It may be that *after* a person has refused to lie he may ask himself when is a statement a "lie," or why he should not lie, or what reason there is to be moral at all, or even what it means to be moral. Ethical analyses are reflective, not activistic; they are critical of the aspects of a moral situation. They reflect upon these aspects using various techniques to bring out contradictions, latent meanings, and generalizations. Such activities cannot be undertaken in the midst of action. They are done prior or subsequent to acting or not at all.

The kind of thing involved in ethical reflection can best be illustrated by indicating some of the questions raised by the ethicist and comparing them with those asked by the moralist. We will use the following example as the nucleus around which these questions gravitate. Suppose someone sided with the doctor who wanted to expose the abortionist and said, "The doctor is right in exposing the one who performed abortions." The ethicist, as ethicist, neither approves nor disapproves the judgment but asks a series of questions.

## Types of Ethical Questions

When someone says the doctor was right, what precisely is meant by "right?" Does it mean, for example, that the action of the doctor is to be applauded? Or does it mean that the consequences of the doctor's act

are better than the consequences that would follow if the abortionist
were not exposed? Or does it mean that the doctor did what God wanted
him to do? There are other possibilities, but these are enough to show
the nature of the ethicist's questions and to hint at the varieties of possible answers. Notice that the ethicist is not challenging he decision but
simply seeking clarification.

The ethicist may continue: "Is it implied that all who perform abortions ought to be denounced?" If the implication is admitted, he might
point to another troublesome word "ought." What does it mean to say
"ought?" What is the relation between the following two statements (if
there is any)?

> "All who perform abortions ought to be denounced."
> "All who perform abortions are denounced."

The second is obviously false; yet even so, we would say that the first
is true. But the first statement is equivalent to saying that it is wrong
that those who perform abortions are not denounced. How may we
know this? If someone were to ask how the truth of sentences that contain the word "ought" or "wrong" could be proved (or established),
what answer could be given? In other words, what kind of evidence
would one accept in support of the statement, "All who perform abortions ought to be denounced?" Many people, no doubt, would probably
insist that abortions are acts of murder or that the consequences of abortions are unhappiness for many people.

But if abortions are called murders, it is possible to ask on what
grounds they are so called. Perhaps this is simply a matter of definition
and whether abortion and murder are or are not the same legally would
be a question of fact to be decided by an examination of the legal definition of murder. At any rate, to reply to a request for a justification of
the "oughtness" of denouncing doctors who perform abortions by calling
abortions murders simply raises another question. Why ought a *murderer* to be denounced on moral grounds? What, in other words, is there
about a murder that makes people call it immoral as well as illegal?

If one appeals to the consequences of an act in support of its moral
character, a host of other vexing questions are suggested. These new
questions are illustrated in the following situation. A person, taking all
precautions, sets fire to a shed on his property. A sudden gust of wind
blows a spark to a neighbor's roof igniting the house. The neighbor is
burned to death. Shall we say the neighbor's death is a consequence of
the fire or the desire to destroy the shed? When is an event that follows

an act a consequence of that act? Furthermore, to what consequences should one appeal? It is not unlikely that the neighbor's death may bring joy to his enemies as well as sorrow to his friends. Is not the selection of the consequences that are to be considered and of the individuals whose happiness is to be given preference already a sort of begging of the question? Even, moreover, if we call the death a consequence of the act of setting fire to the shed, should the owner of the shed be morally blamed for an outcome he did not foresee nor desire?

An appeal to consequences tacitly assumes that

1. It is right to consider consequences
2. "right" and "moral" are definable in terms of certain types of consequences.

Both of these statements have been denied at one time or another. Kant, an important German philosopher, urged that consequences are irrelevant to duty; while G. E. Moore, an eminent British philosopher, argued that "goodness" is an indefinable quality to be recognized as one recognizes, say, yellow, so that the moral is to be defined in terms of this quality, goodness.

An ethical problem of extraordinary importance is made manifest when someone insists: "It is not true that all who perform abortions ought to be denounced. This holds only of those who perform abortions freely."

What does the word "freely" mean? It is extremely difficult to define this word. Yet, as we saw earlier in the chapter, the very meaning of "moral" seems to involve the idea the word "freely" tries to convey. To put the question in another form: What sort of creature is man and what kind of world is required for there to be moral behavior at all?

*Ethics and Philosophy*

The types of ethical questions that may be asked can be summarized in terms of the traditional divisions of philosophic inquiry. Thus, ethics can be said to be concerned with the following groups of problems:

1. Logical problems: Questions concerning the meanings of terms, the logical form of moral statements, the implicative relations between moral statements, the form and validity of moral arguments.

2. Epistemological problems: Questions concerning the nature of the evidence for or against moral statements, how we come to know moral statements, problems of the justification of the principles used to infer conclusions, etc.

3.    Metaphysical problems: whether or not moral predicates refer to anything real, the nature of the moral subject, the nature of the world in which moral decisions are made, whether or not moral principles refer to something in the universe, etc.

Morals, as a study, is concerned with more immediate problems such as:

1.    What are the principles of morality?
2.    What acts are moral?
3.    What is the highest good?

Moral and ethical discussions frequently overlap, but they need to be kept distinct.

BIBLIOGRAPHY

Castell, A., *An Elementary Ethics,* New York: Prentice-Hall, 1954, Chap. 1.
Ewing, A. C., *Ethics,* London: English Universities Press, 1953, Chap. 1.
Garvin, L., *A Modern Introduction to Ethics,* Boston: Houghton Mifflin, 1953, Chap. 1.
Melden, A. I., editor, *Ethical Theories,* 2nd ed., New York: Prentice-Hall, 1955, pp. 1–20.

# CHAPTER II

# THE MORAL SITUATION

*An Example of a Moral Situation*

Since the subject matter of our study is the moral situation, it needs to be analyzed in order to expose those of its elements that deserve our consideration. But if we are to analyze a moral situation, we must be able to identify one. How is it possible to identify a moral situation before a definition of what is meant by "moral situation" is given? Yet a definition of "moral situation" would seem to be impossible until after some specimen has been examined. Of course, we could start with a purely arbitrary definition. This would not do because we are concerned with actual moral situations. Ethics is like a science in this respect. This predicament is not unique to our present study – ethics. Indeed, it is common to all fields of investigation. Even if we had a definition, to the beginner in the field it would be virtually meaningless, or at least misleading. Definition or not, *examples* of what we are talking about are indispensable when an investigation is begun for they serve as tests for what is said.

In ethics the situation is much less serious than one would expect in abstraction from the problem itself. Most people have some idea of what moral situations are like. Few of us have managed to avoid being concerned with them from time to time. Even those who deny that the word "moral" has any real meaning would, I think, agree that it is used characteristically in some situations and not in others. For example, is there anyone who refuses to admit that when an ordinary person is contemplating murder he is wrestling with a problem that is ordinarily called moral, no matter how he analyzes the word "moral?"

We are fortunate, in beginning the study of ethics, because most people have some comprehension, however imperfect, of the meaning of the terms and especially their application to the situations with which we are concerned. The sum total of these everyday notions is often referred to as "common-sense ethics." We must, however, realize that these notions of common-sense ethics tend to be imperfect and need to be corrected and that common-sense ethics is at times nothing more than an attempt at selfjustification. Common-sense ethics may vary with the times and with the place, and, indeed, not be ethics at all.

In order to begin the study of ethics we will describe a moral situation which lends itself to analysis. Here is an interesting one mentioned by Plato in the *Republic.*

> Suppose A loaned his knife to his friend B. After a while B discovers that A has become mad – in fact, a homicidal maniac. A approaches B and requests the return of his knife.

The case is relatively simple but is bears all the earmarks of a moral situation. First, it is evident that the core of the situation is that B is confronted with the necessity of making a choice. He can either return the knife or keep it. Were there no element of choice present one would be tempted to say that no moral problem was involved. For example, if A was stronger than B and was choking B to death and would let go only if A returned his knife, most people would agree that B had no choice but to surrender the knife. It is possible, of course, to insist that even in such a case B had a choice, to die or not to die. But usually in conditions where death is as certain as it is in the situation just described, few indeed would say there was any real alternative. Sometimes, it is true, people do say that death is preferable to certain types of actions. This happens when the act in question is considered to be so wrong, or so evil, in its consequences that death is to be preferred.

## *Logical* vs. *Factual Alternatives*

At this point we need to clarify a type of argument sometimes used to "prove" that no real alternatives are ever possible. This argument involves a confusion of logical and factual alternatives, and goes like this: either B returns the knife to A or he does not and since there is no other possibility he must do one or the other. Therefore, if one or the other *must* be done, there is no choice at all.

One feels intuitively that this argument is fallacious. But why? The argument fails to distinguish a logical dichotomy from a factual possibility. Logically speaking, either B returns the knife to A or he does not. There are no other possibilities. These are the *logical* alternatives. And furthermore, B *must* do *one or the other.* The necessity in this is also logical and not factual. The element of choice is found in the selection of which will be done and why. To say that B either returns the knife or not is to enumerate the logical alternatives, i.e., the *possibilities;* and the same thing is true when we say B *must* do one or the other.

The "must" in this case does not tell us *which* will be done, but that B is confronted with these possibilities – one of which he must choose. It is quite another thing to say that B *must* return the knife or he *must* not return it, then it is false to assert that he *must* not return it. The argument may take another turn and really be asserting that whatever is done is the result of a strict causal scheme. This, however, is a different kind of argument. Logically, then, B must return the knife or not do so, but factually, if freedom is not denied, which act B will do depends on his choice.

So far no attempt has been made to prove or show cause why anyone should believe that choice is or is not possible. All that has been done is to try to point out that choice is an element in a moral situation and to indicate in broad terms what choice involves.

### Choice and Decision

It is very difficult to define what is meant by "choice," but when we say "B has a choice" we mean at least that it is within B's power to decide what to do. If he so desires he can withold the knife, or if he wishes he can return it to its owner. "Choice" signifies that it is up to the person to decide which of several alternatives is to be selected, and that it is possible to make a selection in a significant sense. When we say, "B chose to return the knife," then we seem to imply that he could have chosen the opposite but did not. Moreover, B could have chosen to return the knife, yet failed to do so.

It is quite possible to make an intellectual choice without making a practical one. This is to say that one can intellectually choose one thing rather than another without making any attempt to do or secure what is chosen. People do agree that killing is evil, yet participate in war. A person may intellectually decide that he ought never to steal; yet upon seeing his family hungry he may steal. We often do what we ought not to do; and refrain from doing what we ought to do. This does not necessarily signify either hypocrisy or lying. It may mean a willingness in a concrete situation to excuse departures from the rule. On the other hand, a pacifist may make a practical choice and decide to go to jail rather than betray his intellectual commitments, i.e., his choices. It should be clear that it is assumed that freedom is indeed possible, whether it be in the choice or the act.

Here we may use a nonmoral example to reveal another element in a moral situation. Suppose someone is out for a stroll and comes to a fork in the road. He hesitates because he does not know which turn to take. Just then, another person running blindly down the street bumps him and he is pushed into the left-hand fork. Did he choose this fork rather than the other? Obviously not; he was pushed. A similar sort of situation can occur when someone is hesitating before moral alternatives. Suppose a person sees someone drop a wallet full of money. He picks it up and tries to decide whether to keep it or return it to its owner. However, another passerby sees him pick it up and calls to the owner that the person has it. He is, in a sense, forced to return it. In neither of these cases does a choice appear to occur. But might there be conditions in which one would insist that a choice had been made?

Return for a minute to what happened when the wallet was found. The chances are that when the passerby called to the owner the wallet was immediately returned. If it were said of the finder that he was forced to return it, he might indignantly exclaim: "But I had already decided to return the wallet." He would be offering as evidence that he had chosen to surrender the wallet, that he had *decided* to do so. It would appear that where a decision is made, there has been a choice also.

Common speech also reveals the close relation between decision and choice. Synonymous expressions for "I chose to surrender the knife" are "I decided to surrender the knife" or "I made up my mind to surrender the knife." Although at times the two are used synonymously, there seems to be some distinction between them, since deciding involves making a choice. To decide to expose Dr. A, Dr. B had to arrive at a choice; to decide to return the knife (or not to) equally means to choose that the knife should be returned. Notice that "to decide that the knife should be returned" is chiefly intellectual, whereas "to decide to return the knife" is eminently practical. A choice involves a preference while a decision brings things to a head. So one may choose to act without deciding to do so.

## The Logic of Decision

What elements are involved in making decisions? Let us try to put ourselves in the place of the person trying to decide what to do about the knife. Conceivably he might argue in some such way as this:

> "If I do not return the knife, then I am betraying a trust and one ought not to betray trusts. Therefore, I should return it. But hold a minute! Surely one ought not to betray a trust, but

perhaps there are circumstances (or facts) that make this an exceptional case. If I return the knife to its owner who is insane, he may very well do injury to many innocent people. Certainly, I ought not to do anything that will bring injury to innocent people. The knife is his, but I ought not to return it until its owner is in his right mind."

It will help to rewrite the arguments involved in the foregoing reflections in brief form:

*Argument 1*

> One ought not be betray a trust.
> If I keep the knife, I will betray a trust.
>
> _____
>
> Therefore: I ought to return the knife.

*Argument 2*

> One ought not to do what brings injury to innocent people.
> If I return the knife, I will do what brings injury to innocent people.
>
> _____
>
> Therefore: I ought not to return the knife.

In many ways these arguments look like ordinary logical syllogisms. They contain two premises and a conclusion. *This conclusion expresses the decision.* In other words, a decision is the conclusion of a logical argument. As such, the validity of the argument depends on the nature of these premises. So we need to examine them.

*Nature of the First Premise*

In the two arguments, the first premise – the evidence presented for the conclusion – is a statement containing a peculiar word. This is the word "ought." We shall have occasion to discuss this notion more thoroughly, so all we need underline here is the fact that "ought" seems to involve an element of obligation. There is an evident distinction between

1. One ought not betray a trust,

and

2. People do not betray a trust.

The first statement tells the kind of thing people are obligated to do, the second gives us information about what people actually do. Statement (2) may be, and as a matter of fact is, false. People betray trusts

every day. The courts are full of suits in which the central issue is a betrayed trust. Nevertheless, that people do betray trusts is not ordinarily
taken as evidence either for or against statement (1). Most people know
quite well how to go about proving or disproving (2), but the methods
used to test this statement are not those used to establish (1).

It is important also to recognize not merely that (1) states what ought
to be the case even if it is not, but that in addition, the statement is universal in form. This means that it applies, or is intended to apply to
everyone. *No one ought to betray a trust.* Let us call a statement which
tells what ought to be and whose logical subject is everyone, a *principle*.
We can say as a consequence that moral decisions involve a moral principle. Many statements which purport to be moral principles have been
defended as such by partisans.

Moral principles have another interesting feature which distinguishes
them from principles of other sorts. For example, a person who says,
"No one ought to betray a trust," will usually agree that such a statement
implies a command: "Don't betray a trust!" The command follows from
the principle in a manner that is perculiar to the logic of morality. We
find nothing like it in other areas of knowledge. We would consider it
rather a bad form of humor if one said that since bodies falling from a
height ought to obey the law of falling bodies, $S = \frac{1}{2}gt^2$ – the command, "Fall according to the law," is valid. The "ought" in this latter
case is scarcely a moral one. On the other hand, if one accepts the principle, "No one ought to harm innocent people," the command, "Don't
harm innocent people!" is perfectly significant and may be held validated
by that principle. Moral principles do, in fact, seem to imply commands.
But neither commands nor particularizations of principles are themselves principles. So, "Hitler ought not to have killed innocent people"
is not a moral principle even if it is a moral statement, because it is not
universal in form. It is a moral statement because it can be obtained from
a moral principle, namely, "No one ought to kill innocent people."

### Nature of the Conclusion

The conclusion of a moral argument is most often a moral statement
such as: "*I* ought not return the knife," or "He ought to be charitable,"
and so on. In each case the subject seems to be definite persons who
ought to do or refrain from doing something. Implicit in these conclusions are always commands. In this respect they are like moral principles, but unlike the conclusions of factual arguments. If I prove that my
car can go 100 miles an hour, no command to go that fast is implied.

However, "I ought to return the knife"; therefore, "Return the knife!"
"I ought not to harm innocent people"; therefore, "Don't harm an innocent person!"

Commands implied by moral conclusions are directives – they tell
what to do or to avoid doing. As such, it is possible to disregard them,
or to refuse to obey them. To refuse to do as commanded by a moral
principle is tantamount to a rejection of the principle. In other words,
moral principles are either accepted or rejected by action of some sort.

### Factual Nature of the Second Premise

The statements serving as the second premise, are clearly different in
structure from the moral principle. These statements are conditional in
form, and assert: "if – then –." Their very flavor is distinct from that of
the principle. The second premise does not assert what ought to be, but
describes purported matters of fact, i.e., connections between events. "If
I return the knife, injury to innocent people might result." The denial of
such a statement would be "It is not true because people will stay out of
the maniac's way," or "Innocent people will not be hurt because the
maniac will be taken into custody before he can get away." No question
is raised about the principle which serves as the reason for the decision
or judgment. A rejection of the second premise may involve a decision
not to return the knife not because the obligation expressed in the first
premise is denied, but because the consequences would not be injurious.
The decision to return the knife is challenged on the basis of a denial of
the consequences of doing what the antecedent asserts.

Disagreement over the second premise is basically disagreement about
the consequences of an act and as such should be open to empirical resolution. Whether the consequences asserted to follow when the knife
is returned will in fact follow is a question of fact regardless of whether
or not one ought to return it. The empirical consequences of the return
of the knife can be considered apart from any moral problem. Whether
or not one ought to return the knife may, however, depend upon the
solution of the empirical question.

### Role of Factual Considerations

There are two places where factual considerations may occur in moral
problems. They occur in connection with the second premise when one
tries to assess the consequences of a particular act and in connection
with the first premise when one is asked to justify the moral principle.
For example, if one is asked why he ought not to betray a trust he is

likely to say, "Because if trusts were betrayed then social relations would be impossible." Later when the justification of moral principles is considered, this kind of justification will be critically examined.

Whenever anyone who is faced with a problem tries to decide upon a course of action that will conform to a principle, he must consider the facts of the case. He must, for example, consider whether the situation is the sort in which the principle is to be applied at all. Analogous problems are found in the law also. Suppose John Doe is accused of murdering Richard Roe. The law says that murder is to be punished by death. But John Doe's lawyer pleads that John Doe was not in his right mind at the time of the act; or that John Doe was not guilty of murder because he killed Richard Roe in self-defense. The jury must then decide the questions of fact. Was Doe out of his mind? or was Doe acting in self-defense? If either of these conditions were present, the judge would decide that the law did not apply. In other words, the facts show that act to be one that does not fit the definition of murder.

This relation between facts and moral decision is of considerable intrinsic interest. One expects moral *facts* (if there are any) to influence one's decision. But why should nonmoral facts such as the consequences of any act in any way bear upon the rightness or wrongness of the act? Why, in other words, should it be of any concern that the heavens do fall as long as justice be done? To do justice is to be moral, regardless of the consequences. Perhaps so. This is a question on which there is much disagreement. These comments indicate that there are these two kinds of facts. In argument (2), which was given a few pages back, two kinds of questions are involved:

> Is keeping the knife right or wrong?
> Will keeping the knife prevent injury to innocent people?

The first is a moral problem which concerns a moral fact. The second is a causal problem and involves cause-effect relations.

### Motives and Morals

There is another kind of factual question that does not concern the truth or falsity of the second premise as such, but whether or not it really is determinative in the mind of the person trying to make a decision. Let us suppose that the knife is very valuable and there is some reason to doubt that its owner has homicidal tendencies. However, the person to whom the knife has been entrusted insists that he will keep it to prevent harm being done. In that case, we may suspect that what is of concern is not the welfare of the people, but the value of the knife. What the trustee intends to do, apparently, is to keep the knife and use this presumed tendency on the part of its owner as a pretext. The problem concerns the motives of the person involved and raises, as we shall see, a whole host of questions.

Consider another example. Suppose Dr. B went ahead and exposed Dr A and by doing so prevented the commission of further abortions. Dr. B might very well be judged a brave and moral person. But suppose Dr. B did it not so much because he thought that abortion was immoral as because he hoped that by exposing Dr. A he would ruin his reputation and all Dr. A's patients would then come to Dr. B? Under such circumstances would anyone want to call Dr. B moral and brave? Of course, if you saw someone run over another person your judgment would be definitely affected by the knowledge that the driver had intended to kill his victim. The ambivalence that exists in the minds of people on this point is evidenced by such remarks as "The Road to Hell is paved with good intentions" or "He meant well even if his actions were bad."

People do "good" deeds while under the influence of bad motives, or may do evil for good reasons. There are persons who want to save the world by violence and even murder. Again, there are those who argue that to free people who have been enslaved would lead to disorder; hence, to preserve order these people should not be freed. The motive is good – to preserve order; the means are bad (or evil) – to keep people in slavery. History records many cases of the use of torture to save people's souls from damnation.

Factual considerations seeking to determine motives are of immediate importance when we try to decide not the rightness of the act to be done but the morality of the actor. Is a person moral merely if what he does leads to desirable consequences? If the answer is affirmative, a person may be moral even if his motives are evil. Or are motives the all-important factor, especially since one may not have much control over the consequences of his act? If so, all one needs are good motives no matter how vicious the means and how catastrophic the consequences. The motives of witch-hunters (of all kinds) are quite often good; their actions, injurious. Shall we call them good and moral people?

*Summary*

It is time to summarize the various aspects of a moral situation of importance to an understanding of our subject. Every moral situation involves the following elements: There is (1) an actor who does things of a certain sort. What he does is (2) to act and not merely to respond to stimuli in a mechanical fashion. The act is the result of a (3) choice. In cases where the chief element is approval or disapproval the act may be merely intellectual (an approval) or practical (a course of action). There must be (4) true alternatives so that the choice is a real one. In arriving at a (5) decision that an act is moral, or right, or ought to be done, the actor uses (6) moral principles and considers both (7) motives and (8) consequences as well as the (9) means of achieving his (10) goals or ends.

We do not consider the justification of the moral principles and the consideration of the meanings of terms like "right," "wrong," "ought," etc. as part of the moral situation. These questions arise when one reflects on that situation.

There is no one way or order to approach an analysis of the above elements. It is necessary that we select. Since the most obvious thing about a moral situation is the principle in terms of which one decides whether something is moral or whether an act should be done, it will be most valuable to begin with a consideration of the nature and form of a moral principle and then to turn to an examination of some moral principles. A moral principle is the touchstone for testing moral decisions, acts, motives, and consequences. Moreover, it usually serves as the basis for definitions of moral predicates.

## BIBLIOGRAPHY

Dewey, John and James H. Tufts, *Ethics,* New York: Henry Holt and Co., 1908, Chap. 10, pp. 201–212.
Jordan, E., *The Good Life,* Chicago: University of Chicago Press, 1949, Chapters 2 and 3, pp. 17–58.
Leys, W. A. R., *Ethics and Social Policy,* New York: Prentice-Hall, 1941, Chap. 2.
Macbeath, A., *Experiments in Living,* London: Macmillan & Co., 1952, Chapter 2.
Wheelwright, P., *A Critical Introduction to Ethics,* Rev. ed., New York: Odyssey Press, 1949, Chap. 1, pp. 3–23.

# CHAPTER III

## MORAL PRINCIPLES

The objective of this chapter is to become acquainted with the form and characteristics of moral principles. Later we shall examine their meanings and justification.

### The Forms of Moral Principles

We have pointed out that moral judgments as well as moral decisions are possible only on the basis of moral principles – whether or not these are expressed. If anyone asserts, "Segregation is right" or "John Smith should be treated justly," he does so in virtue of moral principles he maintains tacitly or explicitly. Or to take another example, if someone says, "It is immoral to allow a Communist to teach callow youth," and he is asked "Why?," his answer probably would be, "Communists are sworn to follow the party line, and, therefore, will try to make communists of youth." If he is then asked, "So what?", his reply might be, "Only the truth should be taught and those interested in making Communists do not seek the truth." This quite clearly expresses a moral principle: "Only the truth should be taught."

Suppose we rephrase this moral principle as follows: "All who teach ought to teach nothing but the truth." Since we are concerned only with the form of the moral principle, its justification need not concern us. In order, then, to see what the form of a moral principle is we will list a few more examples:

> One ought to do his duty!
> One ought to be merciful!
> Do God's will!
> Obey your conscience!
> Do not kill!
> One ought not to kill!

These are commonly accepted as formulations of moral principles, even when they are not accepted as binding. These and any other moral principles which may be listed will take either the form, "Do so and so!" or "one ought to do so and so." Let us call the former type "commands" and the latter "obligation-sentences."

## Nonmoral Commands and Obligations

Not all commands, however, are moral principles. There are commands of the sort expressed, say, in the Golden Rule, "Do unto others as you would have them do unto you," and there are commands such as "Shut the door!" Both are directives, but the latter are not moral. The difference is made evident by the fact that moral commands can be prefaced by "you ought to..." and thereby changed into obligation-sentences, while nonmoral commands cannot. If the judge orders, "Silence in the court," it doesn't make sense to say "You ought to be silent in court," unless "ought" is not a moral ought. The command, "Silence in the court" really means "If you want to stay in the court room, be silent." If, however, you say "Love thy neighbor!" it makes good sense to say "You ought to love thy neighbor." There is no condition usually assumed by this command.

In many instances the word "ought" is used where there really is no obligation, but the context usually indicates when this is the case. For example, suppose someone tries to start his car. Repeated pressure on the starter yields no results. To say to the person, "Check your gas," would be to utter an expression that has the syntactical form of a command, but really isn't one. What is really intended is, "I suggest you are out of gas," which is not a command. It might even have been expressed, "You ought to check your gas." The "ought," in this sentence, does not denote an obligation as it does in "You ought to do kind deeds," but rather it indicates that the car may not start because you might be out of gas. The "ought" in such cases could be called a "prudential" ought since it expresses something prudent under these conditions.

Since, as these few examples show, there are moral as well as nonmoral commands and moral as well as nonmoral obligation-sentences, what is the difference between a moral and a nonmoral command? A little reflection reveals that a moral command is justified by, or is a consequence of, a moral obligation, while a nonmoral command is grounded in a desire to get something done. A moral obligation-sentence is related to a moral imperative-sentence as ground to consequence. A nonmoral command is the consequence of a conditional sentence. Its basis is in some cause-effect relation. The obligation-sentence may be said to imply the imperative sentence (or command) in a moral situation, but the goal implies the command in a nonmoral obligation-sentence. This only pushes the question back one step, for we now want to know in more precise terms the difference between a moral obligation and a nonmoral or prudential one.

## Moral Principles as Moral Obligations

Consider the moral obligation expressed by:

"One ought to do his duty."

and the nonmoral one expressed by:

"One ought to eat properly."

Let us call a *moral* obligation, a moral *principle,* or briefly, a principle. A moral principle such as is expressed in the sentence "One ought to do his duty" has a rather interesting aspect. It can be employed significantly in contexts where someone is trying to decide what to do, as well as in situations in which no one is confronted with the practical problem of deciding what to do. For example, suppose war has been declared and a young man about to be married is trying to decide whether to enlist or be drafted. His decision might be announced in the following fashion, "I ought to enlist because one ought to do one's duty, and this is my duty." Suppose, however, war has not been declared but the young man is in conversation with a friend about the hypothetical problem of what people should do when war is declared. Under these circumstances too he might say: "One ought to do one's duty." It would still be significant to assert the principle, even though there is no immediate need to do anything, and there may never be. The point is that this *is* a principle and as such expresses a moral obligation, which is just as binding as it would be if he were about to enlist.

On the other hand, the obligation, for example, to eat properly is "binding" only if one wants to achieve other ends. Eating properly is a means to another goal, in a way in which doing one's duty is not or is not intended to be. It doesn't seem to be quite as appropriate to say "One ought to eat properly" if everyone is doing so, as it appears to be to say "One ought to do his duty" even if everyone is doing his duty. It is possible to say, "I don't want to live by sacrificing my taste for food, and therefore I will eat as I see fit": but is doesn't sound right to say, "I don't want to be happy (or moral, or anything else), and hence I won't do my duty." It is not usual to say "You ought to eat properly no matter what you want," while no one would be surprised at being told, "You ought to do your duty even if it makes you unhappy or brings disaster or anything else."

In brief, nonmoral obligations depend for their force upon the acceptance of some ulterior goal, while principles do not. These carry their obligation in themselves. This is not to say that one cannot question the claim of an obligation to be a principle. If "doing one's duty" were rejected as a moral obligation, this would not mean that moral obligations do not carry their own force. It is also possible to deny that a given act, say, that of enlisting, is one's duty. This, however, is not to deny the principle that one ought to do one's duty, but to question whether what is proposed is one's duty.

### The Unconditional Nature of the Moral Principle

To assert that "You ought not to kill" is a moral principle, is to affirm that killing should not be done under any conditions. In general, moral principles appear to carry this element of unconditionality as integral to their very natures. There may, perhaps, be circumstances under which one may be *excused* for killing, but he is excused and not released from the obligation expressed in the principle. This means that a command such as "Don't kill!" may or may not follow from a moral principle such as "Thou shalt not kill." If it does, ten you must not kill; if it does not then you are merely being told not to kill in the way the police chief may say, "Don't kill. Take the prisoner alive."

If we distinguish a maxim as a prudential rule of behavior in contrast to a principle which involves an obligatory command, we can put the matter another way. It may be said (as people have) that "Thou shalt not kill" is merely a good maxim because doing as it commands makes society possible, or keeps others from taking your life. So those whom we shall later call "hedonists" might urge that "Thou shalt not kill" is moral because refraining from killing brings happiness to the greatest number of people. In this case, "Thou shalt not kill" is a maxim, a rule of conduct, that in general tends to bring happiness. The principle for the hedonist becomes simply "Bring happiness." If this is a way of justifying the principle, its evaluation belongs in the realm of ethics and not morals. But if "Thou shalt not kill" is taken to require justification, it is no longer in strictness a moral principle, for such considerations modify the ought-statement and reduce it to a prudential maxim with the result that the "ought" appears to lose its binding character. It may, indeed, be the case that all apparently moral principles are but prudential maxims, but this is something that needs separate examination and is not our concern at the moment. Even if all so-called moral principles are really prudential maxims, nevertheless the true moral principle is unconditional.

*Moral Principles and Legal Principles*

Moral principles, then, have a binding character. But while they are strict in their admonitions, yet their admonitions are not buttressed with threats of punishments. This can best be illustrated by contrasting them with statute laws. Every statute law contains not merely a prescription of a mode of behavior but also a set of consequences (punishment) which result when the law is violated. As an example let us consider the speed laws. These may define "speeding" as "travelling in excess of 55 miles an hour on open highways." The law, then, takes the form of a statement, "Speeding is prohibited," which since it is a law implies the command, "Don't speed!" The law also states that if one does speed, then a fine will be imposed (or one's license to drive revoked, etc.). If a person speeds he is punished in the way the law prescribes, so the law really says, "Either you don't speed or you will be punished."

Moral principles are, however, different. Consider the commandment, "Thou shalt not commit adultery." Adultery happens to be both illegal and immoral, and will serve to clarify what I am trying to say. As a law, the command says: either you do not commit adultery or you will be punished. A person may, therefore, be deterred from doing this because of fear of the punishment. If this is his reason and we know it often is, we do not ordinarily consider him moral, but rather prudent. As a moral principle, the command is strict and does not carry any threat of punishment (or promise of reward either, for that matter). Not merely does it not carry any sanctions but we do not expect that anyone will punish or reward acts simply because they violate or are not in accord with moral principles. Virtue is its own reward, and vice its own punishment. If you lie, people may frown or, for that matter, under certain conditions even smile. Some people may disapprove and scold or avoid you. No one is appointed or elected to punish lies unless they come within the purview of the law. Bearing false witness is legally punishable, not because it is immoral but because there are laws against it. Bearing false witness is also morally reprehensible but as such is cannot be punished except through disapproval and avoidance. An immoral person may be excluded from certain groups, or lose his job. But these are the consequences of his acts and do not define or even help to prevent them though they may deter him from performing similar acts in the future. The same thing is true of telling the truth, or being honest. We do not expect people who are virtuous to be given medals. In fact, to do so is to run the risk of corrupting the person. The point is that the kind of punishment, if any, that may follow upon violations of moral principles is not a part of that principle; whereas if there is no punishment defined for a civil law, it cannot be said to be a civil law. In this sense moral principles are much stricter than civil laws; sanctions are unessential to them.

## The Logical Subject of Moral Principles

If we turn our attention once again to the form of the ought-statement, we will discern another important feature of moral principles. Consider "One ought to be merciful" and ask to whom the word "one" refers. If the remark was made to a judge about to pronounce sentence upon a criminal, it would be obvious to everyone that what was meant was, "Your honor, you ought to be merciful." In many situations the use of the word "one" in a command serves to soften the harshness of the command. To say outright "You ought to be merciful" connotes an element of evaluation of the person that may be offensive. If this were all that was ever meant by the word "one" in "One ought to be mirciful," it would have no meaning except when used in talking to someone about what he ought to do. But obviously we do use this expression to mean not only "you" but "everyone."

Suppose, instead of being spoken to, the judge were addressing a group of lawyers at a convention. During the course of his discussion of the possible injustice that can arise when there is too strict adherence to the letter of the law, the judge says, "Remember that even in legal matters one ought to be merciful." Now the "one" still means "you" but a plural "you." The judge is saying that everyone present ought to be merciful in the practice of his profession. But when the judge says, "even in legal matters . . .," he seems to be saying much more. He is apparently urging that "One ought to be merciful" is a principle that cannot be disregarded even in a field where it might appear to be proper to do so. In short, he is saying, "You lawyers are no exception – you ought to be merciful." This is equivalent to saying, "Everyone, including lawyers, ought to be merciful."

This reveals a most important characteristic of moral principles – they are applicable to everyone. Moral principles are no respectors of persons and impose themselves on rich and poor, great and small, strong and weak alike. No one is to be an exception because of these incidental and, relative to the moral principle, accidental features. Occasionally, of course, we find someone who, like Nietzsche, will seek to define a group upon whom moral principles are not binding. It was either Lenin or Stalin who said that murder is to be condoned if done in the interest of the class struggle. Those who seek to make such exceptions consider moral principles merely as means towards ends in exactly the same way that one may use a slogan to induce people to buy cigarettes. But this is not how moral principles operate. Most people recognize the universality of moral principles. In other words, "You ought to be merciful" means "Everyone ought to be merciful."

If being merciful is taken to be a means toward an end, then the principle, "You ought to be merciful," is merely prudential. In such a case, the words "one" or "you" would refer only to that person who accepts the end. But as we have seen, moral principles are not intended to be prudential maxims.

Not many would deny that moral principles have these properties of universality and bindingness even when it is denied that there are any moral principles. So one could say that if "One ought to be just" is a moral principle, it would be universal and binding. To one who felt the statement was not a moral principle, this would be a contrary-to-fact conditional of the same nature as "If there is a human who lives on Saturn, he would need oxygen." Or, one could say, "Yes, a moral principle applies to everyone, but this is true only ideally. In practice a ruler, if he acts for the benefit of the state, has the right to be immoral, i.e., to disavow the universality of the principle and pronounce himself an exception." This transfers the element of universality to another moral principle considered to supersede the first, and does not reject moral principles; for now it is said that the assertion "*all rulers* ought to act in the interest of the state" is a moral principle. Or one can say, "Moral principles apply to everyone except the advanced thinkers of the day." Here, too, another principle is placed above the one in question, and the tacit assumption is the principle that "All advanced thinkers have a special character." Somewhere the universality reappears and the locus of its appearance is indicative of what the ultimate moral principle which all others serve is considered to be. All other principles are taken to be maxims relative to this one and to express prudential conditions. So we conclude that a moral principle, when fully expressed, has a form like, "Anyone who is a person ought to be just."

### Moral Principles Timeless

One final characteristic of a moral principle needs to be noted. If we say that everyone ought to be merciful, we mean that this holds at all times and in every place. To assert that "Everyone ought to be merciful" is a moral principle is to insist that even in the wilds of the African jungles where mercy is not a quality that makes for survival, everyone ought to be merciful.

*Moral Principles and Laws of Nature*

If moral principles have the features we have discussed, they do seem to resemble, at least in some respects, laws of nature. But if a law of nature is compared with a moral law, some interesting and important differences are apparent. Consider:

(1)  All freely falling bodies fall in such a way that the relation between distance falling and time covered is given by $S = \frac{1}{2}gt^2$.

(2)  All persons who are moral do justice.

(3)  All persons ought to be just.

The first of these is a law of nature. It affirms that if anything is a freely falling body, then it must fall in the way described. This may be taken as a description of the way a body known by some other criterion to be falling freely *must fall* or *does always fall*. If the law is taken as a description of how the body does always fall, then (1) is simply a generalization and it is possible that a freely falling body may fall otherwise than as described. If the law states how the body must fall, then (1) asserts something necessary about the structure of the physical world. We usually take physical laws to express this sort of necessity-compulsion. A freely falling body cannot fall in any other way. The law may, however, be taken as an analytic statement, i.e., as a statement that defines what it means to be freely falling. If this is the way we interpret a law, then if a body falls in another way, we simply don't call it freely falling. To be freely falling it *must* be falling in this way and cannot do anything else.

Statement (2) may also be a generalization; i.e., it may simply describe the fact that when one finds a moral person, one finds him doing justice. In this respect this is like (1) if natural laws are taken as mere generalizations. On the other hand, (2) may also be taken as expressing a law; it may be taken that if anyone is a moral person, he must be acting justly. If we so interpret it, then there is indeed a relation between doing justice and being moral such that no deviation from justice is possible. One may or may not be moral; but if one is, then he does justice. On this interpretation, moral persons do justice of necessity and therefore are not moral at all, since to be moral implies doing moral acts (of which justice is one) without compulsion or necessity but from the proper motive at least. Compulsion could only give rise to a moral act if (a) the act were the result of one's nature and (b) one can be held responsible for his nature. If, however, we assume that what we are is not our creation, then acts which proceed from our nature are not moral. If at the moment of action the act is a necessary consequence of that nature so that no other act is possible, then the agent cannot be a moral agent.

The point may be illustrated in this fashion. Suppose you promise to lend your friend some money. He appears and requests the loan. Being moral, you, without further consideration, simply from your nature, make the appropriate response – you lend him the money. The act may certainly be "virtuous," but you are not moral. We need not push this further; the point is that whichever way (2) is interpreted – whether as an expression of an empirical generalization or as a law of morality – it is not a moral statement. Obviously (2) cannot be interpreted as a definition. Indeed, (1) and (2) are alike in many respects.

Statement (3), "All persons ought to be just," has the same universal form as (1) and (2) but is otherwise redically different. The form is definitely law-like, but is does not express the same kind of relation as do (1) and (2). Statement (3) is not a generalization in the sense that the others are. It cannot be the result of observing that A is just, B is just, and so on. Nor can we say that "One ought to be just" follows from one's being a person, because persons can and often do act unjustly. (3) cxprcsscs, if it must bc callcd a law, the kind of law that can be violated and often is. In this connection also we notice that if a case of a freely falling body that does not fall according to the ratio $S = \frac{1}{2}gt^2$ or a moral person who is unjust should be found, (1) and/or (2) would be rejected. But, as we have said, if a thousand cases of persons who are unjust could be cited, we might still assert (3), because it says that in all cases one *ought* to be just. Nor can (3) be viewed as a definition since it does not purport to be a definition nor does it have the form of one. And since being a person does not involve being just, it cannot be viewed as analytic either.

We must conclude, therefore, that moral principles are in essence different from legislative acts and from laws of nature.

### Tests of Proposed Moral Principles

All of these considerations are interesting; but, practically speaking, are they important? An ethics which has no bearing on morals is not even an ethics. This is true even though the ethicist is not concerned with actual behavior. The moral situation still remains the place where the ethical theory is observed in concrete form. The things which we have been discussing – the form and characteristics of moral principles – should be of use in deciding whether, for example, an appeal to a moral principle is sincere, or a screen to delude oneself, or to explain away or excuse an immoral act.

Consider our previous example. When your friend to whom you have promised to lend some money, asks for the loan, you find it somewhat inconvenient to keep your promise. So you say, "I shouldn't inconvenience myself in order to keep a promise," and refuse to make the loan. Does your remark constitute a moral principle? If we apply the test of universality, we see immediately that it cannot be a moral principle, because you want it to hold for yourself only. If the tables were turned and you had depended on your friend's promise, you most certainly would say that he should lend you the money since he had promised to do so and everyone ought to keep promises even if they resulted in personal inconvenience.

Or take another example. Suppose in a given society, to kill a weaker neighbor and take his wife was an act universally accepted as the right thing to do. Would it be moral? Since one cannot consider oneself morally obligated to do such things, such acts cannot be considered moral. In other words, our reflections on the nature of moral principles can be eminently practical since they provide criteria for the solution of moral problems and the evaluation of actions, even those approved by a given culture.

### Moral Principles as Universal Premises

This leads us to examine the way in which moral principles are used when moral decisions are being made. When a person is trying to decide what to do, for example to keep a promise or not, he may engage in some such reflection as this: "I promised to lend Bill fifty dollars. Now he wants to borrow the money. Right now, to lend him fifty dollars would mean that I couldn't take that trip I wanted. But then, I did make a promise to lend him the money and *one ought to keep one's promises if possible.* I suppose, therefore, I don't take that trip."

The underlined statement is, quite obviously, the moral principle to which appeal is made, and which provides the basis for the conclusion. The loan must be made, precisely because the promise to do so is seen as an instance of the class of promises and one ought to keep promises. The moral principle stands as a universal premise in the argument. In this respect, it is like the major premise of an ordinary deductive argument such as:

All men are mortal.
Socrates is a man.

_____

Therefore, Socrates is mortal.

The assertion that all men are mortal is the parallel of the assertion that all men ought to keep their promises. And the singular statement, "Socrates is mortal," is the parallel of "This promise to loan money is a promise." Just as the two statements "All men are mortal" and "Socrates is mortal" state something about what is or is assumed to be the case, so also do "All men ought to keep their promises" and "This promise to loan money is a promise."

Whenever, therefore, one tries to arrive at a moral decision, he seeks to subsume some act under a moral principle as an instance of that principle. The situation is exactly identical with what the jurist and lawyer try to do in legal arguments. The moral principle alone, being a universal, does not help us to decide what to do until it has been shown, or in some way it is known, that the act about to be performed (or avoided) is a case to which the principle applies.

Even exceptions to the application of a moral principle bear out this procedure. Consider again the example of lending money to a friend. The person who promises to do so usually feels that he ought to keep his promise. But if he discovers that his friend intends to use the money to buy heroin, (or to bribe a police officer), he might reason as follows: "True, a promise ought to be kept, but not if it violates some other equally valid moral principle. One ought not to keep a promise made under the impression that it will help a friend, if one discovers that the consequences will be worse than those of not keeping the promise. One ought not to do what will bring evil, knowing that it will do so." For clarity this argument might be summed up as follows:

One ought not to do what will result in evil consequences.
Keeping my promise to lend Bill money will result in evil.

_____

Therefore, I ought not to keep my promise in this case.

Briefly, it is being argued that cases where the money to be used for evil purposes are not cases in which the principles to keep one's promises apply. Some other moral principle is given precedence. The new moral principle which is invoked is related to the promise to lend the money as a generalization is to a particular instance in precisely the same fashion as the loaning of money is related to the moral principle, "One ought to keep one's promises." Evidently if there is no statement asserting the existence of a particular instance, there can be no decision on what to do. So, the second premise in a moral decision must be a statement of fact, and then the conclusion will enunciate a decision. The more refined logical considerations need not concern us here.

## Moral Principles as Moral Justification

The converse process to arriving at a moral decision is to justify an act as moral. The moral syllogism as we have just considered it contained a moral principle, a statement of subsumption, and a decision. Moral justification, then, would consist in showing that the act in question was indeed subsumed under the class of acts enjoined by the moral principle.

Suppose someone says, "I ought to do whatever I like. I like to hurt people and to cheat. Hence, I ought to hurt people and cheat." Such a claim if it is intended to be justified morally in this fashion, must be rejected. "I ought to do whatever I like" is not a moral principle, since anyone who proposes it intends it to be true only for himself and would not require it to be true for anyone else. It is not binding upon any other person. Moreover, if the intention is to universalize the statement, it is still not binding because no basis except feeling could be offered to support its universality, and feeling is an individual matter.

Unless, therefore, an act can be subsumed under a moral principle, it cannot be morally justified.

The importance of an understanding of the form and characteristics of moral principles cannot be underestimated.

## Summary

We have seen that moral principles are expressed as
1) statements containing the word "ought" which
2) imply an obligation which connotes
3) command.

We have discovered that moral principles are
4) autonomous, i.e., are independent of ulterior goals, (categorical)
5) unconditional, i.e., involve commands that are completely unconditional and binding
6) independent of rewards or punishments.

In logical form moral principles
   1) are universal,
   2) have as their logical subject "everyone"
   3) are a priori, i.e., their truth transcends space and time limitations.

BIBLIOGRAPHY

Kant, I., *Fundamental Principles of the Metaphysic of Morals,* (New York: Liberal Arts Press), pp. 3–23.

Kneale, William, "Objectivity in Morals," *Philosophy,* **XXV** (1950). Also in Sellars and Hospers (especially Part I).

Lamont, W. C., *The Principles of Moral Judgment,* (Oxford: Clarendon Press, 1946), Chap. 1.

Mandelbaum, M., *The Phenomenology of Moral Experience,* (Illinois: The Free Press, 1955), Chap. 2.

# CHAPTER IV

# MORAL PRINCIPLES: HEDONISM

We have seen that moral principles are principles used as criteria when we are called upon to make moral decisions. A next step in the understanding of moral decisions, therefore, is to find out what the moral principles are to which people do as a matter of fact appeal.

## The Appeal to Happiness

One of the most common of moral principles places happiness above all other things. In the light of the happiness principle, honesty, for example, is considered a moral virtue either because it makes society possible or because in the long run people will be happier by being honest than by being dishonest. If one asks why society is desirable, he will very likely be told that people live happier lives in a society than outside one. To take another example, it is not unusual to hear someone say, "In the case of a man like Hitler, the world would have been happier if he had been killed as a child." If this were challenged on the grounds that killing, even of a Hitler, is immoral, conceivably the challenge would be phrased as follows: "Once you allow killing, even of a Hitler, to be viewed as moral, there is no telling where it will stop. People will go about killing others and life will become brutish and short. More happiness will be achieved if killing is considered immoral." Both antagonists in this argument are appealing to the moral principle which declares that happiness ought to be sought. They differ only in what act they believe will be most conducive to happiness.

## Justification by Consequences

We must be careful to keep in mind that we are not interested at this point in justifying principles as principles, but only in explicating them and examining the ease or difficulty of applying them. So in these examples, we are concerned not to demonstrate that the principle "One ought to seek happiness" is proved to be a valid moral principle by the consequences of acting upon it but to assume that it is a moral principle and show what it means and how one, by means of the consequences, justifies *doing a specific act.*

Let me illustrate the distinction. Suppose someone wants to rob a friend. He may attempt to anticipate the sort of consequences that will result to see whether or not robbing his friend will lead to more happiness than refraining from doing so. He concludes that, the risks being too great, he will refrain. The consequences are evaluated in terms of the degree of happiness they will contain. They are not used to justify the principle "One ought to seek happiness" for this is the criterion in terms of which the consequences are justified. The anticipated consequences justified refraining from robbing the friend, but they did not show the principle to be a valid one.

### The Hedonistic Principle

The principle under consideration may be formulated in the following terms. "One ought to seek happiness." Even a cursory examination shows this to be a moral principle. It serves as a premise in making decisions. It is universal and purports to be necessary and binding. Because this principle involves the notion of happiness, we refer to it as a hedonistic principle, from the Greek word, "hedone," meaning "pleasure." Many hedonists have equated pleasure with happiness. We are here concerned with this form of hedonism.

The following will illustrate how a decision may be made with the hedonistic principle as a premise:

> One ought to seek happiness.
> Being kind promotes happiness.
> _____
> Therefore, being kind ought to be done. (or) One ought to be kind.

It is possible to make the conclusion more specific as follows:

> Being kind ought to be done.
> If I lend you money, I am being kind.
> _____
> Therefore, I ought to lend you money.

Furthermore, if I define "right" to denote the quality which those things have that ought to be done, then I can say "Being kind is right" or "Lending you money is right." All of these conclusions are ultimately justified by the hedonistic principle.

## Empirical Questions

If the hedonistic principle is accepted in some form, then a decision to act or refrain from action depends upon whether or not the act promotes happiness. To decide whether to accept the argument stated above, we need to discover whether or not being kind does in fact promote happiness. This is an empirical task.

In all cases in which the hedonistic principle is used, the decision rests upon some factual statement of the sort described. Should you be honest? Yes, if it promotes happiness. Should you refrain from injuring a person? Yes, if it promotes happiness. Should you sacrifice your interests for others? Yes, if it promotes happiness.

The answer to each question comes rather easily. But consider this question: Should a person sacrifice his own life for another's happiness? Anyone who seriously contemplates sacrificing his own life for another's happiness will surely consider the matter at length. Whoever sacrifices his own life certainly makes it impossible to promote his own happiness any more. In fact, if he dies, his happiness, no matter how small, vanishes and the total amount of happiness in the world is diminished. However, this consideration may be irrelevant because the principle, as so far formulated, doesn't say anything about the total amount of happiness, but only about happiness. The presumably factual statement turns out to be ambiguous.

There is the further complication that the word "happiness" itself turns out to be vague. If I sacrifice my life for the safety of my family, let us say, I might save them, but can one say that they are happy as a result? Perhaps they would have preferred that I live, even though this condemns them to unhappiness, than that I die and they be happy. To say of a man's family that they would be happier if he died, has a rather immoral tone, unless we mean "happy" in a sense rather different from the ordinary one. How then can we say that the second premise is empirical if the key word in the principle is vague and ambiguous?

## Modification of the Hedonistic Principle

These ambiguities in the statement of the hedonistic principle may be removed by giving it one or the other of two more specific formulations. The principle may be altered to read:

> One ought to do what promotes his own happiness.

Or it may be stated:

> One ought to do what promotes the greatest happiness for the greatest number of people.

The first of these is called the principle of "egoistic hedonism"; the second, that of "universalistic hedonism" (or "utilitarianism").

Egoistic hedonism is a rather strange doctrine because we commonly find two contrasting attitudes associated with it. First, there is the widespread feeling often expressed in some such way as, "You must look out for number one" (i.e., your first care is yourself); or, "Self-preservation is the first law of life"; or again, "Why should I give a hoot about anyone else's happiness except as it leads to mine?"

Yet while we do commonly find such expressions used, we also find a tendency to condemn anyone who by his action has sought his own happiness. For example, if John Doe donates a million dollars to establish a library or a hospital, we may praise him. But let it be discovered that he did so because of the happiness he would derive from the gift, and we tend to think of the gift as somehow tainted, and John Doe as of lesser stature.

## The Relation of Happiness to Acts

The difference in attitudes here turns on the question of John Doe's motives. Consider the statement, "John Doe derives happiness from doing charitable deeds." This could mean either of two things. It might mean that John Doe does charitable deeds *because* of the pleasure, i.e., happiness, he derives from doing them. In this sense, John Doe is not so much concerned with doing charitable deeds as he is with getting rewarded with happiness. If he discovered that he could obtain greater happiness doing something else, that is what he would do. Charity is for John Doe, in this case, merely a means to an end – happiness.

But the statement that John Doe gets happiness from doing charitable deeds may have a second meaning. It may mean that John Doe is so constituted that when he acts charitably he is happy. Here the happiness is not the reason why he acts charitably but a concomitant of that kind of behavior. John Doe would (or might) do these deeds even if he did not get from them the happiness which he does. If happiness is the goal he seeks through acts of charity, we would consider him a lesser person than one who admittedly did obtain happiness through such acts but did them because they were charitable acts, or because God commanded he do such deeds, or for some other worthy reason. We ordinarily consider a person who is made happy by doing virtuous acts, but made unhappy when acting immorally, as a fine, upright, moral individual. When the distinction between seeking happiness deliberately and getting happiness as a byproduct of good deeds is thus perceived, the divergence in popular attitudes becomes understandable. A grasp of the distinction will also help us to define egoistic hedonism.

The term "egoistic hedonism" refers to the moral principle that asserts that everyone ought to seek his own happiness. The egoistic hedonist acts charitably so far as he believes that by doing so he will obtain happiness. If being charitable brings happiness to him, the act is moral; if it brings unhappiness, the act is immoral. Acting morally is for him, seeking happiness. Therefore, if he is moral, he is happy – by definition. The converse would also be true; if he is happy, he is moral. In fact, he defines a moral act as one which does lead to *his* own happiness. And he says that an act which conforms to the principle of egoistic hedonism is "right."

## Egoistic Dilemmas

When egoistic hedonism elevates one's own happiness to the highest pinnacle, new problems arise. Consider this sort of situation. A and B are taking competitive examinations, let us say, for admission to some professional school. A is trying to decide whether or not it is right for him to cheat. So he debates with himself in this way: "If I don't pass this examination, I will not be admitted to professional school. This will make my parents and my sweetheart very unhappy for obvious reasons. It will also make me unhappy because my future will be radically altered and because I do not like to see my loved ones unhappy. If I cheat, I will be very happy since these results will not follow. Hence, since it is right for me to do what leads to my happiness, it is right for me to cheat."

Now, it is true that one may retort that A *really* will be unhappy if he cheats because his conscience will trouble him, or his parents may, if they find out, be disappointed, or some other such possibilities. To all of this A may reply, "I'll take my chances; but in any case I think I'll get more happiness by cheating." So his conclusion is that his act of cheating is right, since, in all likelihood, it will lead to his happiness (or greater happiness).

But B says, "If A cheats, then he will get an unfair advantage. In fact, he may get so good a grade that he will be selected for professional school in preference to me. This will make me unhappy whereas if he does not cheat, I will get the appointment and my happiness will be great. Therefore, since an act is right if it conduces to my happiness, A's cheating cannot be right since it leads to my unhappiness."

This is a dilemma. The same act – namely A's cheating – is declared right by A and wrong by B. Since this can obviously be generalized, the principle of egoistic hedonism seems to require that, instead of saving, "The act is right (or wrong)," we should say, "The act is right (or wrong) for ——————," always in a specific case inserting a proper name or definite description in the blank space. One can urge that this is not surprising and would be accepted by anyone who has committed himself to the principle of egoistic hedonism. Why not say that an act is right for some given individual, even if it happens to be wrong for others at the same time. But this will not eleminate the difficulty for the following reasons.

Let us consider more carefully the principle of egoistic hedonism. If it is, as it claims to be, a moral principle, then it is binding upon every-one as a standard. But if I accept it as a standard, I cannot seriously de-fend the proposition that another person ought to act in such a way that his act lead to *my* happiness. If I say that egoistic hedonism is valid, then others ought to act so as to bring happiness to themselves and I to my-self, and everyone to himself. If my happiness also makes someone else happy, that is a fortunate accident, but it is really irrelevant. Therefore, the same deed can be both what ought to be done and what ought not to be done.

True, there may be no real contradiction between the two statements: "The act is right for me (L. O. Kattsoff)," and "The act is wrong for me (John Doe)." But neither is there any possibility of agreement, for even if I say: "The act is right for me (L. O. Kattsoff)," and another says "The act is right for me (John Doe)," the two sentences are differ-ent since "me" refers to two distinct individuals in the two sentences. The same act may bring happiness to me and unhappiness to you. When we disagree, however, on the rightness of the act, we do not disagree on the question whether it does or does not bring you happiness. This could be relatively easy to determine, but a disagreement about the rightness or wrongness of an act is not resolved by the remark that it is right for me. Disagreement about the rightness of an act consists in disagreement about the subsumption of the act under the moral principle used as the major premise. If an act is right, it is justified by the moral principle and the same act cannot both be justified and not justified by the same moral principle. In brief, egoistic hedonism is inadequate even if it might be meaningful, since it makes ultimate agreement in the case of moral disagreement impossible. These reasons may not appear conclusive unless it is recognized that if an act is right, it is right for everyone. This is to say that egoistic hedonism in principle cannot conform to the form of a moral principle. The very nature of a moral principle is such that it implies the resolution of moral disagreements in principle. We shall discuss this later.

### Some Difficulties of the Hedonistic Calculus

But there are still other reasons for concluding that the principle of egoistic hedonism is not as clear as it appears to be. Take a case of this sort. Suppose it is true that deep down in us there lurks a Mr. Hyde, who every once in a while gains control of the Dr. Jekyll in us. Now Mr. Hyde is a peculiar sort of person – he gets a great deal of happiness from inflicting pain on others. Mr. Hyde knows about Dr. Jekyll but he considers Dr. Jekyll to be a strange aberration of his true nature. When Mr. Hyde is questioned about his deeds he replies, "Ah, yes! I am an egoistic hedonist. I believe I ought to do what brings me happiness." Very few people would agree with him. In fact, even egoistic hedonists would, in all likelihood, demur because not many people believe that the happiness obtained by degenerates is the right kind of happiness. There is involved a difference in kind between the happiness of different types of individuals.

The case under discussion enmeshes the egoistic hedonist in a special difficulty. Is an act right (or wrong) when it is conducive to the happiness of Mr. Hyde but makes Dr. Jekyll unhappy? Here the same act is involved and two aspects of the same person, not two different persons.

Lest this seem an extravagantly fictitious sort of example, remember that psychoanalysis tells us that there is a little bit of sadism and even masochism in the best of us. Furthermore, there are individuals who develop dual personalities, like the woman who was part of the time a prim, moral, typical old-maid school teacher, and at other times a flamboyant woman of the streets, who took up with a man at the slightest suggestion of a whistle.

Egoistic hedonism apparently must assume that not all persons are alike and in consequence that only certain, let us say, normal people can legitimately use its principle as their standard. A Mr. Hyde, for example, is not normal and, therefore, cannot appeal to the happiness principle in justification of his behavior. A corollary of this assumption is that we either rank types of happiness on the basis of some principle, or reject some methods for attaining happiness, or consider that what a degenerate calls happiness really is not happiness. But any one of these assumptions involves the surrender of the egoistic hedonist's principle.

All of this may seem complicated, but the point is simple. If egoistic hedonism is to be valid only when certain conditions are met, then egoistic hedonism is not a moral principle, since it is not universal and cannot be considered binding.

In brief, since for a moral principle to serve adequately as a premise when moral decisions are being made it must be precise and complete, the principle of egoistic hedonism is inadequate. This principle is essentially vague and incomplete as is apparent from the criticisms we have levelled against it. If we attempt to modify the principle in the light of these criticisms, it could be rephrased as follows:

> I (John Doe), being the right sort of person, ought to do what brings me the kind of happiness the right sort of person desires.

This evidently changes the principle, because it no longer asserts egoism but rather

> One ought to do what is conducive to the happiness of the right sort of persons.

This form of the principle must be rejected, however, because it appears to violate the principle of justice. Why seek the happiness of the right sort of persons; why not of everyone?

Even if we accept this form of the principle of egoistic hedonism, further objections may be raised in connection with the concept of happiness. Consider a situation in which someone faces the question whether to lie about the quality of his house and sell it at a good profit, or tell the truth and take a loss. Let us assume the owner is anxious to be a consistent egoistic hedonist and therefore wants to decide what to do on the basis of the happiness his action will bring to him. He may list all the consequences of lying and note that many of them will bring him happiness. For example, he anticipates all the happiness he will get out of the car he will buy with the profit. But he recognizes that he must also take into account the uneasiness that he will feel as a result of telling the lie.

Two questions arise: (1) How will the owner weigh the happiness he will get from the profits as against the unhappiness from telling a lie? Moreover, how can he compute the net happiness he will derive from telling the truth in the face of the loss of happiness he will experience from not being able to get a new car? (2) Must he consider the possible eventuality that if he buys the car, he may be involved in a wreck and perhaps be seriously injured? This is to ask, "How do we decide what are the consequences?" Shall we, for example, consider the consequences that occur during the first year or those that occur during the first ten years?

These are not necessarily fatal objections to egoistic hedonism but they do raise significant questions of application and reveal certain points of vagueness. Since egoistic hedonism necessitates a consideration of consequences of a certain sort, it needs to supply criteria for determining how to select among the infinite array of possible consequences; it needs to define how to evaluate consequences in terms of the amount of happiness that will result; it needs to distinguish between the different types of happiness open. (For example, should the happiness that comes from home-ownership outweigh that from car-ownership?) If these questions cannot be answered in a satisfactory fashion, how can anyone use the principle as a guide to action?

### Are Consequences Within the Power of Men?

In order to evaluate the resultant happiness that will follow a given act, the consequences of that act must be anticipated to some degree. The egoistic hedonist makes a tacit factual assumption. We have said that for morality to be possible, the ability to choose must be presupposed. Egoistic hedonism assumes that a man can select what he wants to do in the light of an evaluation of consequences. The determination of a future course of action depends from this point of view upon the assumption that consequences cannot only be predicted but even brought into existence by a present choice.

But are not consequences beyond the control of men – at least for the most part? Suppose the house is sold at a profit. How can one know that the owner will be able to buy the car, or drive it? Perhaps the lie will cause the owner to be mistrusted; or perhaps – so many things can happen. Are we to say that a person is moral when he is at the mercy of events? If, therefore, the principle posits something impossible, is it not thereby invalidated as a principle? In brief, egoistic hedonism assumes that a practical choice is possible that will determine the course of events, and that it is meaningful to calculate the resultant happiness and unhappiness of that choice.

This assumption that choice is possible and events can be controlled are not unique to egoistic hedonism but are implicit in every type of teleological ethics, i.e., in any system that defines moral behavior in terms of consequences of any sort. Nor does the principle provide any clear help toward deciding which consequences will bring the most happiness. In sum, the principle is vague both with respect to what consequences are to be selected as relevant in calculating resultant happiness and with respect to how the greatest amount of happiness may be achieved.

## What is Happiness?

People who maintain that the principle of egoistic hedonism is a sound one may be irritated by the criticisms and objections we have raised. In an attempt to justify its use in the face of what has been said, the hedonist may insist that even though the principle is vague and not clearly understood, yet all people do seek happiness. And in particular he may affirm his own quest for it. We must try to understand what the hedonist is here affirming. His new contention contains the following two assertions at least:

(1) People do seek their happiness.
(2) My happiness is what I propose to seek.

The first is a statement asserting something to be a fact. As such it can only be checked by empirical tests. The statement may be denied, but if it is, the correctness of the denial is established by finding at least one person who doesn't seek his own happiness. We shall consider this point later when we ask how the fact that people do seek their happiness can justify the principle of egoistic hedonism. At this point we remark that if we want to decide whether to steal, or lie, or do something else that is wrong, to be told that people seek their happiness doesn't help at all unless (1) is meant to be identical with the principle. In this case, however, (1) doesn't tell us any more than we already know when we affirm the principle of egoistic hedonism.

The second statement is also a statement of fact – a declaration of the speaker. If he is telling the truth, the statement is true, but again it doesn't help much for we are not interested in what the speaker intends to do but rather in whether he ought to do it.

Even granting that people do seek happiness and the speaker intends to seek his own happiness, we are still confronted with the problem of what it is we are seeking when we seek happiness. What does "happiness" mean? "Happiness" is a noun and as such it presumably denotes something. But when a person has happiness, he doesn't prossess any particular sort of thing at all. "One *is* happy" is a more correct thing to say than "One *has* happiness." To seek happiness is to seek to be in a state of a certain kind.

What kind of state is "being happy"? Many and diverse replies have been offered. Aristotle said that when one is in a state of intellectual activity, then he is happy. Quite possibly many people will deny this, pointing out that when one is deeply involved in intellectual activity, he is unaware of such things as being happy. Some stoics thought that happiness is best described as a state of absence of pain. This too is certain to be rejected, for if happiness is but the absence of pain, a person under deep anaesthesia would be happy. Christians may hold that one is happy only as he is united with God. This would mean that very few people are happy. "Men of the world" often insist that happiness consists in pleasure. But it is possible that one may immerse himself in pleasures and yet by that very fact indicate how unhappy he is.

All of the foregoing attempts to define "happiness" equate it with something else. But it may be objected that what we directly seek is not happiness as such, but some particular way of securing it, e.g., intellectual activity, union with God, etc. We may then prefer to say that happiness is an indefinable psychological state; that these other things help to bring it about but that they are not it.

As was observed previously, the attempt to explain the principle of egoistic hedonism as an assertion of fact does little to clarify the discussion. The egoistic hedonist is not clearer about pleasure or happiness when he asserts that people do seek their own happiness, than he was when he insisted that people ought to seek it. But more to the point, what he has done is to change the problem from one that concerns a moral principle into one that concerns human psychology.

The distinction between the two concerns is indicated by the notable fact that people whom we praise highly as being quite virtuous are often not happy. Nearly everyone would admit that one ought to be honest; yet honesty may lead to unhappiness. And it does no good to say that a person who is honest is *really* happier than one who isn't. He often isn't.

### Transition to Universalistic Hedonism

Actually the egoistic hedonist values happiness not simply because it is his happiness but because he likes happiness. Suppose someone says, "I will kill you because it will make me happy." Now why should he want to be happy? His answer can only be, "Because I like to be happy; i.e., happiness is something I want for myself." If he is asked, "Why do you want happiness?" his answer might be, "Because it is good in itself. I want it for its own sake and not for somethnig else." In technical language he is declaring happiness to be an *intrinsic* good.

If he admits this, then he is really saying that his principle is different from what it appeared to be. If happiness is intrinsically good, then certainly each one of us ought to seek it, and that means everyone ought to. And not merely ought we seek is for ourselves but for its own sake. This suggests that what we are using as our moral principle may be expressed as follows:

One ought to do what promotes happiness.

The egoistic aspect is eliminated since evidently the general happiness may be diminished by seeking only one's own happiness. And conversely by getting less happiness for oneself a greater amount of general happiness may ensue because the increase in the happiness of others may more than balance the loss of one's own. For example, the happiness a soldier loses by sacrificing himself may be more than offset by the happiness he makes possible for his countrymen. If it is happiness that one ought to seek and for its own sake, then the more happiness the better, and the most possible happiness, the best of all.

In this way we arrive at the *Principle of Utilitarianism* enunciated by Jeremy Bentham and John Stuart Mill. It is perhaps best to quote the words of Mill as they occur in Chapter 2 of his book, *Utilitarianism.*

The creed which accepts as the foundation of morals "utility" or the "greatest happiness principle" holds that actions are right in proportion as they tend to promote happiness, wrong as they tend to produce the reverse of happiness. By happiness is intended pleasure, and the absence of pain; by unhappiness, pain, and the privation of pleasure.

And a bit later Mill adds:

... the happiness which forms the utilitarian standard of what is right in conduct is not the agent's own happiness but that of all concerned.

The following illustration will indicate the meaning of what Mill is saying and at the same time reveal some of the difficulties in applying his standard. Mr. A. promises to help his neighbor Mr. B paint his barn on a given date. When the time comes to fulfill the promise and B asks for help, A finds that he had made another important engagement for that same date. To decide which promise to keep, A, as a utilitarian, needs to calculate which course of action would lead to the greatest happiness for the greatest number of people concerned. But, clearly enough, this demands some decisions as to what people are concerned. Certainly B is immediately concerned that A keep his promise to him; but so it the person to whom A made the second promise concerned that he keep *that* promise.

*Difficulties of the Hedonistic Calculus*

That both people to whom A made promises are concerned is obvious, but are there not others who also would be concerned? For example, one might ask whether, in making the decision, A should consider B's son if extra help for his father would mean that the son could then go fishing? And what about the fish-dealer who might lose a sale if the son caught some fish on a trip that was made possible only because A kept his promise to B? This may sound far-fetched; yet there are times when one's decision affects people in distant places as surely as it affects his neighbor.

Technically speaking, utilitarianism presents more difficulties than egoistic hedonism in this respect. If a person makes his decisions simply in terms of his own happiness, that's that. He has no real problem about whom to consider and how to distribute the happiness unless he has a dual personality. But when his decisions are made in terms of an attempt to maximize the happiness of many persons, the situation, as we have seen, may be quite complicated. Utilitarianism offers us no guide in this matter. In fact, when a Utilitarian is confronted with this problem, he tends either to some form of tribalism or to an indeterminate universalism. That is, he identifies the happiness of "all" with that of some limited group, for example, the people of his own church, or state. Or else he includes more or less indiscriminately the Arab peasant, Chinese coolie, and Tennessee mountaineer. In some few instances it may be possible to delimit the group of interested parties without too much difficulty but this does not happen often.

Some other principle than a moral one may at times be invoked to delimit the class of interested parties. The doctor (cited in Chapter 2) who faced the question of denouncing the abortionist might have considered, as the abortionist himself must have done, only the people in town or only the immediate families of the seducer and the seduced, or he might have tried to include in his calculations the happiness of the as yet unborn baby. The man who faced the question of lying to sell his house might have considered only himself and his immediate family, or he might have considered the buyer and his family also. Ought he not to have been mindful of the happiness of future home-buyers as well? The phrase, "interested parties," is so vague as to be meaningless unless areas of interest are defined on the basis of some principle other than a moral one. So the Nazis considered the happiness of Aryans as alone important; Christians consider the happiness of every single person of equal importance. Both of these groups have determined who ought to be considered on the basis of principles which are not moral but rather in the one case racial and in the other theological.

It must be emphasized that these difficulties do not sum up to a refutation of the principle of utilitarianism, but they do throw doubt on its serviceability as a norm for making moral decisions. All of the considerations show that, in general, the utilitarian principle is difficult to apply and its meaning is not always clear.

*The Utilitarian Definition: Happiness = Pleasure Plus Absence of Pain*

Christianity with principles truly universal and Nazi-ism with tribal principles not only define the extent of interested persons differently, they also define happiness in contrasting terms. Mill did try to make the notion of happiness more precise by defining it as pleasure plus the absence of pain. But this definition is hardly more satisfactory than Mill's reference to the happiness of "all concerned."

Consider such an expression as this: "He doesn't have many of the pleasures of life, but he is very happy." Such a remark might be made of a man who goes to a mission hospital in some jungle area and lives among primitive peoples. Why is he happy? Because, presumably, he is doing something he feels is significant and important. More illuminating is the expression: "He has all the pleasures he wants but he is still unhappy." Here what apparently is meant is that the person can and does have certain experiences which are pleasurable. He can eat what appeals to his taste, hear the music that pleases him, and see the pleasant things in life. But despite all this he feels unloved or unwanted. Amidst all his pleasures, he is unhappy.

In common speech we usually associate pleasure with things of the senses. Happiness is different. Although we can say of a person, "He is happiest when eating steaks," we don't quite mean that to be taken literally. It is rather more appropriate to say, "He gets the most pleasure from eating steaks." Happiness is more a matter of a psychological attitude related to a general state of the individual. Intellectual pleasures, so-called, are not really "pleasures" but are enjoyable activities.

In everyday language, there is often no sharp distinction made between these terms because we enjoy both pleasure and happiness. But if happiness is to be pleasure plus the absence of pain, then the two must be different, otherwise all that is being said is that happiness is happiness without pain, which is trivial; or that happiness is the absence of pain, and that is clearly not so. But if they are not the same and if our discussion of their difference is correct, then the equation breaks down because one can be happy even in pain with no attendant pleasure; as when we say of a man that he died happy even though in pain. Martyrs burning at the stake can hardly be said to be experiencing pleasure and evidently the pain must be intense; nevertheless it makes sense to say they died happy in the thought that they were going to meet God.

It is indeed unfortunate that happiness cannot be equated simply with the absence of pain, since then the application of the principle would be easy. All we would need is a sufficient quantity of "pain-killers." This, however, is evident nonsense. We must conclude that, generally speaking, Mill's definition (if it be such) is not adequate for making a decision to do something.

### The Utilitarian Dimensions of Happiness

But if we accepted this principle we still would need to compare and evaluate consequent pleasures and pains. Bentham tried to describe the various dimensions one would need to measure in order to arrive at an adequate weighting of pleasures. These he lists as follows:

1. intensity
2. duration
3. certainty or uncertainty
4. propinquity or remoteness
5. fecundity
6. purity
7. extent

This is quite complex. John Doe wants to kill his neighbor for his money and tries to evaluate his act. He weighs the pleasure he will get from the act and from having the money. Will the money give him a pleasure of greater or less intensity? How long will that pleasure last? Is it certain that he will get that pleasure? Will he have it now or later? Will the pleasure be followed by other pleasures of the kind one gets by having the money. (fecundity)? Will pains result (purity)? John Doe puts a value on the pleasure, then he considers the number of persons affected, and takes that into consideration. If anyone really tried to apply this method to arrive at a decision he never would kill his neighbor, not because the principle prohibited the act but because he would never get around to the act.

In the case of other kinds of acts the problem of choice-making is not so difficult. Someone wants to choose between kissing his wife and kissing his secretary (or neighbor's wife). Here perhaps the evaluation is easier, but the result becomes a function of the particular type of person involved. Some people might get a pleasure of much greater intensity and duration by restricting their kissing activities to their wives – not even taking account of the purity of the pleasure (in Bentham's sense of course). Others might be intrigued by the very fact that pains might follow such extra-marital osculations. Such a consequence, however, may, like the principle of egoistic hedonism, make agreement on moral problems virtually impossible. If the calculation contains a variable that depends upon the calculator, the result can hardly be called objective. In addition, the fact that the decision becomes a function of the person involved brings the principle close to egoistic hedonism.

## The Validity of Utilitarianism as a Principle

Yet, after all is said, there still remains a definite element of truth in the principle of utilitarianism, at least from the point of view of ordinary people. If an act will result in consequences that make for a great deal of pain and unhappiness – other things being equal – we do feel it wrong to commit the act. Of two equally intense pleasures consequent upon a given act, we do feel we ought to seek the one that endures longer. We do feel that people ought to do what makes the greatest number of people happiest. Utilitarianism, in other words, leads people to attempt to live better lives and to improve the conditions of life.

Yet, what Utilitarianism judges is the *act* and not the *actor*. A person, may, on its basis, act evilly and yet do the moral thing. For example, he may have wanted to do harm but, because he was not able to control the consequences of his act, what he did turned out to be beneficial. Thus a politician might spread false rumors about his opponent, but by doing so engender so much sympathy for his opponent that the latter would thereby gain votes. Surely, in this case, even if one wanted to judge the act moral, the person is not.

In this chapter we were not asking whether or not people do always seek happiness. (The theory that asserts that they do is called "psychological hedonism.") We were concerned to explain the meaning of the principle of moral hedonism and see if it could serve as a moral principle. The relation between what people do and moral principles will be discussed later when we consider the possible justification of hedonism as a premise in moral decisions.

BIBLIOGRAPHY

*Primary sources*
Bentham, Jeremy, *An Introduction to the Principles of Morals and Legislation* (Selections) in A. I. Melden, ed., *Ethical Theories,* 2nd Edition (New York: Prentice-Hall, 1955), pp. 341–365.

Mill, J. S., *Utilitarianism* (New York: Liberal Arts Press, 1948).

Schlick, M., *Problems of Ethics,* trans. by D. Rynin (New York: Prentice-Hall, 1939).

*Secondary sources*

Bradley, F. H., *Ethical Studies,* Selected Essays (New York: Liberal Arts Press, 1952), pp. 29–81.

Ewing, A. C., *Ethics* (London: English Universities Press, 1953), Chapter III, pp. 35–51.

Garvin, Lucius, *A Modern Introduction to Ethics* (Boston and New York: Houghton Mifflin Co., 1953), Chapters 10 and 11, pp. 256–314.

Hill, T. E., *Ethics in Theory and Practice* (New York: T. Y. Crowell, 1956), Chapter 10, pp. 152–181.

Titus, H. H., *Ethics for Today,* 2nd Edition (New York: American Book Company, 1947), Chapter X, pp. 153–167.

Tsanoff, R. A., *Moral Ideals of Our Civilization* (New York: E. P. Dutton, 1942), Chapter XXXI, pp. 486–513.

# CHAPTER V

# THEOLOGICAL MORALS

If it were possible to take a poll of the American people on the question, "To what moral principle do you appeal most frequently?" we would probably find that, next to hedonism, the most frequent appeal was made to a principle which referred to God's will. It is quite commonplace to hear such remarks as: "You ought not to steal, for it is against God's will"; or "Murder and rape are contrary to God's will, and no God-fearing people do such things." The Ten Commandments are reverned because they are taken as expressions of God's will. The Golden Rule is authoritative precisely because it too is held to be an expression of God's will.

## The Appeal to God's Will

The moral syllogism that ends in a moral decision for one who accepts a theological morals might look like the following argument:

> One ought to act in accordance with God's will.
> Doing justice is in accordance with Gods' will.
> _____
> Therefore, one ought to do justice.

As before, the second premise subsumes a particular kind of action under the type of actions that accord with God's will. On this basis, the moral person is, by definition, one who acts in accordance with God's will, and the immoral person, one who goes counter to that divine will. So, too, an act is "right" if it accords with God's will, wrong if it does not.

Let us illustrate the application of this principle to the specific problem of suicide. It is conceivable that a potential suicide might try to decide whether he is doing right in committing suicide. People who contemplate suicide do at times refrain because they believe that it is immoral. Let us assume that this would-be suicide believes that acts are right or wrong according as they do or do not conform with God's will, and so he sets about trying to determine what God's will is. Does God will that the suicide be committed? Before the person can decide how to act, he must somehow discover what God's will is in the matter. If he decides that suicide is counter to God's will, then he will also decide that it is wrong to commit it.

### God's Will not a Cause

For an understanding of the principle underlying theological morality, attention must be paid to an important distinction. The statement, "If God does not will the suicide, then the act is wrong," is ambiguous. It may be interpreted in either of two ways:

> (a)  Because suicide is wrong God does not will it.
> (b)  Suicide is wrong because it is contrary to God's will.

In (a) "because" introduces a *reason* or *sign* in evidence of suicide's being wrong. In (b) "because" introduces a *definition* of the *meaning* of wrongness.

Strictly speaking, the principle of theological ethics is represented in (b) but not in (a). To say that suicide is wrong *because* it is contrary to God's will, may be only to cite the fact that God always wills the good – or what ought to be done. Since he does not will suicide, we may take this as a sign of its being wrong. In other words, the morality or immorality of the act does not *consist in* its relation to God's will, but in its relation to some other fact or principle which serves to cause God to will it or not to will it. Reference to this other principle is beyond the sphere of what theological morals asserts. On the other hand, if saying that suicide is wrong is another way of saying that God does not will suicide, then God himself and not something outside him determines the wrongness of suicide. God decides what is wrong or right by his very act of willing. From such a standpoint, morals is but a branch of theology and has no autonomy of its own. The problem is to discover what God wills and not why God wills it. Clearly, however, fundamental to an understanding of theological morals is some comprehension of the nature of God. What God is, will have definite implications for the interpretation of theological moral principles.

### The Meaning of "God's Will"

What does it mean to say that one ought to act in accordance with God's will? The difficult phrase is "God's will." Does this mean "what God wills" or "what God would want?" In other words, when one is told to do God's will, is he being told to act in such a way as to earn God's approval, or to do what God wills that he do? These are not the same.

If a person does what God wills that he do, then he would presumably be doing what God approves. But he might do what God approves without doing that which God specifically has willed unless it is assumed that whatever God approves he also wills that people do. Whoever makes such an assumption may be asserting that at the time a person is tempted to cheat, God wills that he does or does not commit this specific act of cheating. And since what God wills must happen, this is tantamount to saying that everything that takes place does so by God's specifically willing that particular act. If the assumption is not made that God always wills the specific act that He approves, then people can do what God approves yet not what God wills in that particular instance.

What has just been said reveals another important distinction. Consider the two statements: "It is God's will that you do not cheat," and "God wills that you do not cheat." The former uses "God's will" as a noun, the latter treats it as a verb. Since as a noun the word "will" can be considered to be the agency or faculty that wills, we can restrict our considerations to the verb "to will." In ordinary usage the verb "to will" has at least three distinct connotations. It may mean 1) to command 2) to approve and/or 3) to purpose.

To say that God wills that you do not cheat, implies that God commands that you do not cheat; or that God desires that you do not cheat; or that God wishes that you do not cheat. Let us consider the usage of the verb "to will" in the sense of "to command." In this sense to act in accordance with God's will is to do what God commands. So, if doing justice is in accord with God's will, then that means that God commands one to be just. Now this raises difficulties which need to be faced. To say, "You ought to do God's will," seems to imply that it is possible to act contrary to God's will. A person trying to decide what to do – say, cheat or not, needs somehow to discover whether or not God commands him: "Don't cheat!" This discovery would decide the issue, but the decision to obey God's command must remain with the person since, if it did not, the person could hardly be said to be involved in a moral situation. For example, to be so overcome with fear of God's punishment that you obey without really choosing is to remove yourself as a moral agent since no real choice was involved.

If, however, the decision to obey or disobey God's command not to cheat is that of the person involved, then God's commands do not seem to have the force usually attributed to them. If, as we have seen, "God's will" means "God's command," then may we infer from the expression that it is possible to go counter to God's commands? It would appear so. The theological moralist could say, "Yes, man has free will and can choose to disobey God's commands. But if he does so, then God will punish him."

This, however, will not do as an interpretation of theological morals. Surely, when one says, "Act in accordance with God's will," that person does not intend to say, "Because if you don't you will be punished." If this is what he means to say, then he has transformed the theological principle of morals into a teleological one. No longer is his appeal to the principle, "Act in accordance with God's will." Rather, it is to the principle, "Act so as to avoid God's wrath." The latter leads to a different set of considerations. One no longer asks whether or not God commands us not to cheat, but rather whether or not God will be angry if we cheat. The motive of our actions becomes the selfish one of avoiding punishment rather than that of being moral. The outcome would be that it would be all right to murder, cheat, rob, lie, and do other vicious things, provided we could get away with them, i.e., avoid God's knowing what we did, or be somehow able to placate him (say, by sacrifices).

To sum up this part of our discussion, if "One ought to act in accordance with God's will" means "One ought to obey God's commands," then either God, being sovereign, cannot be disobeyed and the principle loses its meaning; or God can be disobeyed and is not sovereign; or God permits men to disobey His commands (revolt against Him in sin) but punishes men for their disobedience, in which case the moral principle may become other than what it was said to be. In this last case the sole difference between this sort of morals and civil codes would be in the source of the punishment.

### "God Wills" as "God Approves"

Let us consider another meaning of "God's will," i.e., "what is approved by God," or "what God would want you to do." Translated into these terms, the principle becomes: "One ought to do what is approved by God" or "One ought to do what God would want you to do." To decide whether or not to rob, this principle requires us to decide, not what God commands, but whether God approves or disapproves robbing; or whether God would want us to rob.

This interpretation of the principle can be illustrated in the following way. Suppose Robin Hood wants to decide whether or not to rob the

rich to alleviate the hunger of the poor. Or consider the case of Jean
Valjean, who in the story Les Misèrables, tried to decide whether to
steal a loaf of bread to feed his starving family. Now, both Robin Hood
and Jean Valjean, as good Christians, could be imagined to say, "Now
look here. God certainly won't *command* me to steal or not to steal this
loaf since, if he did, I would not be a moral agent, being compelled to
obey. But would God approve, or would God want me to steal this loaf?
After all, there are many loaves and my family is hungry. Yet, one ought
to do God's will, do only what God approves or wants me to do."

On this interpretation, the principle can be taken to assert that no
matter what God approves, that is what ought to be done. If this is taken
quite literally it would follow that if God could be shown to approve
injustice, then one would be bound to be unjust, or if it could be shown
that God wanted murder to be done, then one would be bound to commit murder. Quite naturally the theological moralist will insist that
God will not approve nor want people to do such deeds. If he is asked
why not, the theological moralist will produce a theory of God's nature
or else he will appeal to a principle of goodness that makes God approve
whatever has the characteristics required by the principle. If he does
appeal to some principles of goodness, the moralist has abandoned his
theological principle of morals, since such a principle is independent of
God's approbation or desire. The moral "ought" has been made to depend upon this principle and not upon God.

If the principle that one ought to act in accordance with God's will
is accepted and taken to require action in accordance either with what
God commands (along with the consequences of this) or with what
God approves, general principles such as "One ought to act in accordance with God's will in order to attain salvation," or "to avoid punishment," or "to make people happy," and so on cannot be considered moral
principles, except in some indirect sense. To assert any of these statements as moral principles would be to substitute for God's will something else, or to assume that this is what God does will. There may be
criteria that are displayed or possessed by acts that God usually wills,
but they remain criteria and not moral principles. For example, human
happiness may be found in many instances to be a criterion for determining God's will, but God may will some act not obviously conducive
to human happiness, e.g., the sacrifice of Isaac by Abraham, or the destruction of the Temple by the Romans, or hurricanes and epidemics.
All of these things are, therefore, good since they are the result of God's
will. Abraham's act of sacrificing Isaac would have been moral to the

extent that it was God's will, but when God decided to stop Abraham, the sacrifice became immoral. What ought to be done is defined by God's will and not by something to be attained.

### "God Wills" as "God Purposes"

What has just been said leads to the third meaning of "God's will," namely, "God purposes." In this meaning the principle may be formulated in this fashion: "One ought to do what furthers God's purposes." This formulation has implications that need to be made quite clear. To speak of a purpose is to refer to something to be achieved. Hence, the principle tells us that our actions ought to help God achieve something – some goal or other. The difficulty that confronts us at once, and this is true even if we define "God's will" to mean "what God commands," or "what God wants you to do," is to know what is God's purpose. Moreover, the statement implies that we finite, mortal creatures of God can help God attain his purposes. This may not be an unwelcome implication, but it is involved in this interpretation of the theological doctrines assumed. One more implication of this interpretation which one might or might not accept is that God has a purpose and, therefore, desires to achieve something. I do not, however, want to consider this facet of our problem here because it involves us in theological problems to be considered later.

### Meanings of the Principle

We have considered three possible meanings of the theological principle of morals:

> (a)  One ought to do what God approves.
> (b)  One ought to do what God commands.
> (c)  One ought to do what helps God's purpose to be realized.

In each of these, being moral is defined not in terms of something that is true of the act or of one's own goals, but of God. It is either God's approval, God's command, or God's purpose that serves to indicate what ought or ought not to be done.

On the theological view no moral quality belongs to any act in itself but only in its relation to God. This was underlined before, but bears repeated emphasis in order to bring out what is meant by theological morals. There can, in other words, be no act that intrinsically ought to be done, even though some acts, like murder, are acts to be avoided because they are most often found to be contrary to God's will, (etc.).

*Application of the Principle*

This is enough for the meaning of the principle. What about its application? Let us list some of the questions which might typically be involved.

> Does God command (or approve) certain acts?
> (Are certain acts in accord with God's purpose?)
> If God does command or approve certain acts, which or what kind?
> (If certain acts are in accord with God's purposes, which are they, or what kind are they?)
> How can we find out what God commands or approves?
> (How can we find out what acts are in accord with God's purposes?)

Before the principle can be applied, two kinds of questions need to be resolved. One species of questions is about God – what God approves or commands, what God's purposes are; the second species is about the relation of acts to these. In order to answer the first kind of questions we are compelled to seek sources of a somewhat different nature from those which will provide answers to the second kind. The Christian, for example, might say, "We discover God's commands and purposes in the Bible and in the life of Jesus. Sometimes God reveals his approvals or purposes to us directly." To someone who, although religious, does not accept either revelation or the Bible as sources whose authenticity can be guaranteed, an appeal to nature or to God's creatures may be more satisfactory. On the other hand, if we assume that we know what sort of things God commands, or approves, and want to discover whether he approves a particular act, we need only compare the act with God's commandments or expressed approvals. The procedure here is legalistic, i.e., it is like what the judge in a civil court might do. As a judge, he knows what the law says; what he needs to do is to decide if it applies in the case before him.

*The Bible as Source of God's Will*

But in both cases we appear to be asking factual questions, and desire factual answers. To the request to be informed, "What does God approve?" we expect a specific reply: "God approves mercy." To the further query, "How do you know that God approves mercy?" we expect a reply of this sort: "Because the Bible tells us so," or "Because God told me so," or "Because mercy-doing seems to be an ingredient in this world created

by God, and if God didn't approve of it he wouldn't have put it there."
To quote Paley:

> As the will of God is our rule; to inquire what is our duty, or what we are obliged
> to do, in any instance, is, in effect, to inquire what is the will of God in that instance,
> which consequently becomes the whole business of morality. Now there are two
> methods of coming at the will of God, on any point: by his express declarations,
> when they are to be had, and which must be sought for in Scripture; by what we
> can discover of his designs and dispositions from his works, or, as we usually call
> it, the light of nature.

From the point of view of the application of these theological principles, this would be nice if Scripture were precise and definite and if the
light of nature were steady and clear. These questions arise even if we
assume that Scripture does reveal the word of God, something which
non-Christians might dispute. For that matter, even some Christians say
that the Bible is a record of human experiences and not the revealed
word of God at all. But this is not the issue in this chapter. Here our
concern is rather with the applicability of the principle under discussion.

Does Scripture tell us clearly what God's will (or approbation) is in
specific cases? If we assume that the Bible is the word of God, then the
answer to this seems, in some cases at least, to be affirmative. For example, suppose a man is tempted to seduce his best friend's wife. The
Bible clearly says, "Thou shalt not commit adultery" and "Thou shalt
not covet thy neighbor's wife." There is no ambiguity here. The principle
is clear and explicit. But matters are not always so clear. Suppose one
wants to know whether to expose the deceit of his friend's wife; or, to
take a classic example, suppose one has to decide whether to tell a sick
mother that her child had just been killed. Scripture is not as definite
in such matters.

Perhaps the most vivid example of the difficulty of deriving directives
for behavior from Scripture is in the debate over segregation. Pro-
segregationists are apt to quote the Bible in support of their position;
but just as readily do the anti-segregationists find in it support for theirs.
Surely, one or the other is wrong. Yes, but which one? Even the Devil,
we are told, can quote Scripture to support his purposes. The point is
that if the will of God is found in the Bible, it is not always expressed
so clearly that specific deeds find their touchstone by a simple reference
to it.

But this is not the end to the difficulties. What can be said to one who
complains, "How can the Bible express the will of God? The command

is to refrain from killing; yet Joshua is ordered to lay waste the cities he conquers. Is this not a contradiction?"

### World Reveals God's Will

If the Bible appears to be contradictory, to be vague in spots, or even challenged as the source of God's word, what alternative is there for one who bases moral principles upon God's will? Paley, to whom we referred above, tried to meet these objections by saying that God's will can be discerned in his creation, the light of nature. Then Paley tried to prove that when God created the human species, he wished their happiness, appealing for proof to the fact that our senses gave us pleasure and that the world about us ministered to our "refreshment and delight" instead of being such that everything "we tasted, (was) bitter; everything we saw, loathsome; everything we touch, a sting; every smell, a stench; and every sound, a discord." God, then, must have wished human happiness and hence we ought to do what makes people happy. Whether or not this is a sound justification of the happiness principle need not concern us at this point. But what is important is how we can show that Paley has rightly discerned God's will, i.e., he has provided a sound demonstration that God wills human happiness.

Paley's argument simply stated is that, since there is more happiness than unhappiness in life for men, God must have so desired it. The crux of the matter lies in the calculation. If Job finds his life exceedingly distressful, then God must have so desired it and one ought to do what makes Job unhappy. If we can show that all-in-all there is more misery and death than happiness in life, then these must be what God desires or approves – and we ought to do what is conducive to these. The devout Christian might even argue that the misery and death which abounds so plenteously are contrary to God's will, and this is evidenced by the coming of Christ. As a result we must avoid doing what leads to these. In short, there are those who would insist (a) that the light of nature shows us no such thing as Paley claims, or (b) that the light of nature shows that God desires unhappiness, or finally, (c) that no matter what the light of nature shows, one cannot infer simply from that to God's purposes.

This last point (c) can be illustrated in this way. God, it might be argued, could have created the world in such a way as to produce human happiness, but he did not do so because he wanted man to resist the temptation to a happy human existence in order to be worthy of salvation. The point is made that it is often difficult to see from the construction of an implement what its creator had purposed for it. In brief, many theologians would deny that God created the world for human happiness. Rather, they would declare, he created it for his own glory.

These reflections reveal that the most difficult thing about the principle we are discussing is the vagueness of the expression, "God's purposes." What does God want us to do? What does God command? The answers to these questions must be pertinent to living. Factual questions of this sort may be answered in one of three ways. First, a list of specific cases may be given; 2) a general principle (e.g., a law) may be stated to be applied to specific cases; and 3) an example may be given of what is expected.

### The Christian Interpretation

Although the Old Testament does try to list what is forbidden and in consequence is too detailed, the New Testament offers both a principle and an example for aid in doing God's will. What God wills, wants, approves, or commands is expressed in the two great commandments: "Love God" and "Love thy neighbor." God wants us to love Him and our neighbor; this is also approved and commanded. So in making choices between acts we must decide whether what we propose to do is an expression of love for God or love for one's neighbor. Furthermore, the best example of what this means is found in the life of Jesus, and other examples in the lives of the Prophets and the Saints.

So, these commands are not the same sort of things as are commands like "Shut the door!" but are rather to be viewed as moral commands, or, better, exhortations. As a result they can be translated into two cardinal moral principles, expressed as:

> One ought to love God.
> One ought to love one's neighbor.

In a sense, then, the Christian does not in making choices need to discover what God wills or wants or approves. Rather he needs to know whether what he is about to do expresses his love for God and his neighbor. If it does, then he can rest assured that what he is doing does meet with God's approval. In other words, the love of God or one's neighbor becomes a criterion for deciding the morality of the act. It still remains the case that God's approval makes the act right, but since we cannot in ordinary matters have access to God directly we are given, says the Christian, this standard. Ultimately it is God's approval, command, or desire that defines the oughtness of the act.

If the life of Jesus is taken as an example of love, then very concrete maxims seem to follow. Jesus healed troubled souls and bodies; this then, Jesus being what he is, must be what God approves and hence we ought to do likewise. If, therefore, a contemplated act of cheating will be one that troubles one's neighbor or deprives him of something that belongs to him, then the act ought not to be done because it is conrtary to God's will. Jesus forgave his enemies and commanded that no one do harm to his enemies; so likewise we are to know that we ought not to do evil to those who do evil to us. The keynote of this love is sacrifice and self-surrender; such expressions of love are what God wills us to make.

In simple, uncomplicated situations, the problem of application is not too difficult. But, as we saw earlier, cases arise in which it is more difficult to know what it is to love God and one's neighbor. In a case of conflict such as accurs when a doctor is forced to choose between saving the life of a mother and that of her unborn baby, the application is not so easy. Or to take another example, if a doctor knows that a young man (his patient) suffers from a disease and a girl (also his patient) wishes to marry the young man, should he violate his medical confidences and tell her, or fail to tell her and cause her to suffer? What does the principle of love say to do in such cases? But then we cannot expect our moral problem to be resolved by a simple formula. Life is much too complicated, and too tragic, to be like a mathematical equation. Moreover, even with these principles and the example of Christ, humans must reflect and are still free to sin.

BIBLIOGRAPHY

Brunner, E., *The Divine Imperative,* tr. by Olive Wyon (Philadelphia: Westminster Press, 1947).
Castell, A., *An Elementary Ethics,* Selections from Paley (New York: Prentice-Hall, 1954), pp. 20–38.
D'Arcy, M. C., "Religion and Ethics" in *Moral Principles of Action,* ed. by R. N. Anshen (New York: Harper & Bros. 1952), Chapter 24, pp. 512–527.
Dodd, C. H., "Ethics of the New Testament" in *Ibid.,* Chapter 26, pp. 543–559.
Hill, T. E., *Ethics in Theory and Practice* (New York: T. Y. Crowell, 1956), Chapter 3, pp. 39–57.
La Piana, George, "Doctrinal Background of Moral Theology" in *Moral Principles of Action,* ed. by R. N. Anshen (New York: Harper & Bros., 1952), Chapter 17, pp. 378–410.
Muhlenburg, James "Ethics of the Prophet" in *Ibid.,* Chapter 25, pp. 527–543.
Niebuhr, R., *An Introduction to Christian Ethics* (New York: Harper & Bros., 1935).
Thomas, George, F., *Christian Ethics and Moral Philosophy* (New York: Chas. Scribner's Sons, 1955).
Wheelwright, P., *A Critical Introduction to Ethics,* Revised Edition (New York: Odyssey Press, 1949), pp. 195–222.

# CHAPTER VI

# THE PRINCIPLE OF DUTY

The principle of duty, as a moral principle, is not as popular as it once was. People have learned to look upon an appeal to duty with distrust and a feeling of uneasiness. Indeed, even when used in correct contexts, the one who calls others to do their duty tends to be apologetic and somewhat embarrassed. The reason is that the principle of duty has often been used as an enticement to non-reflective action. Political leaders, both good and bad, have called upon citizens to do their duty in causes both good and evil. Invasions have been so often undertaken by armies composed of soldiers doing their duty, that the call has become suspect.

Yet it is equally true that in many ordinary situations we speak with admiration and approval of people who do their duty. We do recognize that "One ought to do one's duty" is indeed a moral principle – if it can be given meaning. Certain aspects of the principle tend to make us feel that the principle of duty has more of the characteristics one associated with true moral principles than any we have so far studied. Indeed, at times we are willing to say that one who does something because it is his duty and not for hedonistic or theological reasons acts with a purer motive and, hence is more worthy of being called "a moral person." Such an individual is worthy of emulation but cannot be because such behavior is beyonds the capacity of most of us. Like so many moral terms, "duty" carries both derogatory and honorific connotations.

## Comparison of Duty with Other Principles

The essential difference between the appeal to the principle of duty and appeals to other moral principles can be exhibited by a kind of caricature. Consider Mr. A, who is confronted with the problem of keeping or breaking a promise to sell his house. Now A is a hedonist, and so he tries to evaluate the consequences of each act in terms of happiness. He proposes to do what will bring the greatest happiness. Mr. B. on the other hand, is a religious man. Facing the same problem as Mr. A, Mr. B searches his Bible, consults his pastor, and looks about to find what God would approve. Mr. B means to keep his promise only if it is God's will that he do so. But Mr. C has a "strong sense of duty" and what he wants to know, since he too has the same problem, is what is it his duty to do. Mr. C wants to do his duty even if it makes him and everyone else unhappy and even if he doesn't know what God's will is. Mr. A says: "I will keep my promise since it leads to the greatest happiness." Mr. B says: "I will keep my promise since God's will is that I do so." Mr. C says: "I will keep my promise simply because it is my duty to do so."

For A, the rightness of keeping his promise depends upon the outcome of a hedonistic calculus and to convince A that he should not keep his promise one would need to show that keeping the promise would lead to less happiness than not doing so. If the same degree of happiness resulted whether or not he kept his promise, A would be in a quandary since he would have no way to decide how to act, in which case he might be forced to say that keeping his promise is not a moral problem at all. Furthermore, unless he could show that keeping a promise *always* resulted in greater happiness than failure to do so, he could not affirm the maxim: "One ought to keep one's promises." Each instance of promise-keeping would have to be considered on its own merits.

Similarly, in B's case, if one could show that God does not will that the promise be kept or that God wills that the promise not be kept, then B would need to say that keeping his promise is wrong. If one could show that God is indifferent to this case of promise-keeping, then B would have to say that this was no moral problem at all or find himself in the same predicament that A was in. Also, this or any other case of promise-keeping would need to be referred to God's will on its own merits unless one could demonstrate that God always willed certain kinds of acts.

In the case of C, however, the situation is different. The only significant question is whether it is his duty to keep his promise. It may be that either it is his duty not to keep his promise or that it is not his duty to do so. If it is his duty not to keep his promise, then he won't; if it is not his duty to keep his promise, he may decide on prudential grounds. In this case, as with A and B, the act of keeping his promise is for him not a moral one.

The major difference between the principles governing the decisions of A and B on the one hand, and those governing the decisions of C on the other, is that whereas A and B must refer to other things than duty, (happiness, or God's will), C can consider only the relation of the act to his duty. In other words, whether or not it is C's duty to keep his promise is a function of the kind of *act* keeping his promise is, rather than of the consequences of the act. Whether or not keeping my promise will lead to happiness tells me nothing about the nature of the act itself, but only whether the consequences will contain certain psychological states. But if I say that it is my duty to keep my promise, then this seems to tell me something about the act of keeping my promise, namely, that it is the sort of thing it is my duty to do. In technical terms, the consequences of an act are extrinsic to the act, its duty-bearing nature is intrinsic to it.

## The Meaning of the Principle of Duty

At the risk of being somewhat repetitious, yet in an effort to make what has been said more concrete, let us imagine the following episode. Mr. A comes before the parole board. He killed three boys wantonly some thirty years ago, and his trial aroused much feeling and received a great deal of publicity. Mr. A has served thirty years in jail as a well-behaved prisoner, even making contributions to his favorite subject, mathematics. Mrs. C is on the board. When Mr. A's appeal for parole is heard, Mrs. C opposes it strongly on the following grounds. First, she says, it is her duty to see that Mr. A pays the full penalty for his crime. Secondly, she insists that it is her duty to protect the parole board from injury that she believes will result if it grants the parole.

Additional light is thrown upon the concept of duty if we ask what sort of considerations could induce Mrs. C to change her mind. Mr. B, another board member, opposes the position taken by Mrs. C., observing that Mr. A has suffered through all these years and that it is, therefore, not fair to keep him locked up any longer. To this Mrs. C replies that where the question is one of duty, as she feels is the case, Mr. A's feelings cannot be taken into consideration. Mr. D., a third member, joins the discussion and points out that Mr. A probably has been punished sufficiently but in any case, as a good mathematician, he could be a benefit to society if granted the parole. None of these arguments move the adamant Mrs. C because she feels that in the face of duty such considerations are irrelevant. In short, for Mrs. C nothing counts – neither consequences, retribution, justice, contribution to human knowledge – nothing except the fact that it is her duty to do a certain thing. Presumably only the recognition that what she was advocating was contrary to her duty could convert Mrs. C.

This little episode brings out an important aspect of the principle,

"One ought to do one's duty," namely, that the consequences of the act, its effects upon the person making the decision or upon others, seem at most to be a minor consideration. If it is one's duty to do something, then that alone is enough to decide the matter. Mrs. C could and probably would say, "To consider whether to parole or not to parole in terms of pleasant or unpleasant consequences is like paying for a good deed. Are we to be bribed into paroling the man by the promise of social benefits; or are we, like children, to be seduced into paroling the man by appeals to our sympathy? No. We must do our duty, and I see our duty to be to refuse the parole." When one says that he ought to do his duty, he means among other things that *nothing else* can function as a motive for doing the act but its being his duty. He cannot recognize an act as his duty by setting up other reasons or motives for doing it. The act in question alone, of its own nature, is sufficient as a motive, precisely because to act in this way is his duty.

## Consequences as Criteria

But there is the difficult problem of recognizing what one's duty is. Perhaps Mrs. C might be converted if she could be shown that the board's influence would be strengthened by a favorable decision. For did not Mrs. C say that she wishes to protect the board? An exceedingly important distinction is involved here. Mrs. C is arguing that it is her duty to protect the board. She will vote against the parole because by doing so she will be doing her duty. In other words, she is considering the consequences of her act – not as the reason for it, but rather as a criterion. What may result from the act serves to indicate to Mrs. C that voting against the parole is what she must do in order to do her duty. She doesn't vote against the parole because the board will thereby be hurt but because the hurt indicates where her duty lies. She is saying this:

> I must do my duty always.
> It is my duty to protect the board.
> _____
> Therefore, I must always protect the board.
>
> But to vote against parole is to protect the board, i.e., to do my duty.
> _____
> Therefore, I must vote against parole.

## The Imperative and Categorical Nature of Duty

This austere characteristic of the principle of duty is matched by another. To say, "It is my duty to report cheating," is to insist that I *must* do so. Wherever there is a duty there appears to be a sort of compulsion. A person who feels it his duty to report cheating will do so. In this respect he is different from one who feels that cheating is wrong and that morally he ought to prevent it, but doesn't. Compare these two statements:

> I ought to report cheating.
> It is my duty to report cheating.

Suppose John says the first and Jim the second. John can then be imagined to continue in this fashion: "Sure, I know I ought to report cheating; but after all, why should I? If I do, my classmates will ostracise me." Now what John is saying is that cheating is wrong and he knows it, but he doesn't feel any compulsion to do anything about it. He may be a "weak" character, if one wants to call him that; more often he is just an ordinary citizen with the knowledge of what is right and what is wrong but without the will to act. We might say, with Kant, that he respects the moral law, although he doesn't act from the motive of respect for it but from some other motive.

Jim, on the other hand, also knows that cheating is wrong, but for him much more is involved. Jim feels strongly that he must do something about it. He is motivated to act by his very respect for the moral law. So we can hear him say something like this: "Cheating is wrong and I am compelled by that very fact to report it and to try to put a stop to it. There is no possible question why I should; I must do so. If my friends ostracise me, then that is too bad. But I must report the act precisely because it is my duty to do so and for no other reason."

The notion of duty, then, carries at least two implications. First, duty seems to imply a disregard of consequences, at least in the way the teleologist considers them. And secondly, duty carries along with itself the connotation of a requirement to action binding upon those whose duty is in question. To put the point in another way, duty involves obedience.

For the sake of convenience (as well as erudition) let us introduce the terms Kant used for these two aspects of the principle of duty. We use the term "categorical," to denote that the principle of duty contains no "if's," or "but's." It is an uncompromising command. This is contrasted with the "hypothetical" aspect of some commands which say "Do so-and-so if you want so-and-so," which is Kant's way of referring to the teleologists's emphasis on results. The compulsory nature of the moral law is summed up in the term "imperative." A moral law states something imperative – a command that must not be disobeyed or disregarded. A moral law is unconditional and expresses such a command.

*Duty and Role*

The discussion to this point has been rather general. Evidently it would be quite meaningless to say of a savage in the jungles of Africa that he had a duty not to cheat in an examination. It would be equally absurd to tell a person who is unmarried that he has a duty to be faithful to his wife. Duties always occur in contexts. "You ought to do your duty" is elliptical. What it leaves out is equally important. We do, however, hear expressions of the following sort: "It is my duty, as a Christian, to worship God"; or "As a father, it is my duty to my family to feed them"; or "As a teacher, I am duty-bound to keep myself abreast of developments in my field."

These expressions indicate that duty is related to specific roles. Mrs. C in our example felt it her duty as a member of the board and as a member of society to do what she did. We must all do things unconditionally because, so to speak, we are what we are. To say, "One ought to do one's duty," means that, being what one is, there are certain things that are unconditionally demanded. It is not that if we want to be Christian, we must worship God; nor if we want to be fathers, we must feed our family; nor if we want to be teachers, we must keep abreast. If we were not Christians, or fathers, or teachers we would not be called upon to do the relevant things. In some cases, our roles are intrinsic. For example, one cannot argue that since he is not a Christian, he need not worship God, since he may have a duty to worship God because he is a creature of God's. The role of creature is one we all have. Being creatures, we have this duty. We may not *want* to do these things, but we are compelled even against our not wanting to do them, being what we are. The duties are involved in the role, hence if we are not in a given role, we cannot have the duties that go with it.

It does not follow, however, that duty involves the notion of constraint, i.e., that duties are not such unless they do go counter to my wants. Indeed, as teachers, we want very much to keep abreast; as Christians, we want very much to worship God; as fathers, we want very much to feed our families. The point is that wants are of little importance where duties are concerned.

*Duties are to Others*

Another respect in which statements of duty are elliptical is apparent if we ask to whom duties are owed. As a father, for example, we have a duty to feed our families. "A duty to whom?" is a sensible question and it has an answer. Some of the most crucial problems and tragic situations revolve around the question of the priority of claims. "Render unto Caesar the things that are Caesar's, and unto God the things that are God's" expresses the problem. It tells us that we have duties to God and to Caesar. But the dictum "A man cannot serve two masters" points up the conflict of claims on our dutiful actions. In any case, every assertion that we have a duty to do something because we are a particular sort of person carries either tacitly or expressly a reference to those to whom we owe the duty. Being a Christian, my duty is *to God;* a father, my duty is *to my family;* a teacher, my duty is *to my students.* In other cases, the duty is owed to one's country or one's friends and so on. Usually if we are to recognize the existence of a duty, it becomes imperative to decide to whom the duty would be owed, if there were one.

This feature of our duties finds expression in our language. In ordinary speech "Duty" is followed at times by the preposition "to" plus an object, and at others by an infinitive of some verb or other. It is one's duty "to worship," "to teach," "to feed," "to obey," and so on. And the act, if in accord with duty, is the right, or moral, thing to do. The import of this is obvious. If a teacher has a duty to his students, then his students can make certain demands upon him. For example, it is his duty as a teacher to have answers to their questions, if answers are available, then his students can demand that he keep informed sufficiently of what is going on in his field to be able to answer their questions. If it is one's duty to keep his promise, then those persons to whom the duty is owed can demand that he do so and he cannot refuse to meet their demand and remain a moral person. In this respect there is nothing as rigorous as this principle of duty.

## Summary

We can now sum up this part of our analysis. To say "It is your duty to do so-and-so" means that

    (1)   there is an act you simply cannot justifiably avoid doing;

    (2)   you cannot legitimately take into consideration any consequences in the form of a principle, in deciding to do that act;

    (3)   you must do that act because you are what you are; and, finally,

    (4)   there are persons who can legitimately demand that you do the act.

The correctness of this analysis is made clear if we consider again briefly what we might say in order to convince someone that it is not his duty to do a certain act. Consider again Mrs. C. If we should simply say to her, "Mrs. C., it is not your duty to vote against parole," it is difficult to see how we could convince her that this is the case. But suppose we said to her, "Mrs. C., you are not a member of the board (or of society) and so you have no such duty." This, if it could be shown to be so, might be an effective approach; but, of course, Mrs. C would surely say, "That is not so."

Another alternative would be to present her with a conflict of duties. For example, one might point out to her that it is her duty as a person to treat others as humans and not as instruments, and that this is in conflict with her duty as a board member. This would not be to deny that she had a duty as a board member, but it would put her in a difficult situation in which one might hope to get her to prefer some other duty to the one she presently feels.

In brief, to prove to someone that he has not a particular duty, one can show:

(1) There is no moral compulsion for the person to act in the manner in question.
(2) He has no role demanding such action as his duty.
(3) Noone has a right to demand that he act in the prescribed fashion.

## Deciding if an Act is Our Duty

Now, all of this may be very well. But there is a difficulty with the principle, "One ought to do one's duty," which does not exist in the case of the appeal to hedonistic principles. In the latter case a criterion is available for determining whether or not a given act ought to be done, or which of two acts ought to be preferred. This criterion consists in the resultant happiness. In theological morals, what God wills is the deciding factor. In each case the criteria may be difficult to apply, but at least what needs to be done is plain. On the other hand, the principle of duty provides no obvious criteria for deciding whether or not a given act is our duty. How do we know whether it was Mrs. C's duty to vote against parole? How do you know whether it is your duty to report a person who cheats? to keep a promise? not to lie?

These are, of course, difficult and controversial questions. Is there any criterion connected with the principle of duty to which appeal might be made in resolving these questions? If no such criterion can be given, then it must be conceded that the principle appears to be vacuous and is virtually useless. Or else, and we mention this alternative in passing because we shall return to it later, the word "duty" is simply an emotive one to which people have been conditioned to react when it is necessary to motivate them to do certain kinds of things like enlisting, or reporting, which are usually unpleasant or undesired. Kant, who faced squarely this question of a criterion for duty, did suggest one that we need to examine.

### Universality as a Criterion of Duty

Kant arrived at a criterion through a series of reflections which we shall outline. Since the morality of an act is not determined by its consequences, we cannot decide that a given act falls within our duty by giving sole attention to its consequences. For example, if in a given case we wish to keep a promise simply because promise-keeping leads to a smoothly operating society, then keeping this promise is not necessarily our duty since whether we keep it depends upon how badly we want a smoothrunning society. If, however, we see that keeping our promise is *demanded* by the moral law itself, then it is our duty to keep the promise. This means that the moral principle (law) is categorical and not hypothetical in character. If this is so then the statement asserting the moral law must be devoid of all reference to consequences, since the introduction of such a reference gives only hypothetical judgments.

Kant's thesis here is connected with what was said before about the nature of duty. That there is a duty means that something is binding on everyone and obligatory. To keep a promise is a duty if we can also assert truthfully that keeping promises is binding upon everyone and obligatory. To help the blind is a duty if helping the blind is obligatory and binding upon everyone. Kant puts it in a negative fashion by saying, ". . . I should never act in such a way that I could not will that my maxim should be a universal law." And he adds, "The shortest but most infallible way to find the answer to the question whether a deceitful promise is consistent with duty is to ask myself: Would I be content that my maxim (of extricating myself from difficulty by a false promise) should hold as a universal law for myself as well as for others?"

Putting it less formally, Kant is saying that the way to decide whether it is a duty to do a certain act is to see if everyone could be held to be obligated to do that act, so that the maxim "I ought to act thus and so" could be willed a universal law. Do you want to know whether to kill your enemy? Then here is the method to be used to arrive at a decision. Formulate the maxim of the act as follows: "One ought to kill his enemies." And now try to decide whether this maxim could be willed to become a universal law. That is to say, ask yourself whether it is possible for this maxim to be obligatory for everyone so that every person is obliged to kill his enemies. If you find that if everyone had to kill his enemies a completely chaotic situation would result then the maxim cannot be willed a universal law and it is not your duty to kill your enemies.

### Which Maxim is to be Universalized?

In the same way, to return to an earlier illustration, if we want to know whether to return a borrowed knife to its homicidal owner, we must formulate a maxim describing our action and decide whether or not the maxim can become a universal law. How shall the maxim be formulated? Shall it be this: "One ought to return property to its rightful owner?", this: "One ought not to help another injure innocent bystanders?", or this: "One ought not to provide people who have homicidal tendencies with weapons they can use to kill others?"

The possibility of choice among a multiplicity of maxims, as in this example, is by no means unusual. In fact, many moral problems arise precisely because persons are confronted with alternative courses of action, each with a claim to be what ought to be done. Unfortunately, in many situations a number of maxims can be formulated each of which taken in isolation would be capable of being willed a universal law, yet such that, if all of them are so willed, conflicting courses of action are prescribed. Thus, there seems to be no reason why I cannot will that everyone return property to its rightful owner, and hence conclude that I ought to return the knife. At the same time, there also seems to be no reason why I cannot will that no one should help another injure a third party, and therefore conclude that I ought not to return the knife. But I cannot both return the knife and not do so.

We might, of course, seek to evade this conflict by saying that the maxim, "One ought to return property to its rightful owner," cannot be taken as it stands but that what is meant is that property ought to be returned to its rightful owner except when he is going to use it for bad purposes. But if we take this course, we are confronted with another problem: When should conditions be added? Is it not true that if enough conditions are added we can always (or at least often) get a principle that we can will to be a universal law? For example, take the maxim,

"One ought not to lie," and add to it this condition, "... except if his life is at stake." Can a person not will that "One ought not to lie except when his life is at stake" should become a universal law? Or consider the maxim, "One ought not to steal." If one adds to this, "unless he is starving and his stealing does not injure the person from whom he steals," surely this could be a universal law!

### Universality and Self-contradiction

But, the question arises, what criteria can be used to decide whether or not "One ought not to lie" could be willed to be a universal law? Is it merely a matter of emotion? Could we will this because we would like everyone to tell the truth, and that is all there is to it? Obviously this cannot be the answer. Nor, again, can the criterion be an appeal to consequences as such. This is indeed a difficult problem. The answer that Kant gives is that if a maxim is to be universalized and be a law, then there must be no contradiction which destroys the law or makes it meaningless.

Although Kant seems to be involved in a consideration of consequences, his view is not really teleological. Consequences are used to test whether of not a given statement (in this case, a moral law) is self-contradictory. If there are cases where the statement leads to consequences that contradict one another, then it is self-contradictory and therefore cannot be meaningful. Thus, Kant bases his criterion on a logical property. Suppose we consider the maxim, "One ought not to lie," and imagine it to be a universal law. No one tells a lie. The situation that results is a coherent one – everyone knows that everyone tells the truth. Moreover, everyone knows what is being asserted. But imagine now that everyone did lie. The situation would become impossible, because although no one would actually be deceived, yet a lie deviates from the truth in an indefinite number of ways and we couldn't know what were the facts in the case. The result would be confusion and chaos. Therefore, the maxim, "One ought to lie," cannot be a universal law and it is one's duty not to lie. But notice how this works when special conditions are added. Surely, if everyone were to lie only to save his life the situation would not become intolerable and lying under such conditions would be moral!

Kant's criterion is not wholly adequate or satisfactory; yet despite the ambiguity and difficulty in applying this principle, there is an element of truth in it. Even criminals will admit that their acts ought not to be universalized; not simply because they fear competition, but because they consider their own situation exceptional and their acts wrong in a moral sense. The fact is that we do mean to assert that if an act is right (or wrong) for me, it is right (or wrong) for everyone under these conditions. Hence, the act that is my duty can be such only if it is everybody else's duty as well provided they are in the same situation I am. But this last qualification introduces a special problem. In a sense no one else is or can be in the same situation I am in if for no other reason than because he would not be me.

There is a second point in connection with Kant's principle that needs to be underlined. In order for a person to be moral, according to Kant, he must act from duty alone and not from a desire for certain goals or from personal inclination. But we know he is acting from duty alone only if we know that he wills the act because it is moral. And it is a person's motives that decide whether or not he is moral. "But motives are after all of essentially the same stuff as desires and inclinations." This point will need more adequate discussion which we shall undertake later.

### Vagueness of Principle of Duty

One is likely to feel not wholly satisfied with the adequacy of an ethical position based on duty alone. In everyday life we do, it is true, feel the notion of duty to be an extremely important one; yet the lack of even a vague method of deciding what is or it not our duty leaves us with the sense that even if the principle of duty is important, it is not particularly useful. A moral principle that offers little guidance for moral decisions and subsequent actions is not a very acceptable one. This may be one reason why it has dropped out of the thinking of many morally reflective persons. Yet, as we have said, if our actions are determined by a desire for certain consequences, can we really call ourselves moral? Perhaps the concept of duty is so basic as to be irreducible, so that when a person says to me, "It is your duty to be just," he is saying nothing more than "Everyone ought to be just simply because of what it is to be just." In other words, may it not be that saying "It is your duty to do A," is a way of asserting that A is the sort of act that must be done and done by everybody? If that is the case, then the only way to find out whether or not it is your duty to do A is to examine A.

But this still leaves us with the question, "What shall we look for?"; a question that perhaps can only be answered by, "Look for the quality of oughtness." But it is not clear what this means, what this quality is. We shall discuss this later when we ask about the nature of moral statements. We simply point out that to say that it is one's duty to be just may mean that doing justice is intrinsically good, and what is so makes a demand on you and me and everyone else.

## BIBLIOGRAPHY

Bradley, F. H., "My Station and its Duties," Essay in *Ethical Studies,* reprinted in A. I. Melden, ed., *Ethical Theories,* 2nd ed., (New York: Prentice-Hall, 1955), pp. 393–425.

Ewing, A. C., *Ethics,* (London: English Universities Press, 1953), Chap. 4, pp. 51–65.

Kant, I., *Foundations of the Metaphysics of Morals,* reprinted in Melden *op. cit.,* pp. 292–341.

Prichard, H. A., "Duty and Interest," reprinted in W. Sellars and John Hospers, eds., *Reading in Ethical Theory* (New York: Appleton-Century-Crofts, 1952), pp. 469–487.

Pratt, J. B., *Reason in Art of Living,* (New York: Macmillan, 1949), Chap. 23, pp. 257–270.

Teale, A. E., *Kantian Ethics* (London: Oxford Univ. Press, 1951, Chap. 6 & 7, pp. 109–148.

Thomas, G. F., *Christian Ethics and Moral Philosophy* (New York: Charles Scribner's Sons, 1955), Chap. 9, pp. 421–447.

Tsanoff, R. A., *Ethics,* Rev. ed., (New York: Harpers & Bros., 1955), Chap. 6, pp. 98–119.

# CHAPTER VII

# SELF PRINCIPLES

No special powers are needed to discern the basic self-centeredness of most human beings. Cynics find it an easy and convenient support of their contentions. Yet quite often people are urged to maintain their integrity as a self, or to be proud of themselves. It is as if there are circumstances where it is praiseworthy to be self-centered. Naturally one tries often to avoid derogatory connotations and replaces the term "self-centered" by "self-expression" or "self-realization."

## The Ubiquity of Appeals to Self Realization

The latter two terms are quite in vogue today. To keep a child from expressing himself is, in the eyes of many a proud (but often misguided) parent, a terrible crime. Misbehavior and deviant behavior are overlooked or excused on the grounds that any attempt to correct such behavior may impose restraints or repressions which will interfere with the development of the child's self. Any action believed to hinder self-development or self-realization is looked upon as immoral – a violation of the personality of the child.

Where once education was supposed to develop the universal nature of man, reason, it now, especially in the secondary schools, aims at the development of "the whole Self." Art, music, baton-twirling, etc. are put into the academic curriculum because they help, so it is urged, develop "the child's whole self." Educators argue for age-grade correlations, no matter how little Johnny knows, so that a twelve-year old boy or girl in the fourth grade should not feel frustrated and not adequately realize his or her self. These illustrations are slightly caricatured, to be sure, but they describe familiar situations.

The appeal to one's Self is often made by oneself. There are evidently times when a person, basically honest, and confronted with a choice between cheating and not cheating will refuse to cheat simply because he

feels he would be betraying his true nature. He may accept all the unpleasant consequences rather than fail to be true to his Self.

The principle that lies behind and serves to justify opinions of this
sort can be expressed in the following fashion: "One ought to realize his
Self." If we use promise-keeping as an example, the moral syllogism
which uses the principle as its major premise would look like this:

> One ought to realize his Self.
> If I fail to keep my promise, I will not realize my Self.
> _____
> Therefore, I ought to keep my promise.

The notion of "realizing one's Self," it may be noted, is often used
synonymously with "being true to oneself" and with the notion of "self-
development." Before we try to give meanings to these expressions, we
need to clarify a related concept, that of "selfishness," because it is basic
to further discussion.

### The Meaning of "Selfish"

A person who does something for himself, or who is always concerned
with his own self-interest, is apt to be condemned as selfish. Yet the
person who seeks to "realize" his Self is rarely criticized. In other words,
when someone is told: "If you act in accordance with your nature, you
cannot go wrong," or "If you seek to develop yourself, you will always
do what is right," the impression is left that this is good advice which
will lead to praiseworthy behavior. At the same time, statements of the
following sort are quite frequently heard: "Nobody is moral. Everyone
is elfish. No one ever does anything which is against his own interests."
Statements of this latter kind present us with two different questions.
One is factual. Is it as a matter of fact true that people do only what is
for their own interests? Are people selfish? The second question is one
of meaning. What is meant by saying: "Everyone acts selfishly," or "No
one ever does what is contrary to his own best interests?"

Let us consider first the cynical assertion "Everyone acts selfishly."
This seems to be a perfectly clear statement, yet we can discover at least
two meanings. In the first sense it is usually uttered with a sneer, while
in the second it is uttered in sorrow as if one regretted the fact. In the
former sense, that everyone acts selfishly is taken as a statement of fact
without moral consequences. In the latter sense what is meant is: "Alas!
All men act selfishly, although they ought not to do so." In both senses
the sentence is supposed to express something true. This is what is the

case, it is urged. And characteristically no appeal to any sort of evidence will cause the one who holds such a view to change his mind. If, for example, someone appeals to the life of Jesus as an example of self-less living, one of two replies is likely to be forthcoming. Jesus being God, it is pointed out, could act contrary to human nature, but mortals cannot do so. Or it is observed that even Jesus must have derived pleasure from acting in the way he did and, therefore, must have acted selfishly.

If, on the other hand, one offers examples of unselfish acts by humans, the examples are rejected with the statement that the actor must have wanted to do what he did and nothing else, or must have derived pleasure from his deed. Since there is a sense in which it is true that a person ordinarily does what he wants to do, this has all the appearance of being irrefutable. Likewise, since people very often do get pleasure or happiness from their acts, the cynic seems to be on safe ground. But closer examination of the statements reveals definite ambiguities.

### Meaning of "Everyone Does What he Wants to Do"

First, let us examine the word "want." We say we want to do something and we mean simply that it is what we desire. We would like to do it. In this sense it is quite evidently not always true that we like to do what we do. There are times when people do what they like to do and other times when they do what they thoroughly dislike. To say that one always does what he wants to do, meaning what he likes to do, is factually false. On the other hand, "I do what I want to do" may be taken to mean "I do what I wish to do." This, too, seems untrue as a generalization. A person may wish to keep his promise, yet not do so because he is afraid of the consequences. Or one may wish to help a drowning person, yet not do so because he cannot swim. In these cases it may, of course, be said that what is really wanted is to avoid the consequences of keeping a promise, or to preserve one's own life. However, this need not be so. Someone may be quite willing to risk his life, but his inability to swim may simply prevent him from even making an attempt at a rescue. It is not uncommon for someone to wish very much to do the moral thing, yet be driven by inclination or habit to do just the opposite.

However neither of these meanings of "want," i.e., "wish" or "like," expresses completely the intention of "Everyone does what he wants to do." There is, in the sentence, the implication that when a person acts in a certain fashion, he has chosen so to act, and has chosen what he desired to do. Suppose a thug points a gun at someone's head and threatens to kill him if he doesn't rob his friend. Under these conditions the temptation

is to exonerate the person from any blame. But the cynic insists that anyone in such a predicament does indeed have a choice and if the robbery
is selected, it is because robbery was chosen in preference to being killed,
what he really wanted to avoid. The tacit assumption is that no one who
is willing to take the consequences can be compelled to act contrary to
his will, i.e., do something other than what he wants to do. In a sense,
the cynic is quite right in what he says, but he is not telling the whole
story. His statement would be more nearly adequate if, in addition to
saying that people do only what they choose to do, he went on to observe
that whether or not that makes them selfish (in the derogatory sense)
depends upon what it is they choose to do. There is most certainly a
difference between two people, one of whom chooses to die rather than
rob his friend and the other chooses to rob his friend rather than die.
Nevertheless, each may be doing what he wants to do, and each may be
selfish but in different senses of the word selfish. If, however, the cynic
were to agree to this, he would surrender his cynicism.

The upshot of these remarks should be evident. The statement,
"Everyone does only what he wants to do," does not give any sort of
support to the statement, "Everyone is selfish" (in the derogatory sense).
In any case it would be ludicrous to insist that a person is unselfish only
if he does what he doesn't want to do. To prove that one was not selfish,
a person would need first to be in the position of not wanting to be unselfish and then proceed to act unselfishly.

There is, however, another subtle confusion in the attempt to prove
that everyone is selfish from the presumed fact that everyone does what
he wants to do. Usually when the generalization that people are selfish
is challenged the evidence produced in support of it consists in attempts
to show that people do what gives them pleasure, or happiness, or satisfaction of some sort. The martyr is said to be selfish because he gets
pleasure or satisfaction from the realization that he has done his duty.
The hero is said to be selfish because he gets pleasure or satisfaction
from the resultant praise. The confusion in this argument rests on an
equivocation

## Happiness as a Cause vs. as a Concomitant

There is no doubt that a person who has a good deal of money builds
a hospital and has it named for himself solely because he wants to enjoy
being praised by his neighbors would be truly called "selfish." His
beneficial act was done *because* of the happiness or satisfaction he would
derive personally. Contrast this case with that of a person who leads his

people in a struggle against injustice, knowing his life is probably forfeit if he is captured. The motive of an underground fighter in Nazi-occupied France was certainly freedom but he must have derived a great deal of happiness from the thought that he was participating in a good cause. In fact, the happiness or satisfaction may help carry him through periods of uncertainty. Possibly no evidence can be produced that will prove or even make it probable that he fought for freedom for the sake of the happiness rather than for freedom itself. Nevertheless, the happiness did accompany his struggle.

It becomes evident, then, that the expression, "All men get happiness from what they do," is ambiguous. The sentence may mean either

> (1) Everyone does what he does because he gets happiness or satisfaction;

or

> (2) Whenever a person does what he wants to do, his deeds are accompanied by happiness or satisfaction.

Only if (1) is true could we correctly say that people are selfish. But (1) may be merely a statement of fact without moral connotation. It is, to repeat, when one's own happiness is deliberately placed paramount to all other considerations that the term "selfish" may be used. On the other hand, a person cannot be condemned for accepting the happiness which accompanies his deed. That person is indeed fortunate who finds happiness or satisfaction in his virtues. In fact, we can go still further and say with Carritt, "It is impossible to conceive of a virtuous or of a moral act, or indeed of any act, which brought no satisfaction to the doer..."

### Selfish or Self-ish

All of these remarks have taken the word "selfish" in its derogatory sense. Since, as is so often the case in English, it is probable that this is not its only sense, we will seek another meaning. It is true that in most cases when someone is accused of being selfish, the intention is to say that he is lacking in consideration for others and will at all times do whatever is necessary to achieve his own ends. Indeed, the expression "accused of being selfish" shows our attitude. A selfish person is not liked by others.

But there are circumstances when the word "selfish" is used in a sort of matter-of-fact sense. For example, when we say "Children are selfish," we mean that they fail to take the welfare of others into consideration.

But this remark about children suggests another connotation. Suppose Johnny, age five, tears a toy from the hands of Susan, age four. Johnny wants to play with it and so takes it. In this case, a child psychologist might very well say, "This is to be expected. Children Johnny's age are selfish." Now, as a scientist, the child psychologist is most certainly not condemning Johnny. He is far from saying that Johnny is immoral, or, for that matter, that the child has done something wrong. Not at all! The psychologist means that a child of Johnny's age sees things from his own vantage point. The child's act is peculiarly a self-referring act. By pointing to this fact, the psychologist wishes to remove any stigma that may attach to Johnny because of what the child did. No scientist passes moral judgment; hence in this case what is being affirmed is that Johnny's act is *his* act – self-centered. It takes maturity to make altruistic considerations possible.

It may very well be that when a person says, "Everyone acts selfishly," he is misleading himself, because what he is affirming is a statement of fact about how people think and act. He is trying to say that people always do acts from their own point of view. Or he may be trying to say something completely obvious, namely, that a person's act is his own act. The cynic, however, feels he is saying something morally significant from which he can infer to the immorality of every person. In brief, to affirm that everyone acts selfishly may be to use "selfish" in a non-moral sense referring either to the reflexive character of the act's relation to the self or to the egocentric focus of the action. In this sense of the expression, whether or not the self which acts is moral or immoral would seem to depend upon what sort of self the act was intended to express. This point is important if we are to understand what the moral principle, "One ought to realize himself," means.

### The *Real Self*

The foregoing considerations show that "self-realization" is not necessarily to be equated with "selfishness" in its derogatory sense. The principle of self-realization may therefore be analyzed in the light of non-derogatory meanings of "self-realization."

We may begin by noting that this principle may be expressed in two forms:

> "One ought to realize his Self."
> "One ought to realize himself."

The obvious difference is that a noun, "Self," is used in the first statement, while in the second a pronoun, "himself," is used. The use of the noun seems to involve reference to an entity which is other than the person who appeals to the principle yet which is at the same time somehow embodied in him. The sentence specifically implies that quite literally the present individual is somehow different from what he should be – his Self. Common speech often refers to a person's "real Self" in opposition to his "apparent Self," as, for example, when we say of a person who committed a crime, "Ah, but his real Self did not approve of that deed," or "It was the alcohol that prevented his real Self from expressing itself." In each case, the Self is taken as something real, something that is prevented from expressing itself through or by means of the body in which it resides.

The second sentence has no such dualistic presuppositions, but does involve the idea of growth or evolution. It presupposes a distinction between a person inadequately or not fully developed, and one whose potentialities have been fully realized. At the present stage of development he is himself, but not completely blossomed. The realized self in this case is to the present structure of the person as the fully developed fruit is to the infolded blossom.

The principle of self-realization thus turns out to be two principles and not one. These distinctions can be illustrated by another look at the doctor who some chapters back was trying to decide whether or not to expose the abortionist. Using the principle of self-realization, he might very well argue in some such fashion as this: "I must, if I am to be moral, allow my Self the fullest latitude to express its very nature. If, then, I exposed the abortionist would my Self be doing something that expressed its nature?" On the other hand, he might conceivably deliberate as follows: "I am trying to become a good physician and a good citizen. If I expose this abortionist, will this help me develop into that which I want to become?" These two questions illustrate respectively the two forms of the self-realization principle. In the first case the morality of the act lies in its conformity with the structure of the Self. In the second case the crucial point is whether the act is conducive towards helping the Self become something other than it is at present. In the former case the Self is held to be perfect, and the present person looks to it as an ideal; in the latter case the concern is with perfecting human nature, or at least this instance of human nature, by developing its capacities.

## What is the Self

One might think that we now understand what the principle or principles we have just discussed mean, and that we should go on to other problems. But there are still ambiguities to be removed. Thus, it is certainly true that often we do not really mean it when we say that people ought to realize their potentialities or express their Selves. Consider, for example, the case of Jesse James, the bandit and murderer. Had people known, when Jesse James was a youth, what his potentialities were, would they have felt impelled to let them develop? Do we, in general, feel that one who is at heart a criminal must be allowed to express his Self? A corresponding mistake is made by many modern child psychologists, who feel that children, to avoid frustration, should be allowed to express their Selves. The result is at times an uninhibited "brat."

In ordinary circumstances when one says that a person should express his Self he means something like the following. Every Self is basically good, but frequently cannot develop properly, perhaps because of the obstructions of daily living, the demands of circumstances, or some other external reason. To surrender to these conditions is to be untrue to one's Self and hence immoral.

In a sense, as the theory of Self-realization has been presented by Bradley and others, there is an evident circularity involved in it. The good (and, therefore, what ought to be done) is defined by appealing to a Self which is by nature good, but no principle for judging the Self is offered. It is simply taken explicitly or implicitly to be good.

It is possible to argue that one cannot say the Self is good since the Self is the condition for goodness. Even so, if we are to use the principle of self-realization to make moral decisions, we need to know much more about the nature of the Self than we have so far learned. If the Self is what Freud says it is, then the kind of acts that will realize that Self will be of a specific sort. If the Self is what Marx says it is, then the acts that will realize it may be of a different sort. If the Self is what the Christian thinks it is, then self-realization will be quite another sort of thing. In brief, the problem resolves itself into another – what is the Self? It may even be that, as some psychologists say, there is no such thing as a "true" Self common to all human beings but only particular selves – personalities – which are respectively a function of the experiences of the several individuals. In that event the self-principle becomes entirely relative to each personality, or type of personality.

The difficulties which may arise in attempting to apply the self-principle as we are now interpreting it are sharply underlined in the following imaginary monologue of a person maintaining a self-realization principle and trying to decide whether or not to cheat his neighbor. He says, "Here. This ought to be simple enough. Am I the type that cheats? Since I believe that I ought to realize my Self, if I cheat when I am not that sort of Self, I will hinder my Self-realization. And if I do not cheat when I am a cheating self, I will not realize my Self." His neighbor then queries, "Yes, but what sort of Self are you?" Our puzzled friend replies, "I am the sort of person who suffers from guilt feelings when he does things like cheating. Even though these guilt feelings are very detrimental to my behavior patterns, my self is a cheating self. Hence I will cheat." Suppose that at this point another person (let's call him "M") intervenes and says, "Friend, your guilt feelings in the presence of cheating are but the responses instilled in you by your social class in its struggle against other rising classes. Your real Self is determined by the structure of the class to which you belong. You realize your Self only to the extent that you remain true to your class. If you cheat, you will aid your class in its struggle to gain power. Cheat and be a true member of your class." To add further to the complications, still another advisor says, "M is wrong and completely so. Man is created in God's image and his true Self is realized as it reflects God's glory. As a true child of God, man can realize his Self only to the degree that he does what glorifies God. To cheat is to do the work of the Devil and is a sin against God. Therefore, you must not cheat." By this time, the potential cheater is completely confused. The apparent lucidity of his principle has vanished in the complexities of philosophical anthropology.

### The Self-principle not Precise

Let us not be misled. No principle, as such, can select from among alternative courses of behavior and tell us what to do. What it does is to provide us with a standard. But our examples serve to illustrate the fact that in this particular principle there is an essential ambiguity and a related circularity. The word "Self" is ambiguous; and the circularity lies in the fact that the principle of self-realization instead of telling us what Self to realize, makes the value of Self-realization derive entirely from the value of the Self which is to be realized. The result is that instead of one principle there seems to be as many principles as there are theories of the Self. It is quite apparent that the principle, "One ought to realize one's Self," has no clear meaning until Self is defined. So if anyone proposes to use this as a moral standard for deciding what to do, it is necessary to find out what he means by the word before any prediction about his judgments or behavior can be made. It would take too much time and not help us a great deal to consider all the moral principles that result from various definitions of "Self." The preceding chapters have offered some examples of the various possibilities. But it will be of value to consider here two concepts of the Self that have particular significance for contemporary civilization.

### The Self as Product of Society

The first of the two theories was proposed by the British philosopher Bradley in a work called *My Station and its Duties*. Bradley's view has many affinities to the Communist doctrine of the nature of man, although Bradley's philosophical position is one much despised by Communists, namely Idealism. Bradley begins with the observation that whatever is done is done by a Self for itself. As a consequence, insists Bradley, the realization of the Self is the highest good for each Self, since this is what all action is ultimately for. What then is the Self? Bradley, at this point, makes the interesting claim that the individual is molded by the society to which he belongs. As he expresses it: "Let us take a man, an Englishman as he is now, and try to point out that apart from what he has in common with others, apart from his sameness with others, he is not an Englishman, nor a man at all; that if you take him as something by himself, he is not what he is ... What we mean to say is that he is what he is because he is a born and educated social being, and a member of an individual social organism; that if you make abstraction of all this, which is the same in him and in others, what you have left is not an Englishman, nor a man, but some I know not what residuum, which never has existed by itself and does not so exist."

This is clear enough. A person is what he is because he is a member of a social organism. Hence, his Self is defined in terms of that social organism just as his arm is defined in terms of the body to which it belongs. It is evident that Bradley uses Englishmen simply as examples and is stating what he takes to be a universal fact. Apart from Bradley's belief that a society is a social organism, what he points out has been widely accepted by social psychologists – except that they usually speak of "personality" rather than of "Self." A Bantu is the sort of person he is precisely because he is a member of the Bantu social organism, and he differs from an American because the American social organism differs from that of the Bantu. But the emphasis on the social organism leads Bradley to say things which few, if any, social psychologists would accept, such as that "... at birth the child of one race is not the same as the child of another ...," and "... civilization is to some not inconsiderable extent hereditary; ..." If you know something about British economic history and are inclined to say, "This is the typical nineteenth-century Britisher talking," notice that in so saying you may be agreeing with Bradley.

Bradley's view leads to an interesting (and at times amusing) consequence. The Self is defined by the social organism of which it is a member. Hence, to say "One ought to realize his Self" really now means "One ought to realize his British Self (or Bantu Self, etc.)." Earlier we pointed out that "ought" statements usually contain implicit imperatives. Therefore, these principles can be translated as: "Be a Bantu!", or "Be British!" Since these can hardly be universalized we might generalize to the tautology: "Be what you are", a clear reduction to absurdity since we are indeed what we are.

One more quotation from Bradley in order to be fair to him: "Leaving out of sight the question of a society wider than the state, we must say that a man's life with its moral duties is in the main filled up by his station in that system of wholes which the state is, and that this, partly by its laws and institutions and still more by its spirit, gives him the life which he does live and ought to live."

On this theory, then, the Self-principle can be applied to a specific case only after one has come to know the "spirit of the community" and its general and special beliefs concerning right and wrong. So that if an American wants to know whether to lie, or cheat, or expose abortionists, or pay debts, he must ask, "Would I be an American if I did this thing?" If the answer is "Yes!" he acts; if not, he refrains from acting. Indeed, the theory reduces to another, namely: "One ought to do as one's social organism dictates," a social relativism.

But there is even less precision than we thought. Bradley admits that social organisms seem to change. Therefore, the Britain of today is not the Britain of yesterday, and to be British in 1896 is not the same as to be British in 1965. The principle really becomes: "One ought to be a twentieth-century Britisher." In other words, the principle is not only relative to the social organism but also to the times. Once again the principle has become vague in its application.

### Self as Unique Entity

Another form of Self-realization morals is illustrated, but not explicated, by A. J. Cronin in a novel called *A Thing of Beauty*. Here the author depicts his hero, Stephen Desmonde, as a person whose actions are determined by his desire to realize his Self as an artist. Alas, Stephen Desmonde is born the son of a clergyman, and the father has an intense desire to have Stephen continue in the Church. But Stephen realizes that his nature is that of an artist. As an artist his impulse is to express himself as a painter in order that as a true artist he will leave something beautiful behind. So when his father throws him out, penniless, Stephen accepts the fact cheerfully and sets out to realize his Self. This is his principle – and his Self is that of an artist. When the war breaks out in 1914, Stephen is confronted with the problem of choosing to serve his country or to continue painting. In the interest of his Self as a painter, he stays in Spain. When his father is in difficulty and Stephen is asked to return and enter the Church, he again refuses. As a result he suffers ridicule, scorn, anger and insult. But he remains true to his Self. Of course, when in the end he dies of tuberculosis, he is triumphantly victorius because he is discovered and declared to be "chère maitre" by a great art dealer.

In this novel the Self is conceived as something unique, not yet realized. Despite the fact that it is an "Ideal Self," it serves as a guide to action. To be true to that Self is the highest principle of morality; and if there is a conflict between it and other principles, the Self-principle, of course, takes precedence. So, confronted by the demand to serve his country (duty), Stephen refuses because it might mean his betrayal of his Self. Or called in the name of loyalty to his family, he again turns away. Sometimes, Stephen appears to be selfish rather than Self-ish. Our sympathies at times go out to Stephen, especially when he is dying, precisely because the Self he is seeking to realize is one we believe to be the sort that ought to be realized. We feel that those who place difficulties in his path, or, like the good people of Stillwater, criticize his art as obscene, are wrong both artistically in their evaluation of his art and morally in their obstruction of his desire to express his Self.

According to the author, Cronin, Stephen's Self was from the beginning that of an artist. Stephen knew this and had framed his life in accordance with his Self. Throughout the novel, too, the assumption is made that this sort of Self is a good one worthy of being a norm for behavior. Somehow to be an artist is to be a Self worthy of realization. Stephen did not need to develop that Self, only to express it. His Self is a unique thing.

### Plurality of Selves

If we consider ordinary people, not in novels but in real life, we are confronted by the difficult problem of saying what Self these people should realize. Ordinarily a person has many "Selves"; Stephen did, even if the author who created him overlooked them. The sociologists speak of "roles" in society. Most people are not merely, say, artists, but also fathers or mothers, members of various organizations, and so on. And, so we are told, all people have self-images; i.e., view themselves as certain sort of persons. It has even been urged that one reacts most violently to what he considers to be threats to his image of himself – even more violently than to threats to his security. Which of these Selves, or self-images, are to be selected when it is decided to govern behavior so as to realize the Self?

These factual considerations do not refute the Self-principle any more than factual considerations refuted the other principles we have examined. But they do indicate the difficulty of its application, as well as the need of finding for it some sort of justification. If the word "Self" in the principle is not meaningful, how can we know what the principle itself means?

If we accept the Self-principle, "right" and "wrong", "moral" and "immoral" will be defined as follows: Those acts are right which help one to realize his Self; those are wrong which do not. And if we define a person who does what is right as moral and one who does what is wrong as immoral, then whoever does what realizes his Self is moral and whoever does what hinders his Self-realization is immoral.

The principle we have discussed in this chapter differs from those with which earlier chapters were concerned in a significant fashion. We do use this principle to make decisions – and moral ones. But the value of the principle for making decisions depends to such an extent upon what we mean by the Self that we are forced to say that the principle leads to moral acts under certain meanings of "Self" and not under others. We certainly would reject the principle if, for example, it condoned torture as being conducive to Self-realization. That is to say, the Self-principle is a moral one if and only if its use leads to acts which are morally acceptable. But such a statement is circular, and reveals the fact that the Self-realization principle really presupposes something else in terms of which it is advanced as moral.

BIBLIOGRAPHY

Bradley, F. H., "Why Ought I to be Moral" and "My Station and its Duties" in *Ethical Essays,* Essays I and IV (New York: Library of Liberal Arts, . .).
Butler, Joseph, *Sermons,* reprinted in A. I. Medlen, ed., *Ethical Theories* (New York: Prentice-Hall, 1955), pp. 206–241.
Carritt, E. F., *The Theory of Morals* (London: Oxford Univ. Press, 1928), Chap. 6, pp. 49–57.

Field, G. C., *Moral Theory,* 2nd ed. rev. (London: Methuen & Co., ..), Part 3, pp. 117–213.

Garvin, Lucius, *A Modern Introduction to Ethics,* (Boston: Houghton Mifflin Company, 1953), Chap. 12 and 13, pp. 320–362.

Green, T. H., *Prolegomena to Ethics* (Oxford: Clarendon Press, 1890), Chap. 2, pp. 189–210.

Hill, T. E., *Ethics in Theory and Practice* (New York: T. Y. Crowell Co., 1956), Chap. 9, pp. 136–152.

——, *Contemporary Ethical Theories* (New York: Macmillan Co., 1950), Chap. 16, pp. 257–273.

Pratt, J. B., *Reason in the Art of Living* (New York: Macmillan Co., 1949) Chap. 9, pp. 85–100, and Part 3, pp. 221–257.

Royce, Josiah, *Philosophy of Loyalty* (New York: Macmillan Co., 1924).

Tsanoff, R. A., *Moral Ireals of Our Civilization* (New York: E. P. Dutton, 1942), Chap. 35, pp. 553–574.

Wright, H. W., *Self-Realization* (New York: Henry Holt and Co., 1913), Part 2, Chap. 5 and 6, pp. 151–193; Part 3 and 4, pp. 193-416.

# CHAPTER VIII

# SOCIETAL PRINCIPLES

When we analyzed the moral situation we discovered that decisions were based on judgments, and that basic to these judgments were moral principles which were used as premises. We are now engaged in an analysis of the meanings of some widely used moral principles and on a consideration of the difficulties involved in applying them. A few more moral principles need to be considered. If the task is becoming tiresome, we must be patient. The clarification of meaning and application is indispensible to an intelligent understanding of moral decisions.

## Social Relativism

In our previous discussions the doctor, confronted with the problem of denouncing the town abortionist, made his decision in the secret recesses of his mind or perhaps to the ear of his attentive wife. In any case, the decision was a personal one the basis for which lay in a principle independent of the attitudes of other people. The principle we are about to analyze differs from the preceding ones by appealing to society as its norm. Let us see how the problem confronting Dr. B appears in the light of an appeal to society. We can suppose that the abortionist, Dr. A, has learned of his possible exposure and has hurried to Dr. B to dissuade him from making the exposure. Dr. A's argument can possibly run along the following lines.

"Look here! You are simply trying to play the noble one. Moral principles have force as such only if people – the society in which you find yourself – consider them to be moral principles. Society approves abortion. Everyone tacitly accepts the practice as something necessary. Hence, abortion is not immoral. If you have an obligation in this matter it is to do what society approves."

Dr. A's argument is quite similar to many used in debating the morality of putting the aged, or the infirm to death, a custom that prevailed in many primitive peoples living in difficult environments. Those who would defend the morality of such deeds urge the uselessness and burdensomeness of the aged in the struggle for survival. Or they may say that putting the aged and infirm to death is an act of kindness since it puts them out of their suffering. Many of those who challenge the morality of such practices do so in terms of the sacredness of human life. Often, however, both of these aspects of the problem are condemned as irrelevant on the grounds that moral principles are functions of the particular society in which acts are performed. In some societies killing the aged is considered moral and the evidence that it is moral is that it is done; in another it is considered immoral and the evidence that it is immoral is that it is not done. If a person lives in a society where the aged are killed, he will, therefore, believe it right to kill them; if he lives where it is not done, he will believe it wrong. All of this, it is urged, demonstrates that there is no way to make an absolute decision. It is not so much that killing the aged is approved by society, but rather that it is done that makes it moral, on this view. The real principle is that one ought to do what his society approves or does because he is a member of that society. Using a quite similar argument, Dr. A could argue that since abortion is the custom, it is moral or at least not immoral.

Now, these two arguments, namely, what is moral is what is approved by society and what is moral is what is done in the society, at bottom involve the same principle. The wide divergence of moral codes in different societies is taken as evidence that moral principles are not absolute. Whether or not the divergence of practices does justify social relativism is not the issue here. We are concerned to ask, "What do those who advocate such moral principles mean to say?" The moral argument presented by Dr. A, in terms of this principle, is as follows:

> One ought to do what society approves.
> Society approves abortion (or killing the aged).
> _____
> Therefore, one ought to do abortions (or kill the aged).

> One ought to do abortions (or kill the aged).
> One ought not denounce what one ought to do.
> _____
> Therefore, it is wrong to denounce abortionists (or those who kill the aged).

This argument is, of course, entirely unconvincing to anyone who lives in a society that disapproves abortion, and for an interesting reason.

To such a person it is simply not true that society approves abortion. He may not deny that another society does, but his does not. So the sentence, "Society approves abortion," as it stands is ambiguous. To clarify the argument, we need to specify "society" as it occurs in this statement more adequately. If we did, the argument might read:

> One ought to do what society approves.
> The society of which I am a member approves abortion.
>
> _____
>
> Therefore, one ought to do abortions.

In this expression "society of which I am a member" denotes a specific society, say Bantu or American, etc. The second premise is then a statement of fact about a particular society, i.e., the one of which I am a member and hence apparently capable of being tested for its truth.

## The Ambiguity of the Principle

But the first premise is also unsatisfactorily stated. If we accept it as it stands, the principle may have two possible meanings: "One ought to do what any society whatsoever approves," or "One who lives in a given society ought to do what that society approves." Each of these interpretations leads to difficulties. That one ought to do what any society approves is obviously contrary to the basic meaning of social relativism, for it sets the dictates of a society as an absolute principle, which is counter to the relativity of morals, in the sense that they vary from society to society. If, therefore, the principle that one ought to do what any society approves is an absolute principle, then even if a society does not approve this principle, it still remains a moral principle. Furthermore, if one ought to do what any society approves, then one would be caught in a net of contradictory obligations, for different societies, and, indeed, the same society, approve quite contrary practices. It is, however, most often the case that when one urges that this principle determine actions, he usually means that what ought to be done is what the particular society in which he lives approves. Few who hold such a view would want to say that *everyone* ought to do what their society approves, i.e., what a particular given society approves, but rather that everyone ought to do what the society to which he belongs approves. The principle can be reformulated in some such fashion as this: "A given person ought to do what the society in which he lives approves."

*Right is What any Society Approves*

As a consequence, if the society in which a person lives approves abortion, then he ought to approve it and not obstruct its performance. If the society in which an individual lives approves mercy-killing, then when needed it should be done. If most people in a given society approve cheating, then for the member of that society cheating is moral. If the Nazi society approves the slaughter of Jews in crematoria, then in that society such acts are moral. The fact that the Jewish society disapproves, or that democratic societies do so also, would merely mean that in those other societies such acts are immoral and would not in any sense indicate that in a Nazi society they were not moral. A Nazi could be immoral in the context of American society for exactly the same deed which entitled him to be called moral in his society. On this view, a person called moral in a Nazi society would be called immoral in an American society – and there would be no contradiction.

*Social Relativism and Sociology*

Acceptance of the foregoing view is tantamount to asserting that the statement, "A is moral (or immoral)", is an incomplete sentence. To complete the statement one would need to specify the society in which A lived and which served as the frame of reference in which the word "moral" was defined. As a result, to find the meaning of the principle under consideration we would need to investigate the nature of the society in which the act was performed and judged and see how that society defined moral acts.

This can bear further illustration. It is usually the case that a boy who wishes to join a gang must show himself worthy of membership in that gang. Accordingly, he, let us say, robs and beats an old man. For this deed he is punished by a jail term. The ambivalent evaluation of this deed is striking. The robbery and beating are "wrong" from the point of view of ordinary citizens. It is "right" from the gang's point of view. Ordinary society considers the jail sentence punishment; it is a badge of distinction from the gang society's point of view.

Although this example illustrates the inherent relation held to exist between moral judgments and a society's mores, it also reveals another important fact. The boy who is a member of the gang-society is also a member of the society of the ordinary citizen. Any given individual belongs to societies of various sorts. He belongs to a church, a club a family, a community and so on almost indefinitely. If the principle is to be useful, somehow the society to which it refers must be more adequately delineated. Until we know the referent of "society" was cannot determine what society approves and therefore what we ought or ought not to do.

## Criterion vs. Standard

But even if we know what society is the norm, how can we decide what that society approves? Since it has often been claimed that the major goal of societies is to preserve themselves, we will do well to clarify a distinction which if ignored can lead to confusion. Suppose someone says that a society approves what helps preserve it. The principle, "One ought to do what society approves," is then equivalent to "One ought to do what helps to preserve society." It is not simply the fact of social approval that makes an act obligatory, but its conduciveness to societal preservation. What helps preserve one society may be destructive to another, so the relative character of the principle is retained. But social approval is now a *criterion* and not a *standard*. A person might in a given instance perform an act socially approved yet injurious to his society In such an event the act would be one he ought not to have done, even though it was socially approved. But if social approval is made the standard then if the deed is approved it ought to be done no matter whether it benefits or injures society. The fact that normally no society would approve what helps destroy it indicates that social approval is a criterion and not a standard. Social approval may be the result of a consideration of consequences but it may also be the manifestation of an emotional state – a passing whim or fancy which disregards consequences. If social approval alone is the standard, we could not call what society approved, not even if it destroyed the society, immoral.

There are other things that society may approve in addition to its survival. For example, society may approve whatever leads to the happiness of its members, or whatever leads to improved working conditions, etc. These, however, need not be taken as standards, but rather as criteria by which to decide what society does or does not approve. If any one of these, however, replaces social approval as the standard, then it becomes the end to be sought. The relativity could still be there in the sense that it is the happiness of a particular society that is sought, but in a given society there would also be a relativity of means. The means of attaining happiness in one society may lead to unhappiness in another – but in both what ought to be done is what leads to the happiness of that society. Under such conditions there is always a way of deciding what ought to be done in a given society through a consideration of consequences. But if one takes seriously the interpretation of the principle simply as referring to social approval, the way to discover what is approved is by looking for what is approved.

## What Is Society?

For the time being, the principle "One ought to do what society approves" will be taken to mean that what society approves is to be done simply because society does approve it. The problem is to discover what society approves. Obviously, if to be moral is to do what society approves, then if we would be moral we need to know what is approved.

The issue between Dr. B. and Dr. A. can be formulated more precisely. When Dr. A says that Dr. B ought to do what society approves and that the act of denunciation would be disapproved, Dr. B retorts that he is doing exactly what society approves since publicly society makes abortion a crime. The issue then appears to be a factual one. Dr. A and Dr. B have each appealed to what society approves or does not approve. Being scientific men, they know that factual questions can be decided only by a consideration of the facts. What could be simpler than to find out what society approves or disapproves? Yet the plain state of affairs is that both Dr. A and Dr. B are presumably appealing to the same thing but are making conflicting affirmations about it. If what society did approve were evident then we would not expect two scientific men to contradict each other so obviously. But there is a second alternative. They may be talking about different things when they appeal to what "society" approves. So let us ask each to say what or whom he intends by the word "society". We give Dr. A the first reply.

"When I say that society approves abortion, I mean the people of this town in which we live and practice our profession." To this Dr. B replies,

"I live in this town, and I certainly don't approve. Furthermore, I am sure that the clergymen of our town don't either. How many have you asked?"

"Since I and a few whom I know," says Dr. A, "do approve, you cannot say that society doesn't either."

To this Dr. B must accede. "Then if by society you mean the people of the town, we cannot say that society approves or disapproves, can we?"

But Dr. A is not finished yet. "I suppose when I refer to society I mean those among whom I practice."

The reply to this is even more obvious. Dr. B replies, "Those among whom I practice do not approve. Certainly they have as much right to be included in our society as those among whom you practice."

The discussion has shown that before we can decide what society approves, we need to know what society is. It should be evident that Dr. A's appeal to "society" is indeed vague. It could be made more specific. For example, Dr. A may be referring to those who have benefited by the practice, or to a selected group of physicians who for realistic reasons feel it to be desirable as a practice. Likewise, Dr. B may be referring to his church group, or to the Medical Society, or to expressed opinions of a representative group such as (say) a welfare society or civic club. But in many cases the use of the word "society" is emotive. It is a word which carries strong authoritative tones so that a reference to what "society" approves has the effect of exerting compulsion on one's thinking. What is often meant, as in Dr. A's case, seems to be "the group to which I belong", so that when Dr. A says "society approves abortion" he means "the group to which I belong," i.e., those who approve abortion. What he is giving us in that case is a tautology: "Those who approve abortion, approves abortion." When the subject term "those who approve abortion," is disguised by the word "society", the tautological character is concealed and the assertion is given plausibility.

### Society is Not the Law

Simple societal approval is rarely something precise enough to serve as a meaningful criterion for moral behavior. Nor are such devices as identifying social approval with legally sanctioned modes of behavior adequate. It is not enough to say, "What I mean by society is its expression in the law." When a mode of behavior is given legal sanction, it may be despite the disapproval of society. So, for example, the prohibition of the sale of alcoholic beverages was extremely unpopular, yet legally sanctioned. The anti-segregation laws are part of the law of the land; yet in some parts of the country they are heartily disapproved. In fact, the difficulty of defining the "society" which approves is well illustrated by these anti-segregation laws. The very societies (Southern) that approve segregation contain within themselves societies that disapprove it, while the country at large has declared segregation illegal. A careful distinction needs to be made between legal behavior and moral behavior. The law is not necessarily moral, nor is the moral yet legal. It should be clear that legally sanctioned behavior is approved by those who make the laws at any rate. Yet, I hardly think we would be willing to call our law-makers our society, nor even to identify their approval with societal approval. The history of revolutions shows the falsity of such an identification.

*Society is Not the Sovereign*

Nor is it possible to identify society with the sovereign on the grounds
that he who can enforce his will makes not only the law but the morals.
A Louis XIV, who proudly asserts, "I am the State (L'Etat c'est moi),"
and thereby intends to identify himself with society and his approval
with societal approval, often winds up with his head under an axe wieded
by an executioner with the approval of others who call themselves the
State (or Society). At any rate, unless we want to say that where there is
no sovereign there is no society, the two appear distinct. When we wish
to learn something about a society, we do not look to the sovereign of
the State. Perhaps in a democratic state the sovereign (i.e., the people)
may be viewed as most closely identified with society.

By this time it is evident that it is not easy to give meaning to the principle that one ought to do what society approves. We have tried a number of substitutions, identifying "society" with more definitely specified
sorts of things:

> "One ought to do what the law approves,"
> "One ought to do what the community approves,"
> "One ought to do what the sovereign approves,"

and none of these was found adequate, either because the identification
was not correct, or the new entity was itself vague.

*The Organic Theory of Society*

Two attempts to define "society" have been historically quite influen-
tial. It will, therefore, be of interest to discuss them briefly. Each of these
two definitions has been adopted by an aggressive political ideology. The
first of these bases its definition on pseudo-biological concepts and defines "society" as "Folk." The second definition relates the word "society"
to economic concepts and defines it as "class." The "Folk" is basic to the
Nazism of Adolf Hitler, the "Class" to the Communism of Marx and
Lenin. In accordance with these identifications, the societal principle
becomes either "One ought to do what is best for the Folk" or "One
ought to do what is best for his class." In each case the obligation to act
or not act in a specific way depends, again, upon the consequences of
the act. If, in the one case, the consequences benefit the Folk
either by aiding it in its struggle for survival and supremacy or
by being otherwise in its best interests, then the act ought to be done.
Likewise, in the other case, if the act being considered is in the best interests of the class to which a person belongs, he ought to do it. Both Nazi

and Communist theoreticians were quick to see that their proposals needed to be made more precise. So the Nazis defined the Folk in terms of race and this in terms of ancestry. The "German Folk" was the "German race." And any person was a member of the Folk in whose veins flowed German blood. However, the Folk was not merely the sum of all those who were of German (Aryan) ancestry but it contained them as organs. The person of German blood was to the German Race as, for example, an arm is to the body as a whole. An arm is an arm only as it is part of the body. In the same way a person is what he is only as a member of the Folk. Further identification of the Folk with its expression in the German State and the Leader (Fuehrer) as its means of making its will known, made the doctrine clear enough for application at least.

The application of the definition of society as the Folk and the result of the elevation of the Folk to the summit are terribly clear and equally horrible. If both Dr. A and Dr. B were good Nazis, Dr. B could say to Dr. A, "You are quite wrong when you say that abortion is approved by society, if you mean the Folk. Only traitors can fail to see that for the Folk to be strong it needs soldiers; soldiers are made from people and the more people the stronger the Folk. Abortion is a practice that deprives the Folk of its potential strength and therefore should not be practiced except upon people not of the Folk." (Lest this seem farfetched, illegitimacy in Nazi Germany was approved on precisely this basis.) Similar considerations would show that cheating, murder, violating contracts, etc., all may at times be obligatory and moral depending upon whether or not the Folk was to benefit by the act. In this fashion, the most horrible crimes were justified as moral because they aided the Folk.

## The Marxist Theory of Society

The Communist takes a different path; yet there is an interesting similarity, as we shall see. He sees society as groups of people organized for the purposes of production. The type of society, i.e., the type of group organization, is a function of the modes of production. So a feudal society differs from a capitalist society because production is carried on in a different fashion. But every economic system contains two chief classes, one working for survival and the other owning the means of production, an exploited and an exploiter class. What a person considers moral or immoral is ultimately based on this class structure and hence depends on the class to which the person belongs. The classes are in constant conflict, and the important and highest goal is the victory of one's class.

Hence, the principle becomes: "One ought to do what serves the class."
For the Communist, of course, "class" means "working class."

What one ought to do, therefore, varies with the person and his class.
So what may be moral to one is immoral to another in a different class,
and there is no way for a person in one class to judge another in a different class. To say "Cheating is immoral" means "Cheating by A in class C
is immoral." Since A can be only in class C, the statement is well defined.
A person in class D can judge the cheating in only one of two ways. He
can either say, "If I belonged to class C, then the cheating would be immoral," or he can say, "If A were in class D the cheating would not be
immoral." The two statements are not contradictory. If A and B are
both in class C, then they can disagree as to the morality of cheating,
but not if they are in different classes. However, what they would then
be disagreeing about would be a factual matter, namely, whether cheating did or did not aid class C in its struggle with other classes. Whether
or not A was a member of a given class – the proletariat or bourgeoisie,
to use the names of the two classes in a capitalist society – depends on
whether A sells his labor or owns the means of production.

How this works out can be shown by giving another twist to the abortionist example. Suppose Dr. A and Dr. B argued in communist terms.
Then Dr. B might say, "As a member of a capitalist society, you should
naturally be anxious to keep the cost of hiring labor as low as possible.
Hence, you should be opposed to abortion, which would help keep the
labor supply down. By practicing abortion you go counter to the interests of your class." To which we can imagine Dr. A's saying, "It is precisely because I do not consider the interests of the capitalist class, but
those of the worker, that I do these things. Why should I not help labor
raise its standards of living by helping to keep the labor supply down?"
Dr. A and Dr. B now disagree about which class is to be benefited, and
if Dr. A and Dr. B were members of different classes, or considered themselves as such, no possible rational agreement could result.

The meaning of "class" would be plain enough if there were but two
or more distinct classes, so that of any person we could say he is a member of one and not of another class. If a class is defined by the people who
make it up, then in American society at least the term is vague because
a worker may own stock in the company which employs him. If "class"
is defined in terms of the ownership of means of production, the meaning is clear, but the application in contemporary America impossible.
The replacement of "society" by "class" in this principle really helps
us very little. Class, indeed, becomes an emotive term.

## Application of the Societal Principle

The question of deciding what society approves, is as difficult to solve as that of the meaning of "society", and depends upon it. Consider the first form of the principle, "One ought to do what society approves." How, indeed, can we find out what society approves? Even if we define "society" as those individuals who are united by certain ties, say, town citizenship, how can we decide what they approve? Shall we take a vote? Or send sociologists with questionnaires? Even if we did, what would be revealed? What most people did approve at the time of the census? There would still be some who would disapprove and hence we are really saying not that one ought to do what society approves, but what the majority approves. Moreover, we would be urging that one ought to do what society (or the majority) approves, or better, approved at a given date. It would be necessary to set up some sort of continuous public opinion survey, on the basis of which we could have nightly tele-casts, like weather reports, on what was obligatory for the day along with predictions as to what would be tomorrow. This begins to sound rather ridiculous.

In the case of German Nazism, what the Folk approved turned out to be what the Fuehrer (Leader) said the Folk approved, and Hitler, the Fuehrer, was at least partly mad. As for the Communists, what the class approves is what the Communist Party says it approves, and the Party is made up of men who seek power.

Another possibility is to say that whatever is not expressly forbidden is approved. It may be satisfactory to say that whatever is not on the statute books is not a law, but an analogous statement for morals is not satisfactory. There are many things not expressly forbidden in a society, yet not approved, such as, for example, the killing of a burglar who does not threaten your life. What is expressly forbidden is put into legal form, and laws are not moral principles even if they serve as a standard for action much as the moral principle does.

Despite these comments, we do often know whether a given act will be approved or disapproved. Most people certainly will condemn unne-cessary brutality on the part of police officers; most people will approve an act of heroism, and so on. We know what is approved by watching people's reactions, by reading our newspapers, by noting what eminent people say about certain deeds, and by considering the literature of the society. We knew that Hitlerite Nazis, in general, approved murder and illegitimacy under certain conditions. But, and this indicates the difficul-ty of applying the principle, it is claimed that many Germans did not approve. All of this reveals that the principle is an inverted one. What is approved by society, as evidenced by these sources, is approved because it benefits society, or is moral for other reasons and is not moral because approved. Of this we shall speak later. At this point, all we need say is that if one is confronted by a moral problem, to do or not to do, then he can apply the principle by first reading what has been said about such deeds, asking people what they approve, and so on. After that has been done, one decides whether or not the act is societally approved. If the decision is in the affirmative, the act may be performed, and, on this principle, is moral.

*Social Approval Implies the Immorality of Individualism*

This may sound strange because it seems to leave all those who revolt against customary modes of behavior condemned as immoral. What sort of principle is it that says, for example, that the person who refuses to exchange wives in the face of the fact that his society (group?) does approve, is immoral? Or that ends in a judgment that when Jesus chased the moneylenders from the Temple, he did wrong since society approved moneylenders in the Temple?

Finally, if society means people, then the principle places the approval of the majority over that of (say) moralists, clergymen, and even psychologists who presumably know more about such matters than the majority of people. Yet it still is true that for most people, uncritical yet confronting a moral problem, societal approval may be a better guide than their own emotional states. One who maintains the societal principle consistently, could accept these consequences. But this would mean that society is not "most people" for they would consider those consequences evidence that this principle is not adequate as a moral norm.

*Summary*

In this chapter, we have considered the common appeal to society as a premise for moral judgments and decisions. Surprisingly, we encountered difficulties quite like those we confronted in interpreting the Self-principle. But there were others very different such as the confusion between morals and customs, as well as between moral principles and legal ones. But a major difficulty was the obscure nature of "society" as well as the sheer multiplicity of societies. All attempts to elevate either a universal society or a particular one to the throne of moral norm, led to difficulties whether it was the approval or the survival of society that was taken as basic. We concluded that, despite the relative ease with which it is occasionally possible to discover what was approved or disapproved by a society, the principle was at best preferable only to sheer emotional reactions and at worst completely useless if not antagonistic to effective moral decisions.

BIBLIOGRAPHY

Durkheim, E. *Elementary Forms of the Religious Life,* tr. by J. W. Swain, (New York: Macmillan Co., 1915).

Garvin, Lucius, *A Modern Introduction to Ethics* (Boston: Houghton Mifflin Co., 1953), Chap. 6, pp. 139-161.

Hill, T. E., *Contemporary Ethical Theories* (New York: Macmillan Co., 1950), Chap. 6, pp. 83-97.

Kattsoff, L. O., *Conflict of Political Ideals* (University of North Carolina Extension Bulletin, May, 1943).

Kolnitsky, P. F., "Communist Ethics and Religious Ethics," reprinted in *Current Digest of Soviet Press,* Vol. 4, No. 28 (August 23, 1952).

Levy-Bruhl, E., *Ethics and Moral Science,* tr. by E. Lee (London: Archibald Constable & Co., 1905).

Stephen, Leslie, *Science of Ethics* (London: Smith, Elder & Co., 1882) Chap. 4, pp. 137-172.

# CHAPTER IX

# SURVIVAL PRINCIPLES

## Survival and Everyday Living

In the twentieth century moral principles that can claim a scientific basis enjoy a special prestige. One such moral principle is based upon the Darwinian theory of biological evolution. A discussion of the scientific evidence for or against the scientific theory is out of place here. But one of its basic statements, the survival of the fittest, has by some been elevated to the rank of a moral principle. The fact, if it is one, of evolution that the fittest do survive, has been translated into the principle: "The fittest ought to survive." In everyday moral thinking this principle is often the last resort of rascals who can find no other justification for their behavior. Treachery and even murder have been justified by an appeal to the principle of survival. "Survival is the first law of nature," we are told by the traitor. "Man's instinct is to survive," is the blasè remark of one who has just refused to sacrifice his own welfare for that of others.

But we must not think that the appeal to the obligation to survive is always made only by scoundrels or immoral people. Perfectly respectable citizens who elevate the survival of others above their own, at times propose this obligation in explanation of their behavior. Many good people, for example, consider social survival of paramount importance. Indeed, even in the theory of evolution, the survival has been actually survival of the "fittest," and the fittest is not always the rascal.

It is interesting that "the survival of the fittest" is not used in support of moral decisions as commonly as most of the preceding principles are. In general the appeal to survival is made in extra-ordinary situations, such as in battle, or in competition (especially business). For example, one would not expect, ordinarily, to hear a young man who is trying to decide whether to lie to his girl friend say, "It is right for me to lie to her because the fittest must survive." Nor would it be usual to call upon the principle of survival in cases involving keeping a promise, unless keeping the promise endangers one's very life. On the other hand, we are not surprised to hear a businessman say, "In business only the fittest can survive. Hence, as long as my act does help me survive, it is the right thing to do." Or again, the use of torture to induce a prisoner to reveal military secrets might be justified in much the same way, "In war only the fittest can survive; therefore, any means may be used to keep oneself alive." In each of these examples, quite obviously it is implied that the businessman in question or the person using torture considers himself to be among those best fitted to survive.

In contemporary civilization it has become not too easy to feel that survival alone is a proper motive for actions. It is difficult to feel that one's survival is threatened by his neighbors in the course of one's daily living, if by "survival" is meant simply "staying alive." We would think it quite strange for anyone to say that he must cheat in order to stay alive. Such a remark would be taken as a sign of possible madness or of a most exceptional situation. Were such a remark made we would still not feel that the act was necessarily justified, or right, but that something needed to be done either to or for the person involved. We do not believe that people ought to be so situated that their existence is threatened. Moreover, should it happen that a person finds himself in such a predicament that he *must* act in a certain way or die, most ordinary people would want to insist that no moral decision was involved.

## The Moral Argument

If, however, survival is to be the key term in a moral principle, a decision to lie could be the result of an argument of this form:

> One ought to do what is necessary for survival.
> Lying is necessary for survival.
>
> ---
>
> Therefore, one ought to lie.

As before we must recognize that the second premise, "Lying is necessary for survival," is a factual statement and, given the meaning of the terms, is to be accepted or rejected on empirical grounds. It may be difficult to prove that lying is necessary for survival, but that is a matter for investigation. Presumably, one may be able in a given case to decide whether telling a lie will keep one alive, while telling the truth means death. Moreover, even if the lie did aid one to survive ,one could insist that survival can be assured by means other than the lie. If this happened the result would be a disagreement about matters of fact. These two factual questions need not detain us now, since they can be answered only by factual investigation, while our concern is with the moral principle used as the first premise.

Let us now construct another imaginary dialogue to illustrate how the survival principle may be used. Imagine John Doe captured by enemy soldiers and put into a prisoner-of-war camp along with others. Life is hard; daily his very existence is threatened by the sentries, by inadequate food, by disease, and all the other horrors of such a place. One day John is taken before the enemy commander of the camp and the following conversation takes place.

"Private, you look like a sensible person. How would you like to have better and more food, and less rigorous work?"

To this John Doe replies cautiously, "Of course, I would. But what do I need to do?"

"We are interested in the welfare of our prisoners. But we cannot help them if we don't know what they are saying. Obviously, they don't trust us, and until they do we must keep conditions hard."

"But where do I come in?"

"We think that if you kept us informed of what they are doing and saying, we could relax and feel ourselves able to improve their lot."

Now, John knows he is being asked to be a spy. He also knows that if he agreed his survival would, at least temporarily, be assured. In fact, he could argue in this way: "Nature made each person such that he seeks his survival, and I am no different from anyone else. I ought to do what is necessary for my survival – this is the first law of life."

It is important to realize that the enemy commander probably expects John Doe to respond in terms of just this principle. He hopes, indeed, that the threat to John Doe's life will so arouse his desire to live that John Doe will do as asked. The commander could have been quite wrong, for John Doe might have reasoned differently in somewhat the following fashion: "If I agree to do as asked, I'll live better. But what a way to survive! Survival under these conditions just wouldn't be worth it. I'd never get it off my conscience. How can I betray my friends?"

## The Ambiguity of "Survival"

The foregoing illustration points to an essential ambiguity in the meaning of "survival." The enemy commander apparently believes that "survives" means "continues to live." If these two terms are taken as synonomous the one may replace the other in the principle which then becomes: "One ought to do what is necessary to continue to live." In these terms, just staying alive is the all-important thing. Whatever one does just to stay alive is, from this point of view, the right thing to do. The second set of considerations seems to say something else. Here the point seems to be that not just staying alive but living in a certain way is what is desired. We do at times speak of a "living death", a most undesired way to stay alive.

If "survival" means simply "staying alive", then we are confronted by a rather paradoxical situation. In advanced civilizations, staying alive is very little trouble indeed. Only extraordinary situations such as crime, or war, or major catastrophes really pose threats to our existence. Most of us, in any case, do not very often find ourselves in circumstances in which we need to choose between acts in order to avoid destruction. We have surrounded ourselves with so many safeguards that most of us arise in the morning with little anxiety about survival. As a consequence, the principle in this form becomes not only useless but to a great degree meaningless because it offers no real alternative. If I am going to survive anyway, it makes no sense to say I must keep my promise if I am to survive.

*Implications of Survival Principle*

To make the point even more concrete, consider the doctor who was trying to decide whether or not expose the abortionist. His survival (ability to live) is not involved. Presumably he will be able to continue to live in the community or elsewhere whether he exposes the abortionist or not. In fact, it could even be argued that if he does expose the abortionist, and were threatened with violence, there exist ways by which he might protect himself, e.g., an appeal to the police. But life in the community could become unpleasant because of the attitudes of the neighbors, or the doctor could find himself inwardly troubled and living a very disturbed life.

We are not concerned with the person who says, "I'd rather die than lie." Such an individual is rejecting the survival principle and, at the moment, we are not considering whether one who appeals to the survival value of an act as reason for doing it, is or is not justified. We are concerned to discover what a person means who says he ought to do what is necessary for survival. If an appeal is made to this principle as a justification for an act, then he who makes the appeal cannot use expressions like "I'd rather die than . . .," because the one who appeals to the survival principle is urging that there is nothing he wouldn't do to avoid death. We may not believe him, and he may in a critical situation refuse to do something even at the risk of his life, but these are matters of action and not principle. He who accepts the principle will cheat, if cheating will enable him to live. Nor will he oppose a crime or hinder a criminal if to do either is to endanger his life. Even acts of courage, such as saving a child from drowning, will not be undertaken if it involves risking one's own life.

### "Survival" Implies a Quality of Life

These remarks do not refute the principle; they point out its significance in various sorts of situations. If these appear to be strange implications of a moral principle, this may be because the implications of this principle are being evaluated in terms of a different principle. We must concede, however, that ordinary people for the most part consider merely staying alive to be insufficient reason for doing all sorts of things. In fact, to judge by public reaction, to give up one's life for something of great value is considered far more noble and moral than merely to continue to survive. People have felt that life deprived of a certain unique factor or factors was not worth the candle. They do commit suicide, whether it be for lack of money, or lack of love, or simply out of fear. Apparently, then, we cannot take the word "survival" in the statement of this principle to mean merely "continuing to live." The quality of the life that is to be preserved is important, but the principle never seems to define that quality.

### Survival of Species

In addition to the ambiguity of the meaning of "survival," there is a vagueness about who is to survive. Darwin, for whom the notion of survival was a scientific one and not a moral principle, referred, so it seems, to the survival of the species and not so much to the individual. He was not saying, "One ought to do what enables the species to survive," but rather, "Everyone does what preserves, or tends to preserve, the species."

If we ought to do what preserves the species, then we need to determine what will enable the species to survive. Since, evidently, biologically speaking, there needs to be individuals in order that there be a species, the principle seems to imply that one ought to assure the existence of individuals of the species. With respect to the human species, this means that what must be preserved are living persons. The difference between this form of the principle and the one with which we started is that on the earlier one each person was obligated to strive to preserve his own existence whereas on the present one he must seek the preservation of certain humans even at the sacrifice of his own life.

## Survival of Superior Individuals

Let us consider a classic illustration. Two men, A and B, are in danger of drowning. Another person, C, can rescue only one of them and in consequence must choose which one he will try to save. Using the present principle he must decide which one, A or B, would do most to preserve the species. If "preserving the species" meant simply "providing for the existence of individuals of that species," it wouldn't matter in the least whether C saved A or B, since saving either would be preserving the species in this sense. However, suppose C knew that A was an atomic scientist on the verge of making a discovery that would extend the use of atomic energy for peace-time purposes while B was, let us say, a cab driver. It would appear that on the basis of the survival of the species principle C would need to save A since A's survival would be of greater value to the species in its struggle for existence. The individual must be viewed as a "means" towards the "end" of the preservation of the species, and whoever is the most useful and fruitful is the one to be saved. To consider a person merely as an instrument for preserving the species, however, seems morally objectionable. Nevertheless, this is an implication of the principle that places the preservation of the species above everything else.

This maxim that persons are to be considered as means to preserve the species leads to the conclusion that "survival of the species" cannot signify merely "keeping as many individual members of the species alive as possible." It must rather signify "keeping those individuals alive who contribute most to the survival of members of the species." If we define "superior individual" to mean "an individual who contributes most to the survival of the species," then the principle: "One ought to do what enables the species to survive," becomes "One ought to do what preserves the superior individual."

Apparently we have reached a precise and well-defined form of the principle. To complete the picture, we need to define the superior individual. If a superior individual is one who contributes most to the preservation of the species, can anything more be said about the kinds of things the superior man does and the type of person he is? In answering this question, we must hold fast to the above definition of "superior." A person may be superior to another in one respect, yet be inferior in another. General MacArthur is presumably superior to Harry Truman with respect to military ability, yet inferior to Albert Einstein with respect to scientific knowledge. John Doe might be superior to Joe Roe in adding figures, yet be inferior in respect to athletic prowess. The survival principle defines superior individuals in terms of the preservation of the species, and this makes matters more precise so far as the principle is concerned. Suppose John Doe is a trained athlete while Joe Roe is a laboratory scientist or an author. Both are drafted as privates in the military forces and are cut off behind enemy lines. John Doe knows how to survive under such conditions; Joe Roe doesn't. Joe may be intellectually superior because he is more educated and able to do abstract work, but he is inferior when it comes to survival.

In many cases, it is apparently easy to decide who will contribute most to the preservation of the race. Won't an industrious person do so more than an anti-social conspirator? And isn't an atomic scientist of more value to the race than the athlete? Perhaps, and perhaps not. Will a strong body preserve the race or a strong mind? The answer often depends on circumstances. In "civilized" warfare, atomic scientists are more important than athletes. In face-to-face combat, athletes are more important than scientists. So at times we feel we need more scientists; and at other times more athletes. What are considered to be "superior qualities" seems to be a function of what is thought to be valuable in preserving the species, i.e., in improving the qualities of individuals that enable the race to survive.

If we try to list those qualities that aid survival, we are faced with a fundamental disagreement between, for example, Christianity and Fascism, or between Hitler and Jefferson. Nietzsche and Hitler saw life as a struggle for survival. Nietzsche taught that those attributes which Christians believe best make for survival were precisely those which made for degeneration and destruction. Nietzsche viewed Christian morals as "slave-morality", a snare contrived by the weak to control the strong – the superior. To be kind, to be generous, to be considerate, these are the qualities that make for degeneracy, for weaknesses and for defeat in the struggle for power. The "superior man" decries and denies the morality of slaves; his code is that of the strong. The strong man is cruel, he is merciless, he destroys his enemie and overpowers his foes. He rules in his own interest; for, being strong, what he wishes he can enforce and what he wants he can get. These qualities may seem abhorrent to a Christian but, according to Nietzsche, if they do aid the superior to survive, they are moral traits. However, the superior must not only survive, he must procreate to preserve the species.

However else the superior excels, he must procreate if the species is to continue. And his offspring must be capable of further procreation. So it would appear that the "superior individual" is the one who can produce offspring and pass on to them his abilities to survive and produce offspring. This may sound rather crude, but it is an implication of the survival principle. If, therefore, offspring can be procured by treachery, seduction, and even rape, then the "superior" man does not hesitate to use these and any other methods to achieve his purpose. The stronger the person, the more ruthless he will be to achieve his success and this is evidence of his superiority. The others, the weaker ones, must serve him.

There are those who will think this is a distortion of the principle of survival. It will be urged that cruelty breeds cruelty; and treachery, lack of trust, and these traits are destructive. Moreover, the argument will run, the history of civilization shows that the principle of survival calls for peace and cooperation, love and kindness. Nietzsche, at least, and Hitler after him, didn't think so. Hitler made a distinction within the human race between inferior and superior peoples, and identified what he called the "Deutsche Volk" (German Folk) as the superior race. For them he saw a future of dominance, of supremacy. To achieve that dominance by any means whatever was held to be valid. The true representative of the Folk, the true Nordic, was a strong, cruel fighter. Only through strength and obedience to the will of the Folk as expressed by its leader (Führer) could the Nordic rise supreme. So for Hitler and his followers, the principle was altered to read: "One ought to do whatever makes for the survival and dominance of the Folk."

*Survival of One's Group*

It is important to be quite clear what the revision of the survival principle to mean survival of the race or Folk, involves. Suppose that in place of judging in terms of its effect on the survival of a particular race, one were to evaluate it in terms of its contribution to the survival of humanity as a whole. Then there would be a kind of universality to the principle. On the other hand, if we consider the survival of our own group alone, whether it be nation, folk, tribe, or church group, the principle suffers a radical restriction of its universality. It is no longer applicable to *all* persons but only to some. To that extent it suffers a lessening of its moral quality and tends to become a strategical slogan.

Furthermore, the primacy of the group means that no one outside that group can claim moral rights. For example, Hitler's followers considered all Jews to be non-Nordics; indeed, enemies of the German

Folk. As a result, the Jew was no longer a person to whom a Nazi had any moral duties at all. So Jews could be cruelly murdered, or deprived of their property, or made slaves with no moral stigma attached to the perpetration of these deeds. In point of fact, nothing evil done to a Jew was considered to be immoral or a crime, while aiding or giving comfort to a Jew was a crime. The extermination of Jews was considered necessary for Folk survival and, therefore, moral.

The Folk-Survival principle is based upon the assumption that there must always be mutual antagonism and constant struggle between various Folks and that in this continual struggle each person is obligated to do what helps preserve his own Folk. Since the Nordic is superior, he alone is worthy of survival. Nietzsche had proclaimed that the weak, seeking to subdue the strong and thereby to avoid the consequences of being weak, had banded together and created the code of Judeo-Christian morality as a check on the rights of the mighty. Hitler too saw Christianity as a Jewish plot to restrain the Nordic and prevent his coming to power. He felt that the Judeo-Christian emphasis upon peace and kindliness was a hindrance in the struggle for existence and power.

Where Hitler explained the struggle for existence in terms of a pseudo-biology and depicted it as one between "racial" groups within the human race, Marx explained it in economic terms as one between economic classes within the economic structure of all society. Should the Communist be confronted with the problem, say, of either committing murder or not, Marx's principle would require him to ask, "Will this murder or, better, killing, aid the class to which I belong in its struggle for survival and power?" If he concluded it would, then he would be justified in killing; otherwise this act would be wrong. In other words, the principle he uses takes the survival and victory of the class to which one belongs as the standard in terms of which to make decisions.

Although we have already discussed the term "class" in an earlier chapter, it will not be wasted to repeat the analysis here. The Communist sees mankind divided into groups determined by the modes of production that exist in the world. There are two major groups. One group consists of all those who produce (the proletariat) and the other of those who own the means of production (the bourgeoisie, in contemporary society). The history of man is a story, and a bitter one at that, of the struggle between these two groups, or classes. Moreover, each class determines the character of its members. A person is what he is because he is moulded by the class to which he belongs. What sort of person is admired or disliked is a function of this very same class structure. What a member of the working class considers the ideal worker, the ideal executive, or the ideal industrialist to be like will be very different from what a member of the capitalist class thinks of these ideal types. In fact, says the Communist, our very moral ideals are the results of our economic system. Compare, for example, what the conception of a moral person is in an industrial society with that of a moral person in an agricultural one. Honesty is the "best" policy for the businessman, but not for the imperialist, while for the worker it is said to be the "only" policy.

The Communist insists that everything a man is and does has its roots and origins in the class into which he is born and by which he becomes what he is. Hence (and this is a strange "hence"), he owes his very existence to the class, and the standard for evaluating his behavior must be the survival of that class. The basic moral principle becomes then: "One ought to do what leads to the victory of the class." However, since the Communist considers himself a member of the proletariat (the class of those who earn their living by their labor), the principle really is: "One ought to do what leads to the victory of the proletariat in the class struggle."

Our previous discussion has revealed that no survival principle can be considered meaningful unless and until there is an answer to the question, "Whose survival?" It is conceivable that a given act may be immoral when judged by one survival principle so far, say, as it involves the death of the actor – and moral when judged by another, so far, say, as it involves the survival of the Folk, or Class, or Race. In order to be able to apply a survival principle, one has to decide which is more important, the survival of oneself, of one's class, of mankind, or of one's Folk. This decision is not a moral one since it is expressed not as an ought statement, but as a statement of the form, "My existence is the most important thing," or "The survival of the Class is the most important thing."

## What is it to Survive?

Another fact needs emphasis. To remove the ambiguity from the term "survival" not merely must there be an answer to the question, "Whose survival?"; but also to the question, "What state of affairs would the survival of a given group involve?" Quite often, those who maintain some form of the survival principle also describe the kind of world that will be achieved if the survival principle is obeyed. Hitler describes the ideal world as one in which the Nordic Folk rules and is served by all other people who are by definition inferiors. Hence, the Nordic Folk not merely continues to survive but survives as master. The Communist dreams of a society in which the proletariat is supreme and lives according to the maxim, "From each according to his ability, to each according to his need," and where class distinctions based on economics are obliterated. For the Communist survival means not merely to live but to live in a classless society.

How these different interpretations affect moral considerations can be illustrated by considering the thoughts of a lawyer trying to decide whether to misrepresent the facts in a given case. He might reflect that if he did so he could win his law case and would be able to live in his community as a successful lawyer. On the other hand, he might realize that, should he be found to have misrepresented facts, life in his community might become impossible. He might lose all his friends, his status, and become an outcast. We might even add that unless he misrepresented the facts he would lose his case and his client would be sentenced to die.

If the lawyer decided that saving the life of his client was above all the most desirable thing, he would misrepresent the facts. Or if to the lawyer the life of his client was far less important than his own position in society, he would not do so.

If the lawyer were a member of a Nazi society, his reflection would be quite different. If his client were Jewish, the lawyer might feel that the life of the Jew was of no importance and, therefore, he could misrepresent without scruple even if it meant saving the life of a non-Nordic. On the other hand, since the good of the Folk was of paramount importance, he could quite well lose his case and yet continue to live in the community.

If the survival of oneself, the Class, the Folk, and so on is of paramount importance, then moral behavior is only a means to be used in the struggle for survival. Morality serves as a "weapon" in a struggle in which each man, or class, or Folk, is against every other man, or class, or Folk. Where "survival" refers to some Class, or Race, or anything other than the individual, the application of the principle may result in a situation in which the individual may need to destroy himself. But given a decision concerning whose survival is to be paramount and the sort of survival to be sought, the survival principle is relatively easy to apply. A person who decides that his own survival is of prime value above all else will seek to ensure it. He will feel free to cheat, lie, murder, steal, or be honest, kind, charitable, etc. whichever serves his survival best, as he judges the consequences. He will then be moral, if his act is right, i.e., if it leads to his own survival; immoral if it doesn't. It is as simple as that, or so it appears.

## Moral Disagreements and Survival

A principle such as this, which places the survival of the individual above all things, would make moral disagreements impossible of resolution. In fact, two people could never really disagree on a moral problem, but only on who is to survive. A, judging an act of cheating, calls it moral because it promotes his survival; while B calls it immoral because it imperils his own survival. Each appeals to the same principle and each is correct on his own grounds. A third person, say, a neutral observer, would then have to say:

> "To cheat is moral, since it preserves A";
> "To cheat is immoral, since it destroys B."

Such an outcome seems quite impossible to accept, unless C has decided that A is more important than B, or conversely. Since an act which benefits one person will usually affect another adversely, no third person not personnally involved can evaluate such an act. So not merely will the egoistic survival principle make for conflict; it will not satisfy a basic requirement of a moral principle, namely that by it *any* person can judge an act. Only the doer of the act can evaluate it, and his judgment is decisive only for himself. The egoistic principle of survival becomes, "One ought to do what makes for one's own survival," and hence since "one" refers to the person uttering the statement, he seeks his own survival regardless of what happens to others. The outcome can only be a "war of all against all", a complete relativism.

However, if "survival" is taken to mean "survival of the Folk," or "Class," etc. then this situation does not arise since C, a neutral observer, can decide on the basis of the cheating whether A's act does or does not contribute to survival. If C decides A's survival will make for the survival of the Folk, or Class, etc. then C can say the act of cheating is moral. If A says the act is moral because it is conducive to the survival of the Folk and B says it isn't, their disagreement is obviously factual. If A could be shown that the act did not lead to Folk survival, it is conceivable he would change his mind about its morality. Given the principle of survival (other than individual), all the resulting questions seems to be factual and of the type: "Will . . . aid survival?", where the blank space is to be filled by a description of a specific act.

The disagreements then concern either 1) what is taken to be of paramount importance or, 2) what does or does not lead to the survival of whatever is to survive. 1) is a disagreement between alternative moral systems; 2) is a disagreement on means.

*Summary*

In this chapter we have examined the principle of survival as a moral premise. We have seen that it can mean survival either of a given person or of something of which the person considered himself a part. Analysis of the meaning of "survival" indicated that it does not signify merely staying alive but tacitly refers to the prolongation of a type of life. Whatever the additional quality life needs to have, the value of that quality seems to be something other than its conduciveness to staying alive. This implies a principle superior to the principle of survival. The application of the principle was also seen to lead, at times, to strange consequences. It was concluded that before the principle could be regarded as meaningful one needed a) to define "survival," and b) to decide whose survival is important.

### BIBLIOGRAPHY

Garvin, Lucius, *A Modern Introduction to Logic,* (Boston: Houghton Mifflin Co., 1953), Chap. 14, especially pp. 380 ff.
Hobbes, T., Leviathan, reprinted in *English Philosophers from Bacon to Mill,* ed. by E. A. Burtt, (New York: Modern Library, 1939), pp. 129-238.
Nietzsche, F., *Beyond Good and Evil,* trans. by M. Cowan, (Chicago: Henry Regnery Co., 1955, Gateway Ed.), Cf. especially "Fifth Article."
Titus, H. H., *Ethics for Today,* 2nd ed., (New York: American Book Co., 1947), Chap. 11, pp. 169-184.
Tsanoff, R. A., *Moral Ideals of Our Civilization,* (New York: E. P. Dutton, 1942), Chap. 32, pp. 503-521.
—, *Ethics,* (New York: Harper & Bros. 1947), Chap. 5, pp. 84-103.
Wheelwright, Philip, *A Critical Introduction to Ethics,* rev. (New York: Odyssey Press, 1949), Chap. 4, pp. 95-124.

# CHAPTER X

# OPPORTUNISTIC PRINCIPLES

When someone makes a moral decision, he bases it on a principle which, he believes, applies not only to himself but to everyone similarly situated, and not only to that act which at the moment he contemplates doing, but to every act of that type. These fundamentals are recalled to indicate that "the opportunistic principle" may at times not be a moral principle at all. To clarify this remark, we will contrast two situations, one in which the opportunistic principle is not involved, the second in which it is.

## Absence of Principle

Some years ago, the then Kaiser of Germany had signed a solemn treaty promising, among other things, not to invade Belgium. When, in 1914, war became the order of the day and the occasion for an invasion arose, the Kaiser is reported to have said something to the effect, "A treaty is but a scrap of paper", and to have torn up the treaty. The first war to make Germany supreme was under way. Even if this tale has no basis in fact, it illustrates the matter under discussion. The Kaiser was about to engage in a war; and there is but one aim in war, to win. The invasion of Belgium appeared to be a necessary step to victory. This situation, however, does *not* illustrate what will be called "opportunism" because it does involve a principle, namely: "Everything that insures victory is right." And this principle was the norm for the evaluation of actions. The Kaiser, in other words, believed he was acting rightly on the basis of a principle.

The second situation is this. Consider a man P who promises to help his neighbor, N, mow N's lawn. When the day for P to fulfill his promise arrives he doesn't show up. When N meets P he inquires why P did not keep his promise. P replies that he just didn't feel like mowing a lawn. If P is told that he ought to keep his promises, he retorts that he has no such principle. In fact P maintains that he does whatever he pleases when he pleases, so far as he is able to do so. This is what will be called an "opportunistic principle," and a person who acts in terms of it will be referred to as an opportunist.

In this case, the principle which directs behavior is the rejection of all principles of the sort we have been talking about. P differs from the Kaiser because the Kaiser did have a principle which directed his behavior and the opportunism was chiefly one of means while P has only the rejection of principles to direct his behavior. The Kaiser keeps a promise if it leads to victory. P keeps a promise only if it pleases him to keep it. The distinction is further accentuated when it is realized that the Kaiser says, "One ought to do what leads to victory," while the opportunist says, "I do what pleases me, and if it pleases me not to do what pleases me, I don't do it." He would not want to say, "One ought to do what pleases one," but only "I do what I please." Evidently, "I do what I please" may be only a statement of fact or even an emotional declaration of independence rather than a moral principle, as may happen when a teen-age daughter informs her worried mother "I'll do as I please." Now it appears that the emphasis here is on the first person personal pronoun, "I". The teen-ager is trying to say that whatever she does will be the result of her own choice. "I'll do what I please" seems to mean "I'll do what I choose to do (and not what you choose for me)." This is a declaration of independence. Yet it may signify something else. Its significance may be as an expression of abandon: "I'll do anything that at the moment I feel like doing" or "I'll do what I want to do, and take what comes."

The implications of a declaration of independence are not our concern at the moment. The person who declares "I'll do what I choose" is not necessarily using the expression, "I do what I please," as a principle for moral decisions, or for that matter for any sort of decision. He (or she) is simply trying to say that the responsiblity for making decisions is one he wishes to bear himself. This is all to the good since, as we saw in an earlier chapter, moral decisions presuppose a moral agent, and one cannot be a moral agent who does not make his own decisions. But one who asserts, "I do what I *choose*," may be saying that he has deliberated and chosen this particular act rather than another. In making this choice, presumably, the person could use some principle or other.

## Doing as One Pleases

We need to do two things; first to analyze the possible meanings of "I do what I please" and, secondly, to see how this assertion functions in a given situation. As we have seen, a person who says "I do what I please" may well deny that he means to say either "I ought to do what I please" or "Everyone ought to do what he pleases." The first alternative is rejected because of the implied obligation which limits action, since it seems to entail that if, for example, I want to kill I must see if that pleases me. If it does, I must kill; if not, I must refrain.

The expression "I do what I please," however, can be taken to convey an absence of obligation or a rejection of all principles. The second alternative is unacceptable because it expresses a universal principle to the effect that everyone is obligated to do what pleases him. But when one appeals to the fact that he does what he pleases, he is not concerned to establish any sort of principle at all. He appears to be simply stating a fact, namely, that what he does he pleases to do.

In summary, a number of interpretations of the statement, "I do what I please" are possible: "I do what pleases me", or "I do what I want to do", or "I do what I, at the moment, am inclined to do."

The following imaginary dialogue will illustrate two of these. Joe has been accused of killing his roommate. The interrogation goes like this:

"Joe, you killed your roommate?"

"Yes, I did."

"Why?"

"Because I do what I please."

"But that isn't an answer. Why did it please you to kill him?"

"I didn't say I was pleased by his death. I merely said I do what I please."

"I dont't understand. You say you were not pleased by his death, yet you killed him because it pleased you to do him to death."

Joe, who may be supposed to have had some philosophic training, replies, "Look here. When I say I do what I please, I do not mean I do what gives me pleasure, but rather I do what is entirely my own action and not something others force me to do. I am not a hedonist; I didn't kill for the pleasure it would bring."

Notice that being pleased to kill is not offered as a justification of killing but rather as a simple statement of psychological fact. And the assertion that one is pleased to kill is not equated with the assertion that one gets satisfaction from killing. He who kills because he does what he pleases may not at all be satisfied either with what he pleases to do or what he does. The point is that at the moment the act is done it pleases the doer of the act to do it. This is one reason why the expression, "I do what I please," cannot mean "I do what gives me pleasure." Pleasure is something that results from the act, while doing what pleases one describes the moment of action.

## The Role of Desire

Suppose that Joe had concluded the above conversation with the remark, "I am not pleased by the death of my roommate. In fact I will miss him. When I say I killed him because I do what I please, I mean I did what I desired to do. Surely, one can desire to do something which he knows will not be pleasant nor give pleasure?"

"You killed him, then, because you desired to kill him. What aroused the desire?"

This question places Joe in a dilemma. He can say that he desired to kill his roommate because of some wrong, or because he simply had the desire. Unfortunately, each of these explanations of the origin of the desire leads to undesirable consequences. If Joe admits he meant that he did what he desired and that he desired the death of his roommate because of some wrong, then Joe is really saying, "I killed because whenever someone wrongs me, I get a desire to kill that person." This will make Joe out to be a vicious person. If he says he means by "I do what I please," "I do whatever I desire to do" so that whatever the origin of the desire, whenever he has a desire no matter how irrational, he does what he desires, then he makes himself out to be something of a dangerous character acting on the impulse of the moment. Yet, surely, the person who asserts, "I do what I please" is not trying to make himself out to be either vicious or dangerous. He is trying to depict himself as a person who is not at the mercy of impulsive desires, a creature not driven to do things because of inner desires over which he has no control. The very assertion, "I do what I please," seems to imply control rather than a lack of it. It seems, if we may repeat, to underline the fact that my actions are mine and they are not determined by some person, or principle, or reason of any sort except my desire. I alone initiate them. I alone will say what I am to do and when I will do it. Perhaps, therefore, Joe is saying that he killed his roommate because he wanted to do so.

Psychologically and physiologically, wants arise when there is something lacking. If a person wants food, it is ordinarily because he needs nourishment. If someone wants to read a book, it is because the book supplies a lack. Usually that which is wanted is only a means enabling one to obtain that which is lacking. Moreover, it is often the case that where there are wants, there is an awareness of a lack even though there is no precise knowledge of what is lacking. For example, a person may want relaxation and, in consequence, want to go to the movies. Or, someone may want to take a trip yet not know exactly why. Now, it may be that when Joe says, "I do what I want to do," he is trying to tell us that he feels a lack of something which will be supplied if he acts in a certain fashion and, therefore, he does so act. If killing his roommate is the result of a lack of something of which he is aware, then he has perhaps chosen unwisely in selecting the means of attaining what he lacks. If it is the result of a lack of something he knows not what, then he is again a dangerous person. Clearly, one who kills another because he thinks that doing so will give him something he lacks, is not socially safe. He would be a rather strange person who finds it necessary to kill (or commit immoral acts) because of a vague feeling of lack. It would, in consequence, appear that the ordinary person who asserts, "I do what I please" cannot be saying, "I do what I want to do" if the word "want" means what we have just been considering.

## Emotivism

Perhaps, after all, the statement "I do what I please" is simply an emotional expression devoid of real meaning. It is conceivable that Joe really doesn't know why he killed his roommate. It may very well have been blind rage, or what people like to call "temporary insanity," or indeed the onset of some form of psychological disease that led to the killing. But Joe is called upon to justify himself, to give a reason for his act. Under these circumstances the poor fellow, feeling quite bewildered yet constrained to say something, exclaims, "I do what I please." His exclamation may be simply an admission that he doesn't really know except that something brought it about that he did what he did. Often enough an exclamation of this sort is used to "explain" a completely subjective act whose roots lie deep within the unconscious of the actor. It is unfair to ask someone in this condition what he means because "I do what I please" under such circumstances tacitly implies that there are springs of behavior not under the control of rational deliberation. To demand a meaning and justiffication, is to ask that the statement be submitted to rational analysis. To ask this under the assumed circumstances is to ask the impossible. If actions originate in non-conscious impulses of one sort or another, then the sentence, "I do what I please," is not directly cognitive at all. It does not really tell us that the act is the result of the "I" being "pleased" to do it. The sentence is an exclamation of bewilderment, rather than a description of a state of affairs.

If all moral principles were of this nature, then morals would be reduced to acts of the unconscious, and ethics would become psycho-analysis. This may be so, nevertheless our concern here is not to ask if this is the case but to explicate meanings. It would seem plausible that, at least in some contexts, the assertion, "I do what I please," is an exclamation, but in other cases it appears to be used as a moral principle.

## Summary of Usages

It should be clear why we said at the start of this chapter that the statement we are analyzing need not be a moral principle at all. We find the statement used in three different ways:

(1)     As a moral principle; i.e., as a universal, necessary, and mandatory statement. "I do as I please" then may be taken to mean "Everyone ought to do as he pleases."

(2)     As a factual statement; i.e., as describing the conditions under which one acts. It may or may not be taken to assert that *all* people do as they please, and it certainly does not imply that anyone ought so to act or that it is possible to act otherwise. It simply says that only when the speaker pleases to do something does he do it.

(3)     As an emotive statement; i.e., as either expressing one's approval of what is done, or as indicating bewilderment, or as a declaration of freedom.

After all these complications, one might suppose it would be possible to indicate without too much difficulty how the principle is used. That this is not easy will become evident soon enough.

## Opportunism and Moral Decisions

Let us consider now how the opportunistic principle is used in a moral situation. Suppose A has loaned B some money and the time has come for B to repay the loan. B, however, simply refuses and, when asked by A why he doesn't repay the loan, replies, "I don't please to do so." A, refraining from punching B, indignantly asserts, "But that is no reason. Surely you ought to repay your loans." To this B replies, "One ought to do what one pleases. I don't please to repay the loan. Hence, it clearly follows that I ought not to do so."

A can pursue the matter in one of two ways. He can treat B's reply as a joke and assume that B intends to pay what he borrowed. If B, however, insists that he is serious, then A can try to convince B of the untenability of such a position by seeking to show that B's principle cannot really be applied. As a point of attack, A asks B how he decides what he pleases to do. A assumes that B knows what the principle means, but A wishes to induce B to reject the principle. B's moral argument runs as follows:

> Everyone ought to do what he pleases.
> Therefore: I ought to do what I please.
> I do not please to repay the loan.
> Therefore: I ought not to repay the loan.

The point of A's question can be formulated in this way: "Suppose I grant your principle; I want to know how you know what does or does not please you to do." How can B discover what he is pleased to do?

It may occur to him that the way to discover whether or not he is pleased to repay this loan is to ask himself. This is a rather curious way to speak. We visualize B trying to decide whether or not to repay that annoying loan and imagine that he says to himself, "B, old boy, does it please you to return the money?" B replies, "B, my good man, it doesn't." So B says, "All right, I won't." Of course, this is absurd. The chances are that B did not even consider the question prior to A's demand for an explanation of how B arrived at his decision. In all likelihood B announced his refusal to pay the loan at the moment he decided not to repay it. But this caricature of the situation shows that we cannot accept the suggestion that one finds out what pleases him by asking himself. Indeed, it is quite likely that one cannot know at the moment of action whether or not doing something, or refraining from it, will be what he pleases. Even if B should protest that he was taken too literally and that what he did was to try to anticipate the future and that he really meant, "I do what I believe will please me after I have done it," there still remain problems that B needs to face up to in deciding what he is pleased to do.

Does B do what pleases him at the time regardless of what it pleases others to do or not? Suppose A were to say to B, "I grant your principle, and accept it. Since you don't please to repay my loan, it pleases me to shoot you, and this would certainly not please you." In brief, would it please B not to repay the loan if by doing so he would cause A to please to shoot him? If B means that everyone ought to do what it pleases him to do, then B cannot object to A's shooting him if it pleases A to do so as a consequence of B's refusal. If B denies that it pleases him to do what would make people react in a way that would be unpleasant to B, then B is considering the consequences of his act in an effort to avoid those that might rebound and cause him to do what he will not later be pleased to have done. It may please B not to repay the loan but not please him to cause A to kill him. In this case B comes very close to saying that what he pleases to do is conditioned by consequences. B then has placed himself in a predicament. If he judges correctly what the consequences will be and acts accordingly, then he has given preferential status to the consequences. As a result he will do this act because its consequences are such that it pleases him to effectuate them. But this is not what he is after. What he wants to do is to discover whether this act is such that it pleases him to do it. In other words, to say "I do what I please" involves a separation of the act from its consequences. This may not be possible. On the other hand, if he judges incorrectly about the consequences of the act, he may decide that it pleases him to do the act; yet the act will be such that if he knew its true outcome it would not please him to do it. In other words, B can be mistaken about what it pleases him to do. He can believe it pleases him to do a particular act; yet it ought not and would not please him to act in that manner if he knew more than he does. An act which pleases someone on the spur of the moment at the time of action may be quite unpleasant after it has been done. But if the consequences are taken into account, the principle is not opportunism.

### The Intrusion of a Prior Principle

The difficulty with this outcome lies precisely in the following consideration. If reason and consequences are to play an important role in deciding what it does or does not please one to do, then the expression, "I do what I please," can no longer make the claim it appears to make. When someone asserts that it pleases him not to repay a loan, or that it pleases him to kill his roommate, he seems to be saying that there is something about the event or deed *as such* that causes him to be pleased to accept it. As we have seen, one can say "It pleases me not to repay the loan"; and when told, "I will sue you for the money," can retort, "Go ahead! I don't care what the consequences are; I will do what pleases me." In other words, the principle as stated really directs one to ignore the consequences and reject reasons.

B, therefore, cannot say simply, "I do what I please" but must rather say something else: "I try to imagine myself doing the deed, and I try to see if the deed in itself is the sort of deed it would please me to do."

Such a modification of the opportunistic principle imputes to some deeds a characteristic which when it is present makes one pleased to perform them. The emphasis is shifted from the "I" to the "act"; the problem is not what sort of "I" am I that makes certain acts pleasing, but what sorts of acts are pleasing. This will retain the taint of opportunism only if the same characteristic may under one set of conditions make a person please not to do it and under another set of conditions to do it. B, for example, may when he has a lot of money please to repay the loan, while when he is in dire straits please not to repay it. This happens not because, having a lot of money, he is better able to do so, but because, say, he is in pleasant humor at the time and so he is pleased to pay A what he owes him. On the other hand, it is conceivable that B may have the money yet feel irritable, say, because of an upset stomach, and not please to repay the loan.

How difficult it is to apply the opportunistic principle is seen when we ask what characteristic repaying the loan needs to have in order that B please to repay it. This is a fair question, because B has said that when confronted by a choice of deeds he seeks to decide which one he is pleased (or would be pleased) to do. But this formulation of B's possible reply is unsatisfactory, because no matter what characteristic B says must belong to a deed he would be pleased to do, he can be accused of forsaking his principle and in reality choosing the deed for the sake of that characteristic. Suppose he says that a deed must be such that one would expect it lo lead to self-assertion, or to self-denial, or to amazement. Then what it pleases B to do is to bring these about and not merely to do what he pleases. The adoption of a characteristic that defines the act that pleases, signifies a surrender of the opportunistic principle.

## The Possibility of a Criterion

We introduced a distinction between a criterion and a defining characteristic in a previous chapter. This distinction can now be made by B to meet the objection we have just discussed. It is possible to urge that B has noticed that whenever he does what he pleases the deed does have this peculiar characteristic (say); people are anazed that that B does it. That is to say that what is involved is not a principle but an empirical generalization. Consequently, B uses this characteristic as a "criterion" in trying to anticipate whether or not he pleases to do the deed. "I do what I please" does not mean "I do what amazes people", but rather 'if the deed will amaze people, then it probably will be what it pleases B to do." Since this is an empirical generalization, it may very well happen that sometimes the deed will amaze people and yet B will not please to do it, or B will please to do it even though it will amaze no one. But as a guide for selecting what B will perhaps please (or not please) to do, this seems useful – if we can learn from the past at all. That an act will amaze people is a sign for B that the act in question will quite probably be what he pleases to do, but does not confer upon the act a property which defines it to be what B pleases to do.

Even though this reply is subtle, it has a strong point in its favor. It does, in fact, give us a means whereby one can select from among alternative courses of action the one that will most likely be selected. The assertion, "I do what I please," being fundamental, must be taken for what it is, a principle which nevertheless leads to criteria at least (i.e., identifying properties) for the selection of courses of action. Moreover, since different people please to do various sorts of things, one would expect (what is the case) that different people would point to diverse criteria. One person may find that whenever an act made him happy he was pleased to do it, another that whenever he made a sacrifice, the act was one he was pleased to perform, and so on. Furthermore, a person at one time may find one thing a criterion of what he pleases to do, and at another a totally different or even opposite criterion. This leads to a situation in which a person's choice is dependent solely upon his state or condition at the moment, unless psychological reasons can be adduced to show that what helps identify what pleases B is a fruition of his past experiences. If there were no regularity, then no empirical generalization would be possible. If there were, we would be compelled to admit that what we are dealing with is psychology and not morals. "I ought not to repay the loan," to be specific, turns out to mean only that as a result of some previous experiences repaying loans never did make me feel that I was being noble, and the feeling of being noble I have found usually accompanied those acts I was pleased to do. Therefore, the chances are that if I repay the loan, I will be doing what it pleases me not to do. So I ought not to repay the loan. Certainly the word "ought" in this context seems to have been pulled out of thin air.

### The Time Element

There is another strange consequence of the use of the opportunistic principle in selecting actions. When one says, "I do what I please," he means at the least, that when he does whatever it is he does, then, *at that moment* he pleases to do it. If one is repaying a debt, then at the moment he is repaying that debt he is pleased to do so. If he tries to anticipate whether or not he will be pleased to repay the debt tomorrow, he tries somehow to see how he would feel at the time he will repay it. Suppose the decision is made that tomorrow repaying the debt will be what the person is pleased to do. He awaits the hour, but now in a state of mind of expectation, he expects to be in the state he calls "being pleased." But the very fact of expectation may destroy the possibility of achieving the frame of mind which enables him to say, "It pleases me to do it." In other words, one cannot, except at the risk of preventing oneself from being pleased, anticipate the fact that it will please him to act in a certain way. On the basis of this principle then, whether or not one ought to do a certain thing cannot be decided except at the moment it is done. At that moment, the person can discover whether it ought to have been done, but it is too late to do anything other than what was done. If at that moment of action it pleases one so to act, then he ought to have done it; if at the moment of doing the deed, it pleases him not to do it, he ought not to have done it. The point is that in advance of actually acting it is not possible to tell whether or not the act ought to have been done, i.e., whether or not it pleases the doer to do it. "It *will* please me to repay the loan" is basically misleading because one simply cannot know in advance whether or not it will. In brief, if this is a true description of what takes place when one tries to use the principle to decide what to do, it turns out that the principle is useless until the act is done and irrelevant at that moment since the act is by then an accomplished fact.

Were it not that many pseudo-sophisticates appeal to this principle, it would be out of place to discuss it. "I do what I please" is either a factual statement, and often false; or, if intended as a moral principle, leads nowhere but is a sort of camouflage for unprincipled behavior.

## BIBLIOGRAPHY

Ayer, A. J., *Language, Truth and Logic* (Victor Gollancz, 1936), Chapter VI.
Freud, S., *Totem and Taboo,* trans. A. A. Brill (New York: Moffat, Yard & Co., 1918).
Hill, T. E., *Contemporary Ethical Theories* (New York: Macmillan Co., 1950), Chapter II.
Hospers, John, "Free Will and Psychoanalysis" in *Readings in in Ethical Theory,* ed. W. Sellars and John Hospers (New York: Appleton-Century-Crofts, Inc., 1952), pp. 560-576.
Pap, A., *Elements of Analytic Philosophy* (New York: Macmillan Co., 1949), Chapter II.
Sartre, Jean Paul, *Existentialism,* trans. B. Frechtman (New York: Philosophical Library, 1947).
Schlick, M., *Problems of Ethics,* trans. David Rynin (New York: Prentice-Hall, 1939).

# CHAPTER XI

## ENDS AND MEANS

We have tried to show the relation of moral decisions to moral principles. But every moral argument that ends in a decision must be supported not only by the principle but also by a factual or empirical premise without which the connection between abstract principle and concrete act could never be realized. This second factual premise must be examined more closely if our decisions are to be intelligent.

In the chapter on hedonism, the following example was used:

> One ought to do what brings happiness.
> Being kind brings happiness.
> Loaning you money is being kind.

---

> Therefore: I ought to loan you money since it will bring you hapiness.

Then in the chapter on theological morals, this was said:

> One ought to act in accordance with God's will.
> To do justice is to act in accordance with God's will.

---

> Therefore: I ought to be just.

In subsequent chapters we used these:

> One ought to do his duty.
> Protecting the parole board is doing one's duty.

---

> Therefore: I ought to protect the parole board.

> One ought to do what expresses one's Self.
> Keeping promises is a method of self-expression.

Therefore: I ought to keep my promises.

One ought to do what makes for survival.
Lying helps me survive.

---

Therefore: I ought to lie.

## The Second Premise

Since at the moment we are concerned with making moral decisions, the second premise is just as important as the first. How, indeed, can we decide what to do if we do not know whether or not what is asserted by the second premise is the case? In order to compare these factual statements, I will list them once again:

> Being kind brings happiness.
> Doing justice is acting in accordance with God's will.
> Protecting the parole board is doing one's duty.
> Keeping one's promises is self-expression.
> Lying helps one survive.

All of these statements assert a connection between specific types of acts and certain consequences. If we are kind, then happiness will result; if we do justice, then we will be in accord with God's will; if we lie, we will survive. None of these sentences contain the word "ought". In structure and apparently in intent they appear to be like the statement "If a match is applied to a mixture of hydrogen and oxygen, an explosion will result." Actually, however, this last sentence has a significance differing quite radically from the others. The following examples which are distinct from those we have used before, will help clarify the distinction.

## Means-end Not Cause-effect

Consider one of Köhler's apes in a cage with a banana just outside his reach and a long stick inside the cage. Evidently the ape can pick up the stick without using it for reaching the banana. If he does use it to reach the banana, then the stick is no longer a stick merely; it is an instrument being used for a specific purpose – to get the banana. In point of fact, for this particular use what is used needn't be a stick at all. An iron magnet or a paper tube would do just as well. The function of the stick as an instrument is the result not of its being a stick but of its relation to the ape who *uses* it. The following statements about the stick reveals various bits of information pertinent to the analysis; "The stick is long"; "the stick is being used to get the banana"; and "the stick can be used for getting the banana." The first tells us something about the stick while the second and third tells us something about the ape and the banana. Insofar as the distance alone is concerned the ape is irrelevant, but since the distance is between the ape and the banana it is the ape which is involved. If the stick is not used to get the banana, it is not an instrument.

The relation between the match and the hydrogen and oxygen mixture is quite different. Someone can *use* the match and hydrogen and oxygen mixture to bring about an explosion, but when fire touches the mixture no one is using these to cause an explosion. If someone says, "John uses the match and the hydrogen and oxygen to cause an explosion," he is saying something about the relation of John to the explosion, that is, that these are the means John uses to achieve an explosion. But the explosion would result even if fire reaches the mixture accidentally. The relation between the fire, hydrogen and oxygen, and the explosion is independent of John.

These two examples show the way in which the words "means" and "ends" are used. If anything is *used* to get something else, it is called the "means" and what is sought is called the "end" (or goal). These words enable is to describe the difference between the examples. Hydrogen and oxygen are not the means to the explosion, unless someone uses them as such. The stick is a means for obtaining the banana. The explosion which results from putting a lighted match to a mixture of hydrogen and oxygen is not the end in view, unless someone is seeking to bring it about. Getting the banana is desired by the ape. The explosion occurs under the appropriate conditions even if no one wants it to happen; the stick doesn't reach for the banana unless an agent takes it up and extends it in that direction. In short, a means implies an agent; a cause does not.

This is a fundamental distinction partially obscured by the fact that both sentences can be put into the conditional form "if . . . then . . ." and express a relation between an event, an act or occurence, and its consequences. In logical terms, causality is a dyadic relation; i.e., its form is "C causes E" where "C" denotes a cause and "E" an effect. "Being a means" is a triadic relation whose form is "M is a means for A to do E" where "M" denotes the means or instrument, "A" the agent, and "E" the end or goal.

*Empirical Verification*

We now can turn to the second premise which asserts a means-end relation. Doing justice is a means of doing God's will. Lying is a means of survival. How can we go about deciding on the truth of falsity of the second premise? Perhaps an analysis of the method of deciding on the truth or falsity of a causal statement will suggest an approach to the verification of a means-end statement. How do we find out whether or not the causal statement, "If fire reaches a mixture of hydrogen and oxygen, an explosion will result," is true? The obvious reply is, "By experience." One observes the conditions described in the antecedent clause, and marks whether the explosion follows. How does the ape discover that the stick truly will reach the banana? By trying it out and noting whether it does. In this respect both means-end conditionals and causal ones are alike. This provides us with a definition of a factual statement. A factual statement is one whose truth or falsity is empirically decided. So, if the second premise is factual, then one discovers, for example, whether or not being kind does bring happiness by examining instances in which people were kind and noting whether or not happiness was a consequence.

Now the second premise in each moral argument states a relation between an end, say, happiness, or doing God's will, or expressing oneself, and a means, say, being kind, doing justice and so on. The principle, in point of fact, tells us what the end is; the situation in which we find ourselves presents us with things, objects or possible actions that purport to be means to that end. If a moral principle is accepted, the end it implies or expresses is also. The problem of making moral decisions then involves making a factual decision, i.e., deciding whether or not the means will bring about the desired end. Suppose a person who accepts the moral principle, "One ought to express one's Self," is trying to decide whether to keep a promise. What he needs to discover is whether keeping his promise is a means of self-expression, and this, as we have seen, is apparently an empirical question to be decided by appeal to matters-of-fact.

That the problem of verification of the second premise is not as simply resolved as that, is strikingly evident when we try, for example, to verify the premise, "Being kind brings happiness." It is immediately apparent that the statement cannot mean that kindness *always* brings happiness, because there are cases where it doesn't. Suppose A had wronged B and come to repent of his deed. B, who is a gentle soul, forgives A readily and to show his sincerity does A a kindness. Upon this, A, who feels badly about his misdeeds, exclaims, "Don't be kind to me!

You only make me feel worse. I am unhappy enough because I did what
I did. Your kindness aggravates my unhappiness." This is no extraordinary situation, it is quite commonplace. If, however, someone were to
insist that A is abnormal and made so by his guilt feelings, then it is
being asserted not that kindness brings happiness but that it is the sort of
thing that ought to do so; and if it doesn't, then the fault lies with the
person who doesn't have his happiness increased by the act of kindness.

### Definition of "Means" and "End"

Whether or not kindness brings happiness to all or to a few persons,
whether it always does so or only sometimes is not the issue, the point
is rather whether kindness is good for bringing about happiness. This is
what we mean when we say, "Kindness is a means for attaining happiness." Similarly, we need to know whether keeping one's promise is good
for expressing one's Self, because "Keeping one's promises is a means of
self-expression." In this sense, the stick is a means for reaching the banana.

If "means" indicates something good for something else, then "end"
must signify that for which it is good. So happiness is that for which
kindness is good; survival is that for which lying is good; and
so on. But is it correct to speak of kindness as a means? May it
not be an end? In our example, kindness was taken to be a means because
it was good for happiness. When one loans his friend money when his
friend is in need, he is being kind. If the kindness is that for which the
loan is good, it is an end. But the kindness may itself be good for happiness, and so it is also a means. Evidently, and we are not too surprised,
kindness is both a means and an end, for one can desire kindness both
because of what it is good for and because of itself. If an end is good
because of itself, we say it is "good-in-itself" or "intrinsically good"; if it
is good as a means to something else, we call it "instrumentally good."
There may be things which are always valued because of themselves, i.e.,
which are always ends and never means.

All of these considerations should help us see what the second premise of the moral argument asserts. The first premise, the moral principle, presents the end. Whether or not this is only an intrinsically good
end or an instrumental one is a further question.

### Discovering Means-End Relations

It has been indicated that the second premise has the appearance
of a factual question. But not all statements asserting means-end rela-

tions are identical in structure. Some differ from other types of factual assertions. Ordinarily one wants to say something like this. Whether or not lying helps survival is an empirical question, and in itself may have little or nothing to do with moral issues as such, except in so far as its truth or falsity enters as a factor in making moral decisions. One can investigate the question, "Does kindness bring happiness?" even if one were totally uninterested in the moral problem whether he ought or ought not to do a kindness. One can ask whether or not kindness leads to happiness without at all accepting any form of hedonism. Even if this is so, it is more difficult to define the empirical procedures for testing some means-end statements, e.g., statements like "Being just is acting in accordance with God's will" than others. The type of evidence one needs to support this last statement appears to be essentially different from that needed for testing a statement like "Lying leads to preservation."

If the problem is whether kindness brings happiness, the obvious thing to do is to examine cases in which a kindness was done. If observation shows that in the majority of situations where a kindness was done happiness did result, one may reasonably conclude that doing kindnesses did bring happiness. On the contrary, if the majority of cases are such that doing a kindness either hinders or is irrelevant to happiness, the reasonable conclusion would be that it does not bring happiness. The process is one of generalization from observations.

Similarly, it is not too difficult to imagine examples where a lie, apparently at least, helped one survive. For instance, if one is captured by the enemy, who demands the betrayal of secrets, then it may happen that a lie will postpone events until help can come. If enough cases can be found, perhaps one could generalize that lying does help survival.

But there is another aspect. Consider the case we mentioned before, and which we left perhaps too hastily, in which an act of kindness leads to unhappiness. Or we can imagine a case where lying leads to unhappiness as well as survival. If someone believes that lying leads to survival, would he necessarily be convinced by a majority of cases where it apparently did not? Or if someone believes kindness leads to happiness, would 50,000 cases when kindness led to unhappiness cause him to change his mind? Would he not be tempted to say that kindness always leads to happiness and that when it doesn't, the situation is an exceptional one which for some obscure reason did not result as it should? Under such circumstances, it may be that when a hedonist asserts that kindness leads to happiness, or lying leads to happines, he may be really making kindness and lying parts of the implications of happiness. In the case of the statement, "Doing justice is to act in accord with God's will," how many and what kind of observations are needed to show this to be so? In part, here too, God's will is taken to imply doing justice. In both cases does it not appear that observations are irrelevant?

In brief, the investigation of means-end relationships is at times either independent of moral considerations or possible only if some moral end is accepted. Means are such only in so far as they are good for reaching some goal.

### The Inadequacy of Induction

This, however, is not the complete picture. Consider an act of murder. Shall we say that if it leads to survival (or any other accepted goal) it is moral, otherwise not? An act of murder is condemned as immoral regardless of the goal to which it may be conducive. Or would we ever ask whether a murderous act was in accord with God's will, and if we decided it was, consider it to be moral? It seems rather that we condemn certain acts at least, no matter how effective they are instrumentally. We tend to say that the very nature of certain acts like murder, is such that they never could be in accord with God's will, or lead to happiness. What acts are so characterized is clearly a function of the moral end, but there are always some at least.

Kant tried to show that lying by its very nature could never be the kind of thing it was your duty to do, while being kind, not overcharging, preserving one's life, and even seeking happiness are acts that are in accord with one's duty. These are not means to doing one's duty, they are instances of doing one's duty. In fact, Kant rejected completely the notion that one can by examining cases decide whether or not the deed in question was a way of doing one's duty. "Nor could one give poorer counsel to morality," says Kant, "than to attempt to derive it from examples. For each example of morality which is exhibited to me must itself have been previously judged according to principles of morality to see whether it is worthy to serve as an original example . . ."

### Moral Traits Recognized, Not Inductively Discovered

In brief, one does not, in order to decide whether or not the second premise of the moral argument is true, always go about seeking instances and trying to generalize from them. Often all we do is examine a single instance, the matter in hand, to see whether or not it reveals itself to be in accord with the moral law. Nor can we decide every case on the basis of an empirical generalization. Quite the contrary, at times, one must somehow either know in advance that, e.g., kindness is God's will, or our duty, or have in mind some criterion which is to be applied to the case under consideration. There may be nothing about an act of kindness which we could discover by an examination that would compel one to say, "This is God's will"; contrariwise, we may approach the act of kindness with a knowledge of God's will, and see that the kind act is in accord with God's will. So murder, or rape, are known to be contrary to God's will, and would be contrary to God's will even if they did bring greater happiness to many. What looked like a simple process of examining cases turns out at times to be dependent upon a prior ability to recognize instances of the kind in question, and this implies that we already have a criterion in mind.

If this is so, then such things as murder, rape, etc. may be evil in themselves, apart from any or all consequences or any end-in-view. That they are contrary to God's will or to one's duty may be a *sign* that they are evil in themselves. In the same way, kindness may be an end; the fact that it is also instrumental in bringing about happiness may not bear on its value as an end. That it is an end is evidenced by its being commanded by God, or by the fact that one has a duty to be kind. That kindness is an end may not be affected by the fact that it may also be a means to other ends, at least for those who maintain theological or duty-principles of morality.

### Means and Ends are Inter-related

The purpose of all this analysis is to show how intricately interwoven are considerations about means and ends. But even more, one cannot always really say at any particular point in the solution of a moral problem that a specific thing or deed is a means, and a means only. For example, if a person considers justice to be a means to something valuable, he will set about trying to do whatever leads to justice. By that fact justice becomes an end. How important it is to recognize that means and ends are inter-related is evident in the following example. Imagine John Doe and Richard Roe engaged in a pleasant discussion. They are trying to decide how to improve the happiness of the people in their city. Says John Doe, "Let us be clear about one thing, Richard, we both agree that people should be happy."

"Yes, indeed. All men deserve to be happy."

"I propose, therefore, that we rob Banker Will, and distribute his money to the people in Hartbreak Hotel."

"But hold on! That's no way to make people happy!"

"It will make them happier, won't it, if they get some money?"

"I suppose so."

"Then why not? You agreed that we ought to make people happy, or at least happier."

"Indeed I did. But robbery is not a proper means for such a worthy purpose."

This may be something of a caricature. Yet variations of the arguments advanced are common enough. John Doe and Richard Roe accept a common end. They may even be willing to proclaim happiness to others as their duty or God's will. Furthermore, they concur in the opinion that the means, namely, the distribution of money, will achieve their goal which is to increase the happiness of others. But although they agree that robbery will provide the money that will bring the happiness, they disagree on the propriety of the method of obtaining the money by such a means. The disagreement is quite clearly upon the rightness of this method of getting the means (which is now an end) to accomplish their laudable goal.

John Doe is obviously irritated. He looks at Richard Roe and sneers, "I thought you agreed with me on the goal to be sought."

"Ah, but I do! I simply don't think robbery is a proper means."

"I don't see what you mean by a 'proper' means. What would you suggest?"

"Well, we could borrow the money instead of stealing it."

"But then you and I would be unhappy whereas if we rob Banker Will, only he might be unhappy."

Here we see the real difficulty. John Doe believes that whatever leads to the end, must be judged only in terms of that end. Richard Roe recognizes that there can be other ways (means) of achieving the end and that one needs to choose among ends. That is, he believes that although the money is a means to happiness, when one acts to obtain the money, then the money is an end and, therefore, only certain ways of arriving at this end are appropriate.

### Means Need to be Judged

This is a rather upsetting revelation. The most striking characteristic about the second premise was its apparent empirical nature. As an empirical statement its truth or falsity was determined by considering whether in actual cases what it asserted was what happened. First, it was seen that empirical generalization was not always involved. Now it is revealed that even if one could establish that (say) kindness did give rise to happiness, or killing one's wife did function as self-expression, this alone would not be enough to lead to the conclusion that one ought to be kind or ought to kill his wife. Not merely must one decide whether the means leads to the end, but also whether the means about to be used are the sort of means that ought to be chosen to accomplish the end.

Should Richard Roe still insist that robbing the banker is not right, John Doe could legitimately ask why it was not right to rob for a moral goal. Richard Roe is, at this point, in a dilemma. He cannot say robbery is not a proper means because it does not lead to happiness since he agreed it would. He cannot appeal to some other end, because he has accepted this one. If Roe did argue, for example, that happiness attained by such methods would offend God, then happiness is for him really only a means, i.e., something good for not offending God. If he argued that happiness attained by such means would lead to unhappiness, he appears to be expressing a hope rather than a fact, or, at least, he is saying something which is contingent, that is, may or may not be so. In this case he can only argue that the robbery is *probably* not right whereas he believes it is categorically wrong. Moreover, if he could be shown that the robbery would not lead to unhappiness, or to a greater total amount of happiness, he would be compelled to accept this means, and this is clearly something he will not do under any conditions. Richard Roe is quite evidently convinced that no matter what the end is, there are, or can be, certain means which are totally unfitting to be used even if they do make it possible to reach the end desired.

The point at issue is an ancient one, namely, "Does the end always justify the means?" Richard Roe said, "No!" while John Doe said, "Yes!" The conflicting answers to this question indicate the complexity of moral arguments. If one says, "No," then the moral arguments so far considered are incomplete. Another premise needs to be added stating that what is asserted in the second premise to lead to the desired end is also an acceptable means for reachting the goal. As a result not only must one demonstrate, for example, that kindness brings happiness, but that kindness is an appropriate method for bringing happiness; or that not only does lying aid survival, but that lying is a suitable method for the attainment of survival, and so on.

In part, at least, the answer to the question whether the end always justifies the means depends upon how one views the desired end. To a devout theologian, doing God's will may be an end such that anything that accomplishes this end must *ipso facto* be appropriate, or fitting.

How, in other words, could anything that accorded with God's will not be fitting? Contrariwise, the theologian would assert that no matter how desirable happiness may be, there are certain things one ought not do to attain it. In the episode described above, this was the essential difference between Richard and John. They both accepted a common end, but John believed that happiness was the sort of condition that justified whatever helped bring it about; while Richard did not.

These comments lead to the following conclusion. If the end, say survival, is but itself a means to something else, say doing God's will, then the means of survival will need to be evaluated in terms of its conformity to this latter end. If the end is an ultimate end and in no way a means, then the means used may be justified only to the degree it aids in the attainment of the end, both quantitatively and qualitatively; or else a new criterion, say appropriateness, may be invoked to judge the means. But if this is the case, it becomes necessary to make explicit the nature of that criterion.

*Summary*

To summarize, then, the cogency of a moral argument rests upon three decisions. (1) Is the second factual premise true (or false); or is the evidence in favor of its being true (or false)? This is possible apparently either (a) empirically, i.e., the premise is taken to be true by reason of evidence, or (b) logically, by reason of definitions which are tacitly assumed.

(2)  Are the means to be used to achieve the desired end appropriate, or fitting, or right? This can be decided either by some new criterion, other than the moral principle expressed in the first premise, or by another moral judgment based on the same moral principle or a different one. In the latter case we have an obvious hierarchy of principles. This leads to the third decision.

(3)  Is the end expressed in the first principle, for which the means is appropriate an ultimate end or not? This can be decided sometimes by asking whether the end is ever itself a means. If it is, then that for which it is a means is a "higher" end, and the given end cannot be an ultimate end.

BIBLIOGRAPHY

Aristotle, *The Nichomachean Ethics,* Book I, reprinted in A. I. Melden, ed., *Ethical Theories, 2nd ed.* (New York: Prentice-Hall, 1955), pp. 88-101.

Dewey, J., *Theory of Valuation,* International Encyclopedia of Unified Science, Vol. II, No. 4 (Chicago: Univ. of Chicago Press, 1939), 33-51.

Garvin, L., *A Modern Introduction to Ethics* (Boston: Houghton-Mifflin Co., 1953), Chapter VIII, pp. 192 ff.

Gomperz, H., "When does the end sanctify the means," *Ethics,* LIII (1942-43), 173-192.

Leys, Wayne, *Ethics and Social Policy* (New York: Prentice-Hall, 1941), Chapter X.

Wright, Henry W., *Self-Realization* (New York: Henry Holt & Co., 1913), Chapter I, pp. 3-15.

# CHAPTER XII

# JUDGING THE ACT

## The Right

In the preceding chapter a phrase was used that needs clarification. This was the expression "appropriate" or "right" means or deed to achieve a certain end. Like so many of the terms involved in moral decisions, this one is also complex in its significance. The following example will help initiate the discussion. Suppose Mr. A, walking along Broadway in New York, is approached by a rather shabbily dressed man who begs for a dime for a cup of coffee. Being kindly disposed, Mr. A digs down into his pocket and hands the man a dime. Mr. B, a friend of Mr. A., walking with him, is displeased and insists that giving the beggar a dime was not the right thing to do. He believes the man will use the money to buy liquor. In all probability Mr. A feels hurt because above all he wants to do what is right at all times. Now, the key term in this disagreement is clearly the word "right." Mr. B judges the act not to be right; Mr. A did it because he thought it was right. Both Mr. A and Mr. B agree the beggar ought to be helped.

The philosophically sophisticated person will most surely realize that there are at least two questions that need to be decided before the disagreement can be eliminated, if it can be. (1) When an act is called "right", precisely what is being asserted? Is something being said about the act, or about its consequences, or about the agent? (2) What conditions need to be fulfilled before one can say of an act that it is the right act? If these two questions can be adequately answered, then one can judge acts with respect to their rightness or wrongness – and this is what people would like to be able to do.

## Meanings of the Word "Right"

In everyday life, the word "right" is used in many different ways. There is an important distinction between its usage in the situation just described, in which the act of giving a beggar a dime is called a "right" act (i.e., the right thing to do) and its usage in the following situation. A student adds up a column of figures and when he is finished his teacher checks his addition and tells him he has exactly the right answer.

When we add up a column of figures and get the "right" answer, we mean, quite unambiguously, the correct one. When we say that giving the beggar the dime is "right" we do not mean that it is "correct" to do so. Giving the dime is only in a vague and analogous sense "correct." The right answer to a sum is the one obtained by following the rules of arithmetic. If there were rules of morality that define the right act in the way the rules of arithmetic define the correct sum, then the word "right" would mean the same in the two cases. However, as we have seen in earlier chapters, this is simply not so. The moral principles need to be *applied* to particular situations. The particular moral problem is never analytic with respect to the moral principle as the sum is with respect to the rules (axioms) of arithmetic. This is to say that a particular correct sum can be obtained by a strictly deductive process from the basic axiom of arithmetic, but a particular act is not deduced in the same way from the moral principle.

The word "right" or "correct" is also used at times to designate something done in such a manner that it leads to the desired end. Extending the example of the beggar asking for the dime for coffee, suppose Mr. A offers the beggar an opportunity to run an errand, thereby earning the money rather than begging it. If Mr. B happened to be a social worker, he might compliment Mr. A and assure him that was the right thing to do because it would tend to make the beggar a more valuable citizen. In other words, given an end which need not be moral, then an act may be said to be right if it lead to that goal. In the original example, the act is judged right because it is the moral thing to do. Nothing need be involved when the question of rightness involves correctness or fittingness of method. To take another example, a mathematics professor who grades a set of problems handed in by his students will give credit for all the right answers (i.e., correct). But he may give some credit for those problems that use the right method, i.e., the method that would have led to the correct solution had no errors been made, even though the answers are incorrect. No moral issues are involved at all. The student may use the right method, but get an erroneous answer because of an incorrect addition. These raise grading problems for the professor, but hardly moral ones.

The preceding discussion has revealed three uses of right: 1) The moral use referring to the right act in a moral sense, 2) the use referring to right in the sense of correct and 3) the use referring to right in the sense of appropriate to reach a goal. Although no general criterion for distinguishing the three usages of "right", has been given we can presumably safely rely on our good judgment to recognize when we are using the word "right" in a moral context and when in a nonmoral one. Our concern is with the moral usage of right.

### "Right" in a Moral Context and Ought

If Mr. A had been asked, "Why is giving the dime to the beggar right?" he might conceivably have answered by saying, "Because this is what ought to be done." In other words, Mr. A would feel inclined to say that an act is right if it ought to be done; wrong if it ought not to be done. Yet there are difficulties in identifying "right" with "ought" even if in many cases this would appear to be exactly what we do mean to do.

The following example illustrates the difficulty into which we might run if he did identify "right" and "ought." Suppose John Smith is a doctor attending a very sick patient. Among the very many things that worry the sick is, of course, the welfare of loved ones. If Dr. Smith lies to his patient about the health of the patient's family, we might indeed say he ought not to have done so, but add that nevertheless we thought he was right in doing what he did. If right is taken to mean simply "what ought to be done" then it would be obvious nonsense to say, "John Doe was right in doing what he ought not to have done," because this would then mean, "John Doe did what he ought to have done when he did what he ought not to have done."

The problem is to decide whether Dr. Smith did the right thing by lying and not whether it is right to lie? In a moral context, the first of these questions is misleading. One of two things can be meant by the questions when we ask if John Smith did the right thing by lying. Either we are asking whether John Smith was moral, or we are asking whether his lie led to the desired results, namely, to give comfort to the patient. The latter alternative is excluded from our consideration because such a question is not a moral but an empirical one. And, in a moral context, we most assuredly would not want to call an act right simply because it led to the desired results unless the desired result was to be moral. For example, John Smith may deliberately kill his patient in order to relieve that patient's relatives of the financial strain. Killing the patient would lead to the desired results, yet would hardly be called right.

As for whether Dr. Smith was immoral when he lied, this is another question we will need to decide later when we consider the problem of

judging whether persons are moral or immoral. But, clearly, an act may
be right in the sense, at least, that it was what ought to have been done
even if the doer is immoral. For example, it surely is right to contribute
to the relief of the needy; yet the person who does so may be making
the contribution only because he wants to get publicity. Dr. Smith is
doing the right thing in alleviating pain, yet he may be immoral because his service is offered only to obtain exorbitant fees .What we would
ordinarilly say in such cases is that Dr. Smith did the right thing but
for the wrong reasons. Such a comment would reflect on John Smith's
character but not on the act itself. In short, that John Smith did the
right thing by lying cannot mean *merely* that he did what ought to have
been done, nor does it mean that John Smith was moral when he did so.

Incidentally, the second question, i.e., whether it is right to lie, if
taken as a moral question raises the problem of the justification of
moral principles which will be considered later in this book. Evidently
"Thou shalt not lie" is a moral principle and if a right act is one that accords with a moral principle, then Dr. Smith's lying is wrong.

*Rightness and Consequences*

Although the rightness of the act appears to be at least in part independent of its consequences, yet if one were challenged to demonstrate
that the act was right, the appeal would in most cases be to consequences.
So, to be specific, if John Doe were called upon to defend his assertion
that giving the beggar the dime was right, he would quite probably
reply that doing so helped the beggar feel better. Or he might say that it
was his duty to help the poor, and giving the beggar a dime did that.
Or he might say that he was doing God's will. On the other hand, if
someone challenged the rightness of the act, he too would appeal to
consequences whether of the hedonistic sort or the kind denoted by the
phrase, "doing God's will." Naturally, he who defends the act as right
will appeal to consequences quite different from those to which the
challenger will point. And the disagreement is apt to be fought out in
terms of contrasting consequences.

John Doe is not saying "The act is right" means "The act leads to
pleasure." The use of the word, "because," indicates that John Doe does
not want to identify the two either logically or factually. It is quite possible that he is perfectly aware that the two statements, "The act is right"
and "The act leads to pleasure," are independent in the sense that there
are conditions under which one could be true and the other false. Rela-

ting them by the word "because" indicates that there are times when the consequent is brought about by the antecedent.

In this sense, we can say that the result of giving the beggar some happiness is a *criterion* for the act's being right. As such it may indeed be that the act may be right even if it sometimes leads to unhappiness, or it may be wrong and still lead to happiness. The former case occurs if, for example, the beggar were sick and contrary to his will he were hospitalized. We would, I think, call the act of hospitalization right, even if the beggar were quite unhappy about it. The second possibility is exemplified if the beggar were addicted to narcotics which he could not get, and someone gave him a goodly supply. Even though this made the beggar happier, we would still insist the act was not right. Consequences may, therefore, serve as criteria for the rightness of the act.

### Disagreements about Ordering Consequences

Joe Roe who argues that the act is wrong because, let us say, the beggar is encouraged to continue in his menial state and, in consequence, has his personality degraded, is appealing to a consequence just as his friend is. We now have appeals to consequences purporting to prove exactly the opposite conclusion.

It is quite conceivable that John Doe might put happiness above a degraded personality while Joe Roe might evaluate them in exactly the opposite fashion. Their disagreement about the rightness of the act would resolve itself into one about the preferential ordering of consequences. Each of them accepts what the other says are the consequences. The debate is not over the empirical question, "What are the consequences of giving the beggar the dime?" The basic disagreement seems to center around a selection among consequences so far as their relative values are concerned. The problem becomes one of deciding which is better, happiness or the maintenance of one's personality, both being desirable.

It is possible that the disagreement might be over whether (say) happiness is always desirable. So Joe Roe might argue that happiness is not necessarily desirable in such cases, while John Doe might insist that to an unhappy person the maintenance of personality is of no value at all.

We are led to the conclusion that the consequences of an act may serve as a criterion for its rightness depending on whether these consequences are or are not desirable. If the consequences are desirable, they do tend to make us feel that the act is right; if they are undesirable, that it is wrong.

Although it is good to have a criterion of rightness, nevertheless a criterion tells us very little about the act as such. Suppose someone asks what an acid is and is told that it is something that burns holes in cloth. Or to the question "What is a sharp knife?" the reply is made, "It is one that has been honed for thirty minutes?" Both replies tell something about what the questioner wants to know, but neither answers his questions very significantly. In the same way, when it is asked, "When is an act right?" and the reply is given, "When it leads to desirable consequences," something is being affirmed about a right act but we are not being told what it is. Since a criterion may sometimes not be applicable nor satisfied while that of which it is a criterion may be present (for example, the knife was not honed thirty minutes, yet was sharp) the problem remains unsolved, or at least simply changed.

## Rightness in Terms of Prior Conditions

If the rightness of an act is not a function of its consequences, what alternatives are left? There are two other possible sources from which the rightness of an act may spring. One is some condition that existed prior to the act, the other some characteristic of the act itself. This is to say that what makes us call an act right may be either something about the way we come to do the act, or something in the nature of the act itself. For example, if we call the act of giving the beggar the dime right, it may be because of something about the way the agent arrives at the decision, or something inherent in the very act of giving a beggar a dime.

Let us examine the first of these alternatives. One of the prior conditions to the performance of an act is the motive of the doer. Can we say the act is right if it is done from a good motive, perhaps the desire to help mankind? If we describe an act as right if it is done from a good motive, then whether or not the act did help mankind would be irrelevant to the question whether or not the act was right. The act would be right, if the person who did it has as his motive doing good to mankind. This implies that the rightness of the act is a function of the agent's motive. Unfortunately, one of the consequences of such an hypothesis would be that the same act could be both right and wrong. For example, in the controversy concerning the rightness of giving the beggar the dime, if he were given the money in order to do him good, the act would be right, but if his enemy gave him the money because he wanted him to get drunk, then the act would be wrong. This kind of relativism could be maintained, I suppose, as we saw in an earlier chapter, but it makes nonsense of all disagreements over the rightness of the act. One could not be sure of the motives of the agent, but given the motives, the act would be correctly judged right or wrong. Yet, clearly, people do disagree even when the motives are quite obvious.

In fact, it could very well happen that two people such as we described above could each have good motives yet disagree on the rightness of the act. Surely to bring someone happiness and to respect personality are both good and commendable motives, yet the disagreement about the act being right remains. And one is often tempted to say, "My friend's motives are quite good, yet his act was wrong." A person may make a bad decision and invest money put in his care in stocks that were not sound in order to enrich the one who had entrusted the money to him. The motive was good. Yet the person was immoral because he used money that did not belong to him, and the act was wrong. He may not have been immoral had the money been entrusted to him to invest as he saw fit. Even so, the act was wrong not because it led to financial disaster but because he ought to have known better. Logically, in any case, since the act may be called "right" whether the doer's motive was good or bad, the motive seems to be quite irrelevant to the rightness or wrongness of the act.

*Right Act One in Accord with Moral Principle*

Another prior condition is the conformability of the act to a moral principle. This situation can be illustrated by examining the intentions of Richard Roe and John Doe, as each attempts to convince the other. Each appealed to a principle; John Doe to the principle that one ought to help others seek happiness, Joe Roe to the principle of respect for the personality of others. Doe urged the rightness of the act because of its accord with one moral principle, while Roe called the act wrong because it violated another moral principle. Perhaps there is a clue here. It is plausible to assume that both would agree that if the act were right it would indeed be in accord with a moral principle.

An example can be used to advantage. A loaned B his gun for a month and B promised to return it. By the end of the month A had developed a homicidal mania and this was known to B. A asked B to return the gun. At first glance the moral thing to do would be to return the gun since it does belong to A and B did promise to return it. Yet would returning the gun to A be the right thing to do? On the surface this would appear to be another of those cases where there is a conflict of principles. If the principle, "Promises ought always to be kept," is taken to be fundamental then B is wrong if he does not return the gun. If the principle, "One ought not to do what will cause needless injury," is given priority then B is right in withholding the gun. But if B does not return the gun when A requests it, is he violating the moral principle, "One ought to keep one's promises"?

Perhaps not. When a promise is made, there are always implicit conditions assumed that need to be fulfilled before the promise can be kept. For example, if someone promises to buy a house, he surely cannot keep the promise if he dies before the time comes to make the purchase. Or, suppose someone promises to meet a friend at a certain place at a certain time. Before the time arrives he is informed that a very urgent meeting is to take place at which his presence is of great importance. Surely, that would be excuse enough to fail to keep his promise. The one to whom the promise had been mede might be angry. He can properly expect to be notified, if possible, and failure to do so would be quite blameworthy but one is not expected to keep a promise at so great a cost. So even if an act is in accord with a moral principle, this is not in itself sufficient to justify calling the act right. Other conditions also need to be present.

We can assume that when B promises to return the gun to A, he tacitly agrees (and A tacitly accepts the conditions) that under normal conditions he will keep his promise. Since conditions can be said to be abnormal B ought not to return the gun to A. B, who is considering whether to return the gun, does not deny that it belongs to A and in fact should, under ordinary circumstances, be given to A. But B believes that *even if* the gun is rightfully A's still A ought not to be entrusted with it for fear of the consequent actions of A. A homicidal tendency implemented by a gun could result in actions that violate the moral principle that one ought not to injure another. B would be quite willing to deliver the gun over to someone else to hold in trust, so to speak, for A. This would be in recognition of the obligation to return the gun to its rightful owner. In other words, B does not deny that although under ordinary conditions it is right to return the gun to its owner, under these present conditions it is wrong to do so.

The upshot of these remarks seems to be this. The statement, i.e., moral principle, "One ought to do as he promises," may be viewed as not in itself defining what is right to do under specific conditions. The word "right" does not mean merely "doing what one ought to do," not merely because of the contradiction previously noted but also because if we did take "right" to mean simply "doing what one ought to do," then it would be right to return the gun since this is what one ought to do if one promises to return it. The word "right" is used in connection with specific acts, and whether or not a specific act is the right thing to do depends not only upon the moral principle involved but also upon the conditions under which the act is to be done. If A were normal, it would be right to return the gun. Since A is not, it may be wrong to do so and in the case described it would be. In other words, before one can decide an act to be right, he needs to examine the conditions under which the act is to be done, to see whether or not they are appropriate. But this again seems merely to change the locus of the problem since we do not know how to decide when the conditions are appropriate.

### Rightness Intrinsic to the Act

Our discussion seems to have led to the conclusion that we should exclude three possible definitions of "right." An act is not called right merely because its *consequences* are good; an act is not called right merely because it is what ought to be done in the light of a moral principle, i.e., because its antecedents are moral obligations; an act is not called right merely because the motives which inspire it are pure. These being eliminated, what is left? The act itself! To say the act is right is to say something about the act and not about other things. But an act does involve consequences and is done in a context. It is, therefore, necessary in judging the act right or wrong to *consider* these as conditioning factors but not as determining in themselves the rightness or wrongness of the act in question. When someone says that B does the right thing in withholding the gun, he is saying not that B is praiseworthy if he does not return the gun (although he may be) but that in the complete context as we have described it, this is the right thing to do. This sounds much like saying that the right thing to do is the right thing to do. And it is saying precisely that, for after all, this is what was said in the first place. This is not precisely a tautology but rather a simple statement of an evident phenomenon. It is like saying "the rose is red" of a red rose seen to be a red rose.

The conclusions to which these considerations lead may be summarized as follows: The right act is the one that would be done by a moral agent who acted on the basis of moral principles in order to achieve an end that is desirable under appropriate conditions. To put the matter in another way, this says that the right thing to do is what a moral person recognizes as the right thing to do. This sounds circular, but the circularity cannot be avoided.

Having provided a summary statement defining a right act does not mean that disagreements will not occur. There are many parts of this definition whose application will be in dispute, and at times the disagreement will be irresolvable. Nor will it eliminate mistaken judgments. No maxim can prevent a finite creature from deciding that an act is right and then, after he does the act, becoming aware of its wrongness, either because he sees more clearly in the light of its consequences that it did not lead to a desirable end but to an undesirable one, or that it was not demanded by a moral principle.

## Criteria for Rightness

To what directives for a concrete situation does the discussion lead? Suppose someone wants to decide what act is right, what questions need to be answered for him to be able to make the decision? There seem to be these:

(1)   Is the act one demanded by a moral principle? (Or, at least, is the act not incompatible with moral principles?)

(2)   Is the end in view desirable?

(3)   Will the act lead, in all likelihood, to the attainment of the desirable end? (or, at least, lead us closer to it than any other act?)

(4)   Are the conditions for the act appropriate? (Or, at least, more appropriate for this act than for any other?)

(5)   Is the act one that would be chosen by a moral agent?

The last may appear to be superfluous since any person who chose his acts on the basis of (1)-(4), would tend to be a moral agent. Sometimes, however, when one cannot decide the questions in themselves, he does appeal to other moral agents. So (5) is a useful question to ask. It takes such forms as: "Is this what Jesus would do?" or "Is this what the pastor would do?" or "Is this what my mother would want me to do?", etc.

If the act is demanded by a moral principle, is projected towards a desirable end, will lead towarda that end, and the circumstances are appropriate, then if it will be one chosen by a moral agent, it may properly be called, "right." This is not simply stipulated, but sums up the conditions under which people do in fact recognize an act to be right.

### BIBLIOGRAPHY

Garvin, Lucius, *A Modern Introduction to Ethics* (Boston: Houghton Mifflin Co., 1953), pp. 142-147, 205-206, 234-239, 388-392, 408-410.
Hill, T. E., *Ethics* (New York: Thomas Y. Crowell, 1956), Chapter XIV.
Lewis, C. I., *The Ground and Nature of the Right* (New York: Columbia University Press, 1955).

Moore, G. E., *Ethics* (New York: Oxford University Press, 1947), Chapters I-V.
Nowell-Smith, P. H., *Ethics* (Great Britain: Penguin Books, 1954), pp. 186-190.
Ross, W. D., *Foundations of Ethics* (Oxford: The Clarendon Press, 1939), Chapters
    II-VIII, pp. 12-168.
—, *The Right and the Good* (Oxford: The Clarendon Press, 1946), Chapters I and
    II, pp. 1-65.

# CHAPTER XIII

# JUDGING THE ENDS-THE GOOD

Making moral decisions is a vastly complicated process. And in great degree the complexity is due to the various meanings that moral terms have. Learning to make moral decisions is, in large measure, learning to use words less ambiguously in order to be able to apply them properly.

## Usages of "Good"

Not the least ambiguous of the terms we use quite freely, and often just as loosely, is the word "good." It is applied almost indiscriminately to all sorts of things. People say, "That was a good show," or "That was a good meal," or "He is a very good person," or "This is a good deed," or "This is a good knife," or "He is a good driver." At times the word "good" is used also as a noun, as when we say, "Happiness is a good," or "Money is a good." The list of examples of ways the word is used can be continued indefinitely but this would not throw any more light on its meaning. But the length of such a list shows why there can be so much endless debate over whether or not something is good without any real issue being involved.

Consider, for example, the following disagreement between two persons, John and Joe, who have just seen the same theatrical show. John feels that it was a good show, while Joe, disagreeing, insists that it was not. John bases his opinion that it was a good show on the fact that he enjoyed it. Joe insists John's enjoyment of the show is no evidence in favor of its being good. Joe counters John's remark that the purpose of a show is to provide entertainment, with the statement that in his opinion the show was quite immoral and evil. At this point in the argument John realizes that the disagreement is based on his rejection of the notion that a show to be good needs to preach moral virtues. He is willing to concede that even if a show doesn't need to provide enjoyment, it ought to express aesthetic qualities and not moral ones.

This brief conflict of opinions reveals at least three of the ways in which "good" is used. First, it may be used in a purely instrumental fashion and applied solely to means. This is what John means by it – "to be good" is "to provide enjoyment." So when John says, "This is a good show," he is really saying, "This show provides enjoyment"; and if he were to say, "There should be more good shows," he means to assert, "There should be more shows that provide enjoyment."

The same meaning is intended when we say of a knife that it is good, namely, that it is an effective instrument. It serves well for doing what needs to be done, i.e., to cut. All such cases simply tell us that in such instances what we call good is something conducive to the achievement or attainment of some goal.

The other two meanings of good in the dialogue are involved in Joe's assertion that the show was immoral and in John's insistence that aesthetic qualities need to be exemplified. We often do mean by "good" simply "moral," or better, "conducive to morality." "The show is good" then signifies that the show is moral, or is inducive to moral behavior. The second sense of "good" is intended when, e.g., an art critic pronounces a book containing descriptions of immoral acts to be nevertheless good because it is well-written and aesthetically satisfactory. Plays, books, art may all be good in either or both of these senses.

### "Good" as Applied to Ends

Now, all of these various meanings of "good" are interesting to consider but really not relevant to our discussion, chiefly because we are trying to discover what is meant when someone says that "the end he sought is good." This problem arises at this point because in the preceding chapter we had finally agreed that, in a moral sense, when it is said, "The act is right" it is meant that the act leads to desirable and good ends. We are assuming that "desirable ends" is synonomous with "good ends" and will conduct the discussion in terms of the less psychologically tainted expression, "good ends." We will not concern ourselves with what is meant by a "good means." When one says of something that it is good because it is an efficient means to a good end, he will be taken to mean that it is right to use that means.

It is best to carry on the discussion in terms of a specific end, say happiness. Accordingly, it is assumed that happiness is the end we seek and that happiness is good. Therefore, any act that is conducive to happiness, other conditions being met, such as eating or doing good deeds, would be right. But since happiness is taken to be the end and it is called good, we cannot mean that happiness is conducive to something else. It may be so, but this is quite irrelevant at the moment.

## Good or a Good

Furthermore, it is important to note that the sentence under consideration is not "happiness is a good," but "Happiness is good." This is significant because happiness has been assumed to be the end sought and not one of a number of desired or desirable goals. Moreover, to say that "Happiness is a good" would mean that it has qualities which are good (so that it can be classified as one of many goods), but also some which are either indifferent, or, in fact, evil. So if happiness is a good, it may also function as something else, for example, a soporific, an incentive, or other things. But if happiness is taken as good, it cannot be viewed as a soporific even if being good to experience, is to be lulled by it, and it may therefore function as a soporofic.

Consider another example: "Money is a good." This means that this thing which is called "money" has attributes which enable one to procure things he desires. It remains money, however, and as such may, even though it is a good, be the cause of conceit or miserliness. Hence, money may be a good, yet be evil also. But to say that "Money is good" would mean more. Indeed, it would signify that it always gives rise only to beneficial effects. Once it is asserted that "Money is good" money could not be taken to lead to something evil. To say that money could lead to evil would be to deny that it is good.

So for happiness. No one would deny that happiness is a good to be sought after and shared with others. But there can be wide disagreement when happiness is called good.

With this distinction in mind, we can resume the discussion. What is meant by saying, "Happiness is good," assuming that happiness is the end sought and not a means to something else? One thing is clear: whoever maintains that there is a *summum bonum* must be prepared to say of it that it is good and not merely a good. In fact, the *highest good* cannot be a means at all since there is nothing for it to be a means for. Moreover, to be the highest good must entail that it cannot possess any traits that cause evil consequences. There are, indeed, hosts of people who nominate various things as the highest good: "To do God's will is good"; "To express oneself is good"; "To do one's duty is good"; and so on.

## Happiness is Not the Same Thing as Good

To come closer to the meaning of the expression "Happiness is good" we first note that the sentence "Happiness is good" does not assert an identity. No one really would mean that happiness, which describes a state or condition in which humans may or may not be, is the same as good. "Good" is not "good-ness." This is to say that "happiness" is a noun, and, therefore, if it is to be equivalent to something, that too must be expressed by a noun. But "good" is adjectival. If happiness and good are equated, or even tacitly identified, the sentence would have read, "Happiness is goodness." But they are not equated and most people would refuse to do so.

*Good and Approve*

Nor is it possible to say that "Happiness is good" means merely that people approve of or like to be happy, i.e., in that condition, since "good" tells us something about happiness and not about the person. Happiness is a state or condition of a person. The person called "happy" is in a definite kind of condition. "Good," on the other hand, refers, at least in the context in which we are talking, to something about happiness and, therefore, not about the person as such but about his condition. In saying "Happiness is good" the intention is that "this sort of condition in which a person is, is good." True, if happiness is good, then by all means it ought to be approved. But happiness ought to be approved because happiness is good, and its goodness therefore is not the same as approving of it. If it were, then the assertion, "Happiness is good," would be strange since that would make nonsense of any assertion that one ought to approve it. Surely, happiness being good, one does approve of it and one does like to be happy.

But there are occasions on which one might conceivably not want to be happy even though he approved of being happy. For example, a person could be quite happy if he possessed much more money. Yet if the possession of that money could only come about by doing a good deal of harm to people, the person in question might quite well decide to remain in his present state of unhappiness. This is to say, that when the meaning of "Happiness is good" is identified with "I approve of happiness" what is asserted is not that happiness is good but that happiness is *a* good, because if happiness is good and not merely a good, its acquisition could not be the result of evil. Nevertheless, when it is said that happiness is good, the intention is to assert at the same time that specific attitudes are also involved. Everyone ought to approve of it, for whatever is good is *ipso facto* to be approved. Everyone ought to like happiness, for that same reason. Happiness ought to be sought. One ought to help others attain it. And so on. Notice that these statements are not offered as defining characteristics at all. Not for a moment is it meant that "Happiness is good" means "I ought to help others attain it", or any of the other things. These sentences all express what one ought to do or what sort of relation one ought to be in with respect to whatever is called good. The resultant obligations are due to the fact that whatever has the characteristic of being good also carries an authoritative demand that it be sought.

If A returns B's gun and B now becomes a menace to his neighbors, the return of the gun would be condemned as wrong because, although keeping one's promise is good, in this case the act would lead to unfortunate consequences, namely, to its use as a weapon to injure other people. Under these circumstances is it not good for A to keep the gun longer? By keeping the gun, would A not prevent B from harming other people? This example, as in the case of happiness, shows that the word "good" is used as a predicate, and hence tells us something about the end sought.

*Good as a Quality*

If "good" is a predicate when applied to the name of a goal, then the goal must have the property denoted by that predicate. Since "good" is applied as a predicate to the names of many things, it may be that they all have some property in common that compels us to predicate good of their names. What this is which all good things have in common is extremely difficult to say, because there is apparently nothing one can identify which happiness, returning the gun merely as the act of doing so, and doing God's will, for example, have in common. If, to take one of these, happiness is a state of a subject accompanied by the feeling of pleasantness, neither the state as a psychological phenomenon, nor the feeling of pleasantness as a neurological one, carries characteristics to which we can point and say: "Behold, there is its goodness-quality."

Perhaps the difficulty is that we are looking for a quality like the yellow of the paper, or the slowness of a motion, or the manifestation in a smile of the feeling of happiness, etc.; and goodness is not that sort of quality. If the goodness quality is not like these things, then it is misleading to look for that sort of quality. What other possibilities are there? It may be that some synonym of "good" might point the direction in which to look if we wish to recognize what things can be asserted to be good and what not. Or it may very well be that, with a term as fundamental as good, we may not be able to give a definition, because it may

have none, in the ordinary sense of a "definition". If there is no definition for "good", all that can be done is to indicate what is good and what
isn't and try to learn to identify the two sorts of things. To clarify these
last remarks two kinds of explications need to be made. We must explain
the nature of a definition and that of a basic quality.

### Nature of a Definition

A definition in its classical form contains two parts:    a) the definiendum – the term being defined and    b) the definiens – the term giving
the definition proper. Hence when we try to give a definition we try to
find a definiens for a definiendum. We need, however, to be quite familiar with the terms used in the definiens. To take an example: suppose we
define "triangle" as "a three-sided plane figure." If this definition is to
be significant, we need to know what it is to be three-sided and a plane
figure. If we do not know, then we may ask for definitions of these. If we
give a definition of three-sidedness, then this definition will give other
terms that either need to be known or themselves need definition. At
some point we will reach a set of terms whose meanings must be known
because they are simple and indefinable in the context in which they
occur. Suppose "three-sidedness" is a simple and indefinable term, but its
meaning is unknown. Then all that can be done is to show objects, figures, etc., which have three sides until three-sided figures can be recognized when seen.

In the same way as there are simple and indefinable terms in a context,
there may also be simple and indefinable properties of objects. When
we reach simple and indefinable things or qualities such as yellow, for
example, all we can do is to indicate them. This is indeed what we mean
when we assert they are indefinable, that we cannot reduce them to
other things but must know them as they are in themselves. This makes
communication about these simple qualities difficult, because if no
matter how hard we try, we cannot get people to recognize the indefinable for what it is, then we will be unable to convince them of its existence. To a person who cannot see yellow, the color, no amount of convincing or arguing will serve to enable him to identify it. This would
seem obvious enough. If, in consequence, "good" is a predicate denoting
a simple quality, then both it cannot be further defined and it must be
recognized when present or be beyond the comprehension of those who
fail to "see" it.

*Physical Qualities vs Non-physical Ones*

The recognition that something is good is, however, made difficult by a characteristic which good has which does distinguish it from other simple qualities like yellow. Consider the color of this paper to be yellow. If the paper is dyed, it gets to be a different color, say, blue and one says that the paper has changed its color. That the color has changed is something one recognizes. In a sense, one can consider the blue piece of paper to be a different piece of paper from the yellow one since a physical characteristic has changed. The same thing is true when we talk about the shape or the size of this piece of paper. Alter its shape (or size) and one has a different piece of paper. Each of these aspects of the paper that was changed tells something about the paper itself. Moreover, every piece of paper must have a color, and a shape, and a size, etc. Changing a physical quality, changes the object but there can be no physical object without physical qualities.

Let us apply these considerations to the act of returning the gun. The act is, in a sense, the same act if A returns the gun, or if some other person who may happen to have the gun does so. Happiness is happiness whether it is intense or mild, had by A or by B by someone else. To say that the act of returning the gun is good does not imply anything different about the act as such. It is still essentially the same act if instead of good we call the act bad. In other words, the act of returning the gun is in no way affected in its nature, whether it is good or bad. What one does when he tries to decide whether or not the act is good is to look at the act as a unique single entity and not as its defining characteristics as a mere act. If A decides to return the gun to B, knowing B to be insane, the act is not good; but if, unknown to A, B regains his sanity, the act becomes now good. But it is the same act, even though the quality of being good or bad has changed.

*Good as a Function of Context*

This, however, is not the case with, for example, happiness as an end. Whether or not happiness, as a means, is good is evidently not a function merely of the happiness. A person who is happy but for whom happiness is bad would experience quite the same sort of thing that one did for whom happiness was good. But his being happy in a given context might induce us to pronounce happiness bad (or good). But this we can only do if happiness is a means. It appears that when we judge something to be good and transfer, as we seem to have done, the adjective "good" to the means we are judging in a complete context.

Ends are held by their advocates never to be bad precisely because of the context in which they must occur if they are to occur at all. For example, the Christian would maintain that doing God's will is never bad. It is intrinsically good. In fact, if one maintains that there is something intrinsically good (or the highest good in the sense of intrinsically so) and in the present case this is doing God's will, then he might urge that even if what it is to do God's will would be unaltered if it were bad, still to do God's will is intrinsically and inherently the sort of thing that cannot but be good; to do God's will couldn't possibly be bad. Now why not? Why cannot one ever say that to do God's will is bad? There can be no other reply but the simple one, "Because it is God's will. It is good to do God's will not because it is an expression of a will, but because it is an expression of God's will. In brief, if one's end is to do God's will, then that end is good because of God and his relation to all there is. The goodness of God's will is not in its characteristics of being a will but in the relation of the will to the Greator. How do we know that the goal of doing God's will is good? Precisely by our knowledge of God. God being what He is, His will must be good because it is His will.

In the same way each advocate of a particular good would insist that the goodness of his end is intrinsic to its very nature. Happiness is good, not because it is a means or because it is sought after, but precisely because it is happiness and in the contexts in which it occurs always, for it to be bad is impossible. Self-expression is good for exactly the same reason, because self-expression is what it is. Doing one's duty is good because it is that sort of thing. When someone argues that a given end, as an end, is good, he is not trying to defend its utility or anything else, but he is simply asserting that by its very nature it has that characteristic. In this respect the relation of the quality of good to the moral end is different from the relation of the color of the paper to the paper. Where the yellow is not involved in the nature of the paper, the good-quality is in the nature of the moral end.

### Good as an Indefinable Predicate

These reflections provide a foundation for insisting that although an end is good in the same sense that the paper is yellow, nevertheless to be good is not all the same sort of thing as to be yellow. The good-quality and yellow-quality are both properties but different types of properties. Yellow is the color quality of a material object or of a light. Goodness is the moral quality of an end. Both are, however, qualities of that which possesses them. Just as the paper would appear different if it were blue rather than yellow, so the end would appear different if it were bad rather than good. By the very nature of definition, if good is an indefinable, simple quality it must be irreducible and be what it is. Moreover, since good is not a physical quality it cannot change its object when the object or act became other than good. Good must be intrinsic to the end it modifies in a context.

## Criteria of a Good End

Perhaps enough has been said concerning the meaning of the term "good end." The crux of the discussion is that the end has a unique character when seen in a context. In this context the character of the end needs to be recognized but cannot, perhaps, be further defined. It is an ultimate quality of the end as a unique total unity. Such comments, however, are entirely too vague for this to be a satisfactory final word. Fortunately, the impossibility of giving a definition does not eliminate the possibility of enumerating a set of criteria for identification of ends as good or bad.

The first criterion that comes to mind is the following: if an end is good, people will tend to choose that end in preference to others. This is not to say that "The end is good" means "The end is chosen." To assert that it did would be false since people at times do choose bad ends, such as, for example, to conquer the world, or amass a fortune simply to have power, or to end one's life, etc. But the fact that many people do praise or choose an end is some evidence that it is probably good.

Empirically speaking, if a group of people were presented with alternative ends, then that which most selected would properly have some claim to be called good. This assumes that under normal conditions people do choose good ends rather than bad ones. This assumption could be justified either historically or by a study of man. This is much like the case where one presents a group with a set of colors and asks them to select yellow. The color selected as yellow by most would be claimed to be yellow, even though it is possible that in a given population the majority may be color-blind. So happiness is indicated to be good since (not because) so many people choose it as such and even if it may not be the highest good. The question, "Why is happiness good?" cannot be answered by "Because it is chosen," but only, "Because it is." In short, choice is a criterion of a good end, and not part of its definition.

Evidently, even if one chose happiness one need not act in accordance with the choice. A theoretical choice limited to an expression indicating what was chosen is enough since it may not be expedient to try to attain the end at the moment. It is not odd to say that happiness (or some other end) is good but no effort will be made to attain it, because to make such an effort in a given situation might very well lead not to happiness but to disaster. The happiness of the Jews in Nazi Germany may have been a good end, but to effectuate it apparently necessitated war and, hence, unless one were prepared to engage in a war it would have been ill-advised to try to bring it about.

A second criterion closely related to the first may be stated as follows: an end is good if it is approved. If happiness is chosen, it is most likely because it is approved, but a nation faced with a choice between happiness or freedom may choose the latter even though it approves happiness. Indeed, in an historical situation, a nation may choose war rather than peace even though its people disapprove of war because only in this way could they avoid a greater evil, e.g., slavery. Evidently, then, to choose and to approve are related but not the same thing. Conversely, if an end is rejected or disapproved by many people, that would indicate that there is at least some doubt as to its goodness.

A third criterion is: it is better for a good end to be rather than not to be. One asks oneself: "Would it be better for God's will to be done always, or not?" In a sense, the process involved is one of universalization and the attempt to universalize an end may serve as a criterion for its being good. This could be done by imagining the sort of world that would result if everyone did God's will, and contrasting it with the sort of world there would be if no one did God's will. If one could say it would be a better world if God's will were done, then this would indicate that to do God's will is good. Or if someone asks whether self-expression is to be considered good, then if one contrasts the result of universal self - expression with its absence, and concludes that it would be better to have a world in which self-expression were universal then self-expression would be good.

## Autonomy of Good

The final criterion we shall mention is: the good end is worth having for its own sake. If it is not worth having for its own sake, then either it is bad or else it is a good. This underlines once more the distinction between good and a good. For example, if money is said to be good and the question is raised whether money is worth having for its own sake, the answer would have to be in the negative. Money is worth having but not for its own sake. In fact, anyone who values money for its own sake is considered to be abnormal. This shows that money is a good since it is worth having but not good (except in an instrumental sense of "good").

But if one asks, "Is happiness good?" the answer would depend upon whether one considers it to be worth having for its own sake. The hedonist says, "Yes, it is"; the person who values duty retorts, "It is not." Both might agree that it is a good. The hedonist takes happiness as a good end because he feels that happiness, being what it is, is good not because of what else it leads to, but in itself. The person who values duty would accept happiness as a good if it helps him do his duty, which to him is good, i.e., worth having or doing for its own sake.

There is a temptation to conclude that "good" may be defined as follows: "The end is good" means "The end is worth having for its own sake." The chief reason for rejecting this definition and accepting the statement as a criterion is that it seems quite possible to ask, "Why is it worth having for its own sake?" To this the only answer is, "Because it is good", and the result is a tautology. If the definiens, however, is considered to be clear in itself then the two statements may be viewed as logically equivalent, since if "The end is good" is true (or false), "The end is worth having for its own sake" is true (or false). Or to put it another way "Any end that is good is worth having for its own sake" or conversely.

## Experience in Recognition of Good Ends

There may be other criteria that can be used to recognize an end as good. Those we have indicated may at least help us decide whether or not a specific end is good. But in the last analysis the only way we can know an end to be good is to recognize it as such. This means that experience in making such decisions, presumably under the guidance of moralists, is the best way of learning to recognize the good when we are confronted with it. To modify Prichard, but completely in harmony with the spirit of his essay, "Does Moral Philosophy Rest on a Mistake," we can say: If we do doubt whether an end is really good, the remedy lies not in any process of general thinking, but in getting face to face with a particular instance of the manifestation of good-ness and then directly appreciating the good-ness in the end in question – if it is good.

### BIBLIOGRAPHY

Ewing, A. C., *The Definition of Good* (New York: Macmillan Co., 1947), especially Chapter IV, pp. 112-120.
Green, T. H., *Prolegomena to Ethics* (Oxford: Clarendon Press, 1890), Book III, Chapter I, pp. 160-189.

Hill, T. E., *Ethics in Theory and Practice* (New York: Thomas Y. Crowell Co., 1956), Chapter XII, pp. 205-229.
Moore, G. E., *Principia Ethica* (Cambridge: University Press, 1903), Chapter I, pp. 5 ff.
Nowell-Smith, P. H., *Ethics* (Baltimore: Penguin Books, 1954), Chapter XII, pp. 161-185.
Ross, W. D., The *Right and the Good* (Oxford: Clarendon Press, 1946), especially Chapter III, pp. 65-75.

# CHAPTER XIV

# MOTIVES AND CONSEQUENCES

## Motives in Moral Decisions

It is not difficult to illustrate the obvious fact that a consideration of motives and consequences does play a very important role in making moral decisions. In all the preceding pages there has been a constant appeal to consequences and occasionally to motives. In judging, for example, whether it was right to expose the abortionist consideration was given to the effect of exposure on the various people involved. In arguing whether or not it is right to lie, extensive appeals were made to consequences. If one tries to decide whether or not a person who said something false was lying, his motives would be carefully examined. Suppose, for example, Mr. A in New York tells Mr. B in Philadelphia, "It is snowing in Boston." Mr. B, who has just spoken to Mr. C in Boston, replies, "It is not. You are lying." Mr. A in all probability might be indignant and could say, "Perhaps what I said is false. But I did not lie. I did not intend to deceive you or mislead you by deliberately falsifying what is the case." Mr. B might argue in this fashion: "Anyone who tells an untruth is lying. Whether or not your motive was to deceive, you did tell an untruth. Therefore, you are lying."

The disagreement between A and B undoubtedly involves the definition of lying. More specifically, it is centered around the role of motives in the definition of lying. Mr. A insists that motives must be considered whenever one is trying to decide whether someone is lying, while Mr. B wants to remove any consideration of motives and define a lie to be the telling of an untruth. The injection of the question of motive in a moral argument focuses attention upon the agent and, in fact, away from the act. Agents have motives; acts do not.

Up to this point attention has been centered on the act. We have considered the part moral principles play in deciding what we ought to do, the way in which we make up our minds what act is right in a given case, and what ends are good. Now we are changing our orientation. Our discussions have made it evident that a person's motives in doing an act have very little bearing on the question of the rightness of the act in a moral sense, or on that of the goodness of the ends. One may do the right thing for good ends out of either purely selfish motives or altruistic motives. We may commend one who does the right thing out of altruistic motives, and censure the one who acts wrongly for selfish motives. Or we may even praise someone who does the wrong thing for altruistic motives, and censure one who does the right thing but for selfish reasons.

In a similar fashion, the consequences of an act (assuming we know what they are) appear to be independent of the motives which inspire the act. The consequences of an act may be highly desirable or extremely undesirable, while the motives behind the act may be moral or immoral. Yet because we do at times judge a person moral on the basis of his motives, and do classify motives as moral or immoral we need to consider their role in making moral decisions.

A person's motives are something that, in a sense, are definitely and uniquely his. This fairly obvious remark is further evidence that when we discuss motives our concern is with the person involved, and with him as a responsible agent. Since motives concern the agent, two kinds of questions are at issue: the problem of deciding what were the motives in a given case; and the problem of the relation of motives to moral judgment. The first of these is an empirical question of a sort which invites examination for its intrinsic interest as well as for the light the analysis of the problem sheds on the *difficulty* of judging someone moral or immoral. The second problem assumes we know what the motives are in a given case and we ask, "Given these motives, is a person so motivated moral or not?" An evaluation of motives is a condition for the moral evaluation of a person.

## Discovering Motives

How can we decide what motives a person has? If John Smith keeps his promises, if he aids the poor, if he never lies, or if he does any of the thousands of things for which one ordinarily is praised, what are his motives? Why does he do what he does? What is he really after? These three questions indicate what information is sought when motives are questioned. They imply that to know motives is to know what the person really is after. The use of the word "really" is an indication that what someone is after is not always obvious. To ask for a motive is to ask for a "why" – a goal, an aim. The goal may or may not be evident; it may or may not be an ultimate good. Whatever it is, the motive is what brings the agent to act. In brief, a motive is never present unless there is behavior and the behavior is oriented by the motive.

The word is ambiguous. "Motive" may refer to one of two things: either the goal or the psychological "starter," so to speak. To say that someone has motives is to say either that he keeps before himself certain things he wishes to achieve or that there are certain psychological factors that stimulate him to act. If people always told the truth, then the best way to find out what a person's motives were would be to ask him, "When you contribute to your local Community Chest, what are your motives?" Given an honest individual we would believe him if he replied, "To obey God's law and be charitable." The motive would then be clearly expressed.

But even if people did always reply truthfully, they may still be unaware of their true motives. Contemporary psychology has demonstrated that to assume that people know what their motives are is in many cases completely unwarranted. John Doe may intend to give his wife a vacation; his motive may be to get her away from home so that he can be unfaithful. And more than that, he may not, at the moment, be aware that his motive is unfaithfulness. Indeed, if one even insinuated that he meant to be unfaithful John Doe would react angrily. Nor does it follow that John Doe is a hypocrite, as would be the case with someone who says his motives are one thing, knowing quite well they are not. John Doe may not be aware of the discrepancy between what he says are his motives and what they are. In point of fact, he may be fooling himself and be doing it quite successfully.

### Motives as Desires or Impulses

One cannot then assume that a person's motives are what he says they are unless the stipulation is made that nothing will be called a motive which is not consciously known to be such. If this assumption is made, a careful distinction would need to be made between motives in this sense and something else which resembles motives but is not in the person's consciousness. We will call these latter phenomena "impulses" even though this word has additional connotations. Impulses then refer to non-conscious forces that often come into consciousness as motives.

With such a distinction, the problem of discovering what motives a person has divides into two problems:

    (1)   What are his motives?
    (2)   What are his impulses?

Such a division will help clarify the problem of discovering motives as well as that of the role of motives in making moral judgments about an agent. We will need to recognize, for example, that when it is said that A does not know what his motives are, that it is his impluses of which he may be unaware. The distinction also indicates that there may be a basic clash – sometimes conscious, sometimes not – between impulses and motives.

The following incident may serve as an illustration of how important the distinction may become. Joe Roe risked his life to save his child. He jumped into very swift waters when he saw his child fall into the stream, and he did it knowing he was not a strong swimmer. This was a very praiseworthy thing to do. Certainly he was brave. Yet, perhaps, his real motives were simply selfish, because Roe was quite well aware that if he did not take the risk, he would be thoroughly disliked by his friends and relatives, and roundly condemned. Joe Roe knew he could not bear such condemnation. So, he was brave and for his bravery he should be praised, but one cannot consider him a virtuous hero. In this case, what Roe said were his motives, namely, to save the child, were not. His true motive, i.e., his impulse, was to avoid public condemnation.

To this Joe could insist that he didn't know what his motives really were, i.e., what his impulses were, but that all he knew was that he wanted above all else to save the child. He did not calculate the consequences either to himself or to his friends. The only motive of which he was aware was to save the child's life.

If we make use of the distinction between motives and impulses as defined above, then the issues become clearer. Joe is being accused of having self-regarding impulses. And, in fact, he may very well have. Joe's defense is not so much a denial of the existence of these impulses as an insistence that consciously there were other motives and desires. Both motives and impulses may quite well have been present. Joe may be fully justified in insisting that he desired the safety of the child, as someone else might be in urging that his impulse was the avoidance of censure.

## Impulses

A rather intriguing point may be made here. If the statement that all people have their own self-interest or something else as their basic impulse, is correct, then there is nothing one can do about that impulse except perhaps to control it. If such an impulse does exist, then no one in any sense chooses his impulse. It is what it is and it functions to motivate us in all we do or refrain from doing. Motives, on the other hand, seem to differ from impulses precisely at this rather significant point. One can and does choose his motives, or at least which one to act on.

If impulses are part of his nature, then a man cannot necessarily be expected to know what they are. What impulses trigger behavior can only be discovered by considering what man is. What, indeed, the nonconscious forces are that spark one's behavior becomes a problem for those who concern themselves with the "nature of human nature." It may be that these impulses are innate or developed. Whichever they are, a person is not often aware of them, nor of their powerful effect.

Yet, despite the fact that impulses may be intrinsic to human nature and cannot be chosen there may be a choice, and a valid one at that, connected with them. For example, a person may have an impulse to kill and another impulse to rescue anyone drowning. If both of these impulses are made conscious, and therefore motives, then it is possible to conceive of making a choice between one or the other impulse. There is reason to believe that people can be trained to control their impulses. A person can be praised or blamed for allowing one or the other impulse to have free reign, but not for having these impulses. People with kindly impulses are preferred, those with brutal ones rejected. But if they are born with these impulses and cannot alter them, they cannot serve as the grounds for calling people moral or immoral.

These are interesting by-paths, but the discussion at the moment is centered around the following questions. What are motives? And if one knows what motives are, how are they to be discovered? The analysis of these questions showed that motives refer either to those goals a person tries to attain, or those psychological drives that constitute a person's inner motivational orientation. And neither of these can be discovered simply by asking. Finally, the evidence indicated that if motives are impulses, there really is no question of their bearing on moral behavior, for they would have none.

## Motives and Behavior

Can we determine a person's motives by observing his behavior or by means of psychological testing? Let us first consider whether behavior reveals motives. The attempt to determine a person's motives by observing his behavior has a tremendous appeal because it seems to offer an "objective" approach to the problem. All we need to do, apparently, is to keep our eyes on Joe and watch what he "goes for," i.e., what he does, and that will reveal his motives. If, for example, he donates to his community chest, and then gets angry because his name is not included in the list of contributors, one might suspect his motive to be something other than to do charity. If John loans Joe money when Joe is in need, and then expects Joe to vote for him when he runs for office, it would seem plausible to assume John's motive is not Joe's welfare at all.

The general structure of such a method is easily outlined. If A does B and then C, the relation of C to B somehow indicates A's motive in a way B alone or C alone does not. But this is curious. Act C seems to throw light on A's motives because it came after B. Could not Joe's anger at not being included in the list of contributors be due to his feeling that his contribution may have been mislaid, or stolen? What if, as a result of Joe's anger, he doubled his contribution; or exposed a fraud. It may not be true that C rather than B reveals A's motives.

Cases in which disagreements are present are more illuminating. If Joe denies his motive to be what someone says it is, he can support his denial by reference to other things or by showing that his later act does not reveal his motive at all. This indicates that two assumptions are made when one endeavors to discover what a person's motives are on the basis of his subsequent acts. First the assumption is made that there is an ulterior motive, and secondly that an inference from subsequent acts to the true motives is possible.

Inferences are always risky enough; to try to infer (or impute) motives is even more dangerous. In some instances, of course, the problem is easily solved. If, for example, a married man showers gifts and attention upon a woman other than his wife, one would hardly say he is doing it simply out of the motive of making others happy, or of respect for womanhood. But people outside of the motion pictures, television, or novels are not so obvious and their subsequent acts would take more subtle forms so that outsiders could not easily discover the true motives. We must conclude that behavior consequent upon an act may, indeed, throw some light upon, or hint at, the motives of the preceding act, but an inference is involved which is often quite risky. When motives are imputed to another on the basis of such an inference, it is possible that more is revealed about the character of the one making the inference than about the one to whom the motives are imputed.

As for the discovery of motives by psychological testing, this is no place to consider the value of such methods. In everyday living, moreover, where people are called upon to make moral decisions, they rarely have the chance to use such tests upon those whose actions they are concerned to evaluate. It, therefore, is of little consequence to the present problem to try to determine the value of such tests. They simply do not advance the solution of the problem under consideration.

## Summary

In this section of this chapter we were concerned briefly with an elucidation of the notion of motive which plays so important a role in judging agents either as moral or immoral. Motives are reasons why a person does what he does, and we know that an agent who acts for some motives rather than others may be moral or immoral depending upon his motives, or reasons why. It is possible to do the right thing on the basis of bad motives, or the wrong thing with the right motive. Both possibilities raise moral problems. We saw, however, that it was very difficult to discover motives, either as desires or impulses, because of man's ability to hide his true thoughts as well as his ignorance of himself. Nevertheless, we can often discover motives by watching behavior, past as well as present. We, however, take the risk of being wrong in our inferences from behavior to motives.

One final set of considerations to clarify issues. A motive is a psychological fact, and such facts cannot really be held to be moral or otherwise, since clearly psychological facts or phenomena are like physical phenomena in not being what can bear moral predicates. Yet we have continually spoken of moral motives or immoral ones. This is so; but the reference has always been to the agent who has the motives. We may call happiness a motive moral (perhaps); or the desire to do God's will may be said to be a moral motive, and so on. What we mean, of course, is that the person who has these motives is moral; the person who has other kinds of motives is immoral.

## Moral Evaluation and Consequences

Whatever a person's impulses and desires may be, whenever we evaluate his character or his actions we point to the consequences of what he does. So we say, "John D. Rockefeller must have been a most virtuous man. Look at all the good he has done with his money – libraries, hospitals, research grants – all are made possible by his generosity." Since we cannot tell what his motives were, the consequences of his acts become the primary factor determining our evaluation of his character.

To take another case, we often say, "Hell is paved with good intentions. When he did what he did, he brought great misery into the world. How can such a person be moral?"

Or we say, "Sure he lied; but by doing so he saved the country from disaster. This shows that his intentions were good and he was moral."

In fact, at times we seem to be ready to say this, "Indeed he did tell the truth, but as a result he brought great sorrow into his family. How can one refrain from calling a person who will do this sort of thing, just in order to tell the truth, immoral?" Here it is evidently not the motive that is the object of censure but the person is condemned because, despite his laudable motive, the consequences were so unfortunate.

A person whose acts lead to unhappiness may be called "evil" or "malicious," while one whose actions lead to human welfare may be called "moral" of "altruistic". There are many difficulties in the way of precise and clear usage of consequences in making moral decisions. For example, since the consequences of any act are many and varied, one can select some consequences that make condemnation possible, or others that call for praise. This is illustrated quite plainly in the case of lying or, for that matter, in cases of murder for money. If A kills B and uses the money he gets from B's body to buy food, C can call the death of B a consequence and call A a murderer or the happiness B's death may bring to B's relatives a consequence and call A an unfortunate victim of circumstances, and so on.

The importance of the consequences of an act is, perhaps, best indicated by the degree to which moral debates center around an evaluation of the consequences or, better, around the empirical issue of deciding what the consequences are or will be. Consider every example used in this book, and it is quite apparent that this has been one of the basic issues every time. Even Kant could not avoid making consequences at least a criterion of action in accordance with the moral law.

A debate concerning the morality of a person who lies, quite often revolves about the consequences that will result. The question, "Should a doctor lie (and be immoral thereby) to save his patient from mental depression, or should he tell the truth?" is ordinarily discussed in terms of the consequences of lying. Those who insist that the doctor should not lie urge that, if he lies, other patients will not believe him and this is an undesirable situation. Those who take the contrary position insist that the doctor should lie because it will bring happiness to his patient.

*What are Consequences?*

A second difficulty in the way of making moral decisions on the basis of consequences arises when we try to decide what we mean by "consequences." Most people feel it is fairly easy to decide what the consequences of an act are and fail to see the difference between the following two questions: "What are the consequences?" and "What are consequences?"

If one knows what consequences are, he can more easily decide what *the* consequences of an act are. The simplest and most obvious answer is entirely inadequate. The consequences of an act are what takes place after the act is performed. This is evidently of little use. After A kills B, A may go off to eat his supper; this takes place after the act, and yet we would certainly not want to call it a consequence of the act of killing B. A second suggested definition is: Consequences are what result from the act. But many things may be said to result from the act. One of the things that results from A's act of killing B is (say) the expenditure of a bullet. Another result of the act is a series of shock waves caused by the fall of B's body. Still another may be the general condemnation of A for taking a life. Finally, a result of the killing of B will be the diminution of the world's population by one. All of these are "results" of the fact that A kills B. Are they also consequences?

Of course, the two words could be equated by stipulation and "the results of an act" asserted to mean precisely the same thing as "the consequences of an act." Yet one must admit that the meaning of the expression, "consequences of an act," is incomplete in a sense in which that of "the results of an act" is not. If one is asked what resulted from the act, he would be somewhat at a loss where to begin and where to end the enumeration. The results may be thought to include A's condemnation, the shock waves, the expenditure of a bullet, and so on and on.

But if the question is "What are the consequences of the act?" the reply would very likely be, "To whom?" "Consequences" implies an indirect object and, therefore, before a reply can be given to the question, "What are the consequences?" a prepositional phrase needs to be added. Consequences are evidently the results of an act, but with particular reference to some one individual or thing. If, for example, someone says, "The consequences of his act were to make people happy," he means that what was done made John, Mary, Joe, etc. happy. This explains what the act "did for" these people. If Benedict Arnold reveals the secrets of the campaign of his army to the enemy, then a consequence to his own army will be its defeat. It would be strange to say, "A consequence of Benedict Arnold's betrayal was that history books recorded his deed."

Recording Arnold's betrayal was a result of his act but not a consequence.

Perhaps we are over-working a distinction. But the chief point is that when one talks about the consequences of a moral act he refers to something that happens after the act, and which is somehow related to the act and which involves a definition of the subject of the consequences and in particular a *person* or *persons*. Even this is not yet adequate for moral decisions, since not all consequences, even in this sense, are to be taken into consideration when judging a person moral on the basis of something he has done.

Not all results are consequences, but neither are all consequences relevant to moral considerations. In the case of murder, the sorrow of the wife of the murdered person is a consequence of the act, as is the anger of a citizen incensed that anyone should kill another. Yet in trying to decide whether A who killed B was moral or immoral we would not consider the anger of an aroused citizen. Since not all consequences are relevant to moral considerations, some criterion is needed for the selection of those consequences that are to be called "relevant" and "appropriate" when making moral decisions.

Moreover, since teleological moral principles assert that consequences are always relevant to moral decisions, and even attempt to provide a criterion for selecting among consequences, it is important to examine the meaning of "relevant consequences" in some detail.

## The Calculus of Consequences

Suppose A is a hedonist (an egoistic one at that) who maintains that moral decisions must be made in terms of the happiness resulting to him. What he does he judges to be moral or not by considering a part of the total set of consequences, i.e., the resultant happiness that the act brings him. This seems simple enough until he tries to calculate the happiness. First, it frequently happens that a given act produces both happiness and unhappiness. For example, if A cheats, he may pass the examination. This makes him happy, or could. But the cheating may prevent him from learning the material. This brings unhappiness, or could. As stated, this is an extremely simple illustration; real cases are more complicated and involve complex situations in which happiness and unhappiness are inextricably interwoven.

Perhaps this predicament can be avoided by saying not that A is moral if he does what brings him happiness, but that he is moral if he does what brings him the greatest amount of happiness. This, of course, necessitates some principles by which A can compare and give "weights" to the kinds of happiness as well as the degrees of happiness that may be consequential to an act. So it becomes necessary to establish a "hedonistic calculus." But this is an extremely difficult, if not impossible, calculus to define. One needs rules not merely for the selection from the possible relevant consequences of those that will bring happiness and of those that will not, but also rules for separating those that bring more and more intense happiness from those that bring less and less intense happiness. Moreover, we need rules to tell us how much one type of pleasure is "worth" and finally, rules for "adding" pleasures to get a resultant.

## Present or Future Consequences

Before these selections can be made, another problem needs to be faced. Some deeds result in happiness if one projects only a week in advance, but if the time is extended to two weeks the happiness changes to unhappiness. For example, suppose someone decides to buy a car. This may, he calculates, bring happiness in terms of the trips to the country, the convenience in shopping, and so on. However, it is possible that on one of the trips this person may be involved in a wreck. This will bring him unhappiness. But after the wreck, and as a result of it, he may collect heavy damages, and so on in time. This may sound quite ludicrous, but very often it is the way life works out. Where, then, is the time series to be stopped and a decision made not to go beyond that moment in considering consequences, and what criteria will be used to select the time at which to stop? In other words, what, temporally speaking, are the consequences of the act? How long after the act should one cease calculating the value of the consequences?

The same kind of difficulty is encountered when we try to take into account the number of people affected. If the principle is universalistic hedonism, should all one's neighbors be considered, or all one's countrymen, or all people on earth? If, for example, a beggar is given a dime, is he not depriving another beggar of that dime? Should the effect of an act in the United States on a native in Asia be considered in evaluating the act? If this sounds far-fetched, we can restrict our concern to our neighbors. Should the effect on them be considered in every case a consequence of the act? And should every one of them be taken into account? Is an act that brings great happiness to a few and misery to many of greater or less value than one that brings a little happiness to a great many but misery to a few?

*Actual and Intended Consequences*

One final set of difficulties needs to be indicated before concluding this part of our analysis. Should a person be judged on the basis of consequences he did not intend? Not all consequences are intended by one who does something. The distinction between actual and intended consequences is an important one, as the following example shows. A farmer, John Smith, wants to destroy the old shed on his farm and decides to burn it. He takes every possible precaution. However, unknown to John Smith, during the preceding stormy night a tramp had taken refuge in the shed. Early the next morning when John sets fire to the shed, the unfortunate tramp is killed. How should John Smith be judged? Surely, he did not intend nor, perhaps, could he be expected to foresee the tragic situation. He anticipated the possibility of the fire's spreading and took precautions to prevent that. But he could not be expected to know that it would rain nor could he be expected to foresee that a tramp would seek shelter in the shed, and be burned to death. Although this is not necessarily a moral situation, it is a legal one and does illustrate how important the distinction between actual and intended consequences can be.

The intended consequences of an act are those the actor wanted to effectuate. What a person may want to bring about does not always happen. No one has complete control over the future if, indeed, one has any at all. So much of what one intends to have flow from an act may not come about while other things that one may not at all desire may happen. The actual consequences of the act may or may not include what was intended. At times, too, a person is praised for something he did not intend and so it is necessary to distinguish between intended consequences and praiseworthy ones. It often happens that a result of one's act is something completely unintended yet decidedly to be applauded. And the actor may be treated as if he did quite consciously intend these laudable consequences. The inverse often happens also, for an act may lead to highly undesirable consequences never intended or approved by the actor, for which, nevertheless, he may be held responsible.

A person who commits a felony is often held responsible for the consequences of his act even if they were unintended and condemned by the criminal himself. Suppose someone tries to rob a bank and locks a teller in the vault making sure, or feeling certain, that the vault would be opened in time. Should the lock jam and the person inside be suffocated, the robber would be held responsible for the death even though he tried to avoid its occurrence. The situation may be even more complicated. If a bypasser sees the robbery and dies of a heart attack brought on by the excitement, I believe most of us would feel the robber is not responsible for this death even though, in a sense, it too is a consequence of the act of robbery.

## Determinism and Intentions

The problem of the relation between intended and actual consequences leads directly to the question of determinism. When we speak of intended consequences, we must realize that one can intend consequences completely outside his power to bring about. It does not follow that to have intentions implies a world in which one can work towards their realization. Can a person ever realize his intentions? The world may be such that no matter what one intends the consequences to be, actual events go their own way and it is a fortunate accident when what happens corresponds to what is intended.

The moral implications of the metaphysical problem are clear. If the consequences of an act are independent of what the doer intends them to be, then neither can he be judged in terms of the actual consequences of his act, nor can his act be judged right or wrong in any significant fashion. If the act is right it is not "because" it leads to desirable consequences but only "since" it does. Furthermore, the consequences can be said to be desirable only in the way in which one says that rainfall is desirable. There is in this no real significance, morally speaking, for right or wrong. Moreover, the act itself cannot be attributed to the actor as his act except in a possessive sense, since it too occurs independently of his intentions. These comments indicate how close the relation is between metaphysics and ethics. Obviously, since we have defined a moral act in terms of choice, everything we have said is based on a rejection of determinism. The justification of this assumption is a task for metaphysics.

## Conclusions

Let me conclude this chapter on a more positive note. We do in our ordinary daily living infer what people's motives are. If we did not, we could hardly protect ourselves against evil-doers. "Intent to kill," "intent to commit assault," "intent to save someone's life," "intent to defraud," etc. – these are all good expressions used not merely in legal contexts. That we make mistakes when we infer intentions is indeed part of our experience also.

If we consider an intention to be a state of psychological readiness to act in a given way, and a motive what triggers the act, then we can and do infer motives from intentions and these from a number of factors. We consider a person's past deeds, his character, his possible vested interests, his utterances, his efforts and so on, to be clues to his intentions and motives. It would be quite absurd to say that a robber with a loaded gun in his hand ready to be fired, did not intend to use it. He may not have had the motive to do so, but the intent is presumably there and is evidenced by the possession of the gun under those circumstances. Yet he may not really have intended to use the gun; he may merely have intended to frighten his victim. But this latter intention is less credible than the former in most such situations. Still, if we knew that he was desperately hungry, had never robbed, and was known to be a gentle soul, would we not perhaps give him the benefit of the doubt and say, "Perhaps he really didn't intend to use the gun.?" But notice how the inference is supported by facts. This indicates the way we do arrive at intentions and also motives. There is no simple and direct syllogistic inference leading to the conclusion, but there seem to be at times reasonable beliefs about intentions and about motives.

Much the same sort of thing can be said about consequences. In most cases we do seem to be able to differentiate between relevant and irrelevant consequences. Moreover, we are quite often capable of saying what consequences were intended and what were not. Intention is vectorial; that is to say, that it does select from a region certain things. And we can and do know what is selected and what not. A person who shoots at a target wants to pierce it. The fact that he sets up a chemical process that explodes the powder that bursts the bullet is irrelevant. Indeed, if the bullet hits a rock, ricochets and injures the family cat, it is clearly not an intended consequence. Under other conditions, one may intend to kill the cat, but this too we can infer.

If neither motives nor consequences were determinable, not merely would moral judgment be impossible, but also legal ones. For the law does make distinctions between intentional and unintentional killing, and between foreseeable and unforeseeable consequences even, in the latter case, to the extent of constructing a mythical individual, "the normal person." So a foreseeable consequence is one, legally, which a normal person under ordinary conditions might be expected to anticipate. This, however, is law, so we leave it.

## BIBLIOGRAPHY

Ewing, A. C., *Ethics* (London: English Universities Press, 1953), Chapter V, pp. 65-86. (Also, pp. 59-62).

Kant, I., *Foundations of the Metaphysics of Morals,* Preface, First, Second, and Third Sections, in A. I. Meldon, ed., *Ethical Theories*, 2nd Edition (New York: Prentice-Hall, 1955), pp. 292-341.

Ross, W. D., *Foundations of Ethics* (Oxford: Clarendon Press, 1939), Chapter XII, pp. 290-310.

Sharp, F. C., *Ethics* (New York & London: Century Co., 1928), Chapter IV, pp. 52-65.

# CHAPTER XV

# JUDGING THE PERSON

## To Be Moral and To be Virtuous

Means and ends, motives and consequences, play quite important roles in moral judgments when the subject of the judgment is the agent and not the act or the ends. The discussions of the preceding two chapters have laid the groundwork for an examination of such judgments as "John Doe is moral" or "John Doe is immoral." What do such statements mean and how, if at all, can they be confirmed?

For many people statements like "John Doe is honest", or "John Doe is kind," or "John Doe is just," etc., are taken to mean the same thing as "John Doe is moral." If such characteristics as kind, honest, just, etc., are called "virtues", then the statement, "John Doe is virtuous," is equated with "John Doe is moral." This identification is not correct.

When one asserts of John Doe that he is virtuous, he is quite evidently saying something about John Doe. Presumbly, too, if one says this of John Doe, the implication is that this is something nice. To be virtuous is to be worthy of emulation. But suppose the compliment is paid John Doe and a friend looks at John Doe and says, "John Doe looks just like everyone else. I don't see any virtuousness anywhere about him." Of course, the friend would never say such a thing unless he had been a student of philosophy. If he is saying anything at all by that remark, he is trying to underline the fact that virtue is not a quality in the sense that, for example, white-skinned is. The predicate "virtue" tells us something about John Doe, to be sure, but what it signifies is not one of his physical properties. If we try to decide what we would say to someone who made such a comment, we will see what the word implies. "Look here, my friend, what I said about John Doe is, most evidently, not something about his skin-color, or eye-color, or height, or any other physical property. What I am trying to call to your attention is how John Doe acts."

## Virtue is Behavior

This seems to be a most promising comment. Surely, if one wanted to decide whether or not to call John Doe virtuous, he would look at what John Doe does. If he tells the truth, does what he promises to do, and so on, we are forced to concede that he is honest, keeps his promises, and so on. He may also be thought to be foolish, but that introduces a non-moral consideration, perhaps. If John does not abuse animals, gives alms to the needy, helps old people cross highways, he is called kind. Since ordinarily one does not expect people to possess all virtues, a person will be said to be "virtuous" if he exhibits at least one of the virtues. So if John Doe is honest, i.e., acts honestly, it will be said that he is a virtuous person. If he is charitable, he will also becalled virtuous.

It sometimes happens that people will say of someone, "John always tells the truth, but he really is dishonest," "John always acts virtuously, but at heart he is really not virtuous at all." Unless such remarks are blatant contradictions, they must contain different meanings of the terms. Consider: if John Doe always tells the truth, then he must be truthful since that is what is meant by "truthful". How can we then say that he "really" is not honest? Only if we mean that merely to act honestly does not constitute being honest because something more is involved. If one who made such a remark were pushed to say what he meant most certainly he would reply in some such fashion as this.

"John always does what the honest man would do under the circumstances. But he does it because he believes he can profit most by being honest." And this is, clearly, to return us to the discussions of the previous chapter about motives. But another distinction is in order. If it is agreed that to be virtuous is to act in a fashion indicated by such words as "honest," "kind," "upright," "chaste," and so on, then, by definition, he who acts in this way is virtuous, and he who does not is not. It makes no difference why the person so acts, the only requirement is that he do so Hence, to impute motives is really to talk about something else. If "to be honest" means never to lie, for example, then the person who never lies is honest regardless of why he never lies. We cannot say that the person who is honest because he never lies is also dishonest, if we stick by our definitions. So a person who is said to be virtuous because he acts as a virtuous person does, cannot be said to be vicious or un-virtuous because of his motives.

Evidently being moral is different. A person who is virtuous because he acts virtuously need not necessarily be considered a moral person. If honesty is viewed not as a virtue but as a moral trait, motives become important. One can be virtuous without being moral, which is to say that one can be virtuous for the wrong reasons. In any case, there seems to be little difficulty in deciding what we mean by the judgment, "John Doe is a virtuous man." The statement means that John Doe acts in the manner defined by the predicates denoting virtues.

Indeed, it is not too difficult either to define what the expression "John Doe is more virtuous than Joe Blow," means. To be explicit, the relation of being "more virtuous than" means that in the case of a given virtue, e.g., honesty, John Doe practices it more often or with greater intensity than Joe Blow. Or, John Doe acts in accordance with more virtues than Joe Blow since John Doe is not merely honest but kind, while Joe is only honest. It is also not too difficult to set up an ordering of degrees of virtue. So John Doe could be said to be braver than Joe Blow if John Doe risks his life to save a child in a situation where he is more apt to lose it and in which Joe Blow would hesitate to act.

### Morality and Moral Principles

The expression "A virtuous person may be immoral" needs to be explained. If John Doe had all possible virtues, one would be compelled to concede that he was moral since he could not then be thought of as being hypocritical, or acting selfishly, and so on. Short of having all possible virtues, or of being known to have them, for John Doe to be moral involves more than simply acting in a certain way, such as telling the truth, or giving alms, etc. One may do these things yet be acting in a fashion contrary to moral principles because of the motives. It is clear, therefore, that one may *act morally* in one sense, yet not *be* moral. A person may *act* morally if the act happens to be in accord with a moral principle.

However, since motives are so very difficult to discover, we tend to rely completely on behavior. As a consequence, if a person is seen always to act in accord with moral principles and his reasons are unknown one is tempted to say that "John Doe is moral" means "John Doe acts in accordance with moral principles." This I shall refer to as a legalistic definition. That this legalistic definition is inadequate is demonstrated by the following considerations.

Ordinarilly, the expression, "John Doe acts in accordance with moral principles," implies that John Doe deliberately tries so to act that his actions do accord with moral principles. The result is not a chance agreement between act and principle but a deliberate one. But, as we have seen, it is possible for the outcome of an act to be other than what was intended. Shall we then say John Doe is immoral because his act turned out not to accord with moral principles, i.e., because John Doe made a mistake? Or shall we call him moral even though the act did not accord with moral principles? Perhaps we should rephrase the definition in the following fashion:

"John Doe is moral" means "John Doe desires and tries to bring it about that his acts be those dictated by moral principles."

On this definition if John Doe were a Kantian, he would be moral if he desired and tried to bring it about that his acts were those commanded by the moral law which dictates the maxim: "So act that you could will your act to be a universal law." Or, in the eyes of the Old Testament theologian, John Doe would be moral if he desired and tried to act in accordance with the Ten Commandments. The following analogy will help clarify this point of view. A person who obeys the law of the land is law-abiding; so one who obeys moral principles at times is said to be moral. Nevertheless, there is a difference. A person who does not break the law, i.e., obeys it, cannot be said to be lawless no matter why he obeys the law. One who obeys moral principles may be immoral if his reasons for so acting are not of a certain sort. A person who obeys the law may be praiseworthy, no matter why he obeys it, even though one who obeys the law out of respect for it rather than out of fear of it is more praiseworthy. But one who obeys moral principles for unworthy reasons is not considered praiseworthy at all, even though he might be preferred to one who violated them.

The reasons why a person obeys the moral law are important in judging a person in more ways than one. Not merely need we take into account motives but also the relation of the person to the moral law itself. If the obedience to the moral law is the result of a compulsion similar to what the stone undergoes when it falls, then the statement, "That person is moral", merely expresses a state of affairs analogous to "That stone is falling." To conceive of a moral law as analogous to a physical law is to rob persons of their freedom, and hence to make meaningless all moral decisions. A purely legalistic definition of "John Doe is moral" suffers from this apparent dilemma involved in the phrase "obeys the moral law." Here again we are confronted with a metaphysical problem which needs resolution but which we will simply assume to have been discussed elsewhere. A moral law may be viewed as inherent in the universe, yet basically different from physical laws. Indeed, it may be desirable not to speak of "moral laws" at all.

## Moral Rigidity

Contrariwise, the person who adheres to the very letter of the law and who takes care to dot all the i's and cross all the t's in the law appears to become unworthy of being called moral. Here is a most interesting paradox. We would not call one who violates moral principles a moral person; but we may refuse to call John Doe moral simply because he lives in accord with that law. The reason is clarified when we recall the two meanings of the expression, "live in accord with the moral law." First, the phrase may mean that one's acts are those dictated by the moral principle but accidentally so, as when the criminal robbing a house calms the fears of the sick, or saves the life of an invalid in a burning house. Secondly, "to live in accord with the moral law" means "to direct one's actions deliberately so as to do what the moral law commands." In this second case, the rigidity of one's adherence to the moral law may be a measure of moral determinism and not of morality at all. We are all acquainted with the picture of the moral purist who is cruel and merciless in his insistence on obedience to the moral law. The common stereotype of the Puritan or moral "Do-gooder" is evidence of what is meant here.

## The Yoke of the Law

The import of these considerations is that the moral principle cannot be a law but must remain a principle. John Doe must direct his actions by the moral principle of his own free will and accord, realizing at all times that he can do otherwise and taking into account all the relevant circumstances. Kant recognized the need to retain the full exercise of free will, when he insisted that the moral person acts in accordance with the categorical imperative out of *respect* for the moral law, and not because of the consequences of the act or its binding character except in so far as he takes the obligation upon himself. But it may happen that a person who tries to be moral by taking upon himself the obligation of a moral law loses his character as a person and becomes nothing but a poor lost soul obsessed and driven by the moral law to which he has subordinated his very life. The law becomes a yoke and a hindrance rather than an aid in living the moral life, i.e., in being a moral person.

Imagine, if you will, John Smith, who has accepted the yoke of the moral law. He has freely chosen to submit his every action to the test of the hedonistic principle, to act so as to maximize pleasure taking into account both the quality and quantity of pleasure. When he seeks to decide whether to keep his promise, he endeavors with all ingenuity to compute the resultant pleasures and see what will lead to the maximum. Or if he wants to decide whether to be charitable and give the starving beggar a dime – again he produces his scales and weights to compute the pleasure resulting from the act. Indeed, he is so occupied trying to obey the moral principle, he tortures himself by his continual insistence on maximizing pleasure. The desire and attempt to live by the moral law become obsessions driving John Smth to excesses. An observer watching a John Smith trying to live under his obligation feels pity tinged with sadness for the mistaken hope that to submit to a moral law is in itself to be moral.

We have seen, I hope, that merely to abide by a moral law is not enough to warrant the adjective "moral." True, if one violates moral principles, he cannot be called moral, but to be moral involves more than submission to a moral law.

### Morality and Good Will

Our discussion of motives and consequences leads to two other possible definitions of what it is to be a moral person. The first is that the moral man is the man of good will; the second that the moral man is the one who acts so as to bring about the best of the possible consequences of his actions. Let us discuss the first of these – the moral man is the man of good will. This definition is unsatisfactory for two reasons. In the first place, one can have a good will and yet do evil things; the second reason is derivative from this, namely, to be moral is not the same as to be a man of good will.

To be a man of good will is to will what is good. This obvious remark indicates that "man of good will" tells us something about the ends sought rather than about either the means used or the rightness of the act. Indeed, the world offers numerous examples of people who will what is good yet do what is evil. People kill (an act indubitably wrong) to free others from slavery (an end worthy to be sought). Or, a person robs, as did Jean Valjean in Hugo's *Les Misérables* (an act wrong even if justified) to feed his family (an end laudable indeed). All rulers of countries arming themselves with atomic weapons insist they have the will to peace. And it may quite well be so.

One can argue that a man of good will not merely wills good ends but also good means (which are, approximately speaking, ends). This may be so, but in ordinary life we do speak of people who will what is good, yet do what is wrong, and who for that reason cannot be called moral. But even if we stipulate that a person who wills both a good end and a good means will use that means to achieve the end. But, unfortunately, we do that which we do not want to do as well as that which we ought not to do, and do not do that which we want to do as well as that which we ought to do. In brief, willing and acting in accordance with the will are two distinct operations in human life. The argument that a person does what he really wills to do, and if his acts are contrary to what he says he wills, then he is either a liar or else is unaware of what he wills, cannot be easily gainsaid. But neither can it be proven. By stipulation, the act rather than the words is taken to express the will. Yet one can just as easily assert the converse. Is it not quite as simple to insist that the act is beyond my control but my words are not, and, therefore, I tell you what I do actually will?

Clearly, then, if a wrong act can be chosen even by a person with a good will, knowing that it is wrong, we cannot equate "to be moral" with "to have a good will." When I say, "To refrain from injuring someone is indeed a moral act," it does not seem to me that I am saying, "To refrain from injuring someone is to have a good will."

This brings out an essential difference between being a moral person and having a good will. "To be moral" is an expression that tells us something about the way in which John Doe lives, while "to have a good will" tells us something about John Doe's motives or intentions and very little about how he conducts the business of living. In logical terms, the two are not equivalent since it appears that it may be true to say, "John Doe has a good will" and yet false to say, "John Doe is moral."

*Morality and Consequences*

Let us return to the second alternative, namely, that "John Doe is moral," means "John Doe always acts so as to bring about the maximum beneficial consequences." That this definition too has its limitations is evident in the light of the following possibility. A pharmaceutical laboratory manufactures Salk vaccine. Due to a defect in the experimental controls, the vaccine is contaminated without anyone's being aware of it. When a polio epidemic threatens, the owner of the laboratory, out of concern for mankind, offers this vaccine free. It is loaded on a truck driven by a man who maliciously and deliberately wrecks the truck and destroys the vaccine. This complicated illustration contrasts in the same situation the man who could be called moral but whose good deed unknown to him could have resulted in great evil, with the man who deliberately does evil but whose deed unknown to him did have beneficial results. Surely, the driver's act brings about the maximum beneficial consequences; yet the driver can hardly be called moral, as he would of necessity be if we accept this definition. Nor would anyone seriously call the owner of the pharmaceutical laboratory immoral even if his contaminated vaccine had reached its destination. He might be called careless but surely he would be considered more moral than the truck driver.

To meet such objections, it may be suggested that the consequences were not those intended either by the owner or by the driver and hence we need to modify the present definition to the following: To be moral is to *intend* the maximum beneficial consequences. In criticism of this definition there are other comments to be made in addition to those already mentioned when we discussed the nature of consequences. If intention is a factor, then social reformers are the most moral of people, and busybodies too, running about doing good. Women who devote their days to "charity" and "charitable organizations" must certainly be conceded to be moral. Even a dictator may intend maximum beneficial consequences. If the moral person is the "do-gooder", then why the scorn for the "do-gooder" and the "social reformer" as well as the fear and hatred of the dictator? Precisely because in their zeal for maximum beneficial consequences, they may disregard basic human considerations and ignore those who unfortunately will not stand to benefit by the act in question. A violation of essential human dignity is often far more significant than all the beneficial consequences that may flow from some act. Sometimes the integrity of one single lost soul is of greater importance than the happiness of a whole mass of high priests. The high priests always aim at the maximum beneficial consequences in their condemnation of new prophecy that offends the ear of Caesar.

At times the moral person does, in fact, stand up to confront evil even in the face of catastrophe. When a dictator is challenged the result may be widespread misery. Shall we, therefore, say that a person who challenges a dictator is accordingly immoral? Quite the contrary seems to be the case, for if to be moral were to do whatever is necessary to achieve the maximum beneficial results, then the moral person might well turn out to be the person who causes the least disturbance. And this is quite often not so. Great moral leaders did not accept evil because to challenge it would entail disturbances. Liberty, at times, comes only after great upheavals. Nor is it an objection to say that such an argument is possible only in terms of the lack of a definition of "maximum beneficial results." This cannot be accepted as an objection because, however one defines the term, it may still be immoral to act to achieve it in those cases where a minority (even one) needs to be injured to realize that maximum. In

brief, the mere insertion of intention does not help to make the definition any the more acceptable.

### Morality is Behavior

Two kinds of definition have been rejected. The type that tries to
define "to be moral" in terms of action (either in terms of motives or in
terms of consequences) and the type that tries to define the expression in
terms of a good will. Both were found to be inadequate. We have
also seen that the predicate "moral" where conjoined to "John Doe" does
not signify a peculiar kind of attribute which is related to him as is his
bravery, or other virtues. The virtues do, quite clearly, characterize John
Doe's actions so that to be brave is to disregard one's own safety, or to be
honest is to act openly and not to conceal, to be charitable is to give alms,
and so on. We can, therefore, try another approach. Let us say that an
expression such as "John Doe is moral" tells us something about the
kind of person John Doe is which reveals itself in his total life pattern.
The two best known examples of this sort of definition are:

(a)  "to be moral" means "to be rational";
(b)  "to be moral" means 'to be like Christ."

The first of these is in many ways the ideal of the Greeks and was expressed clearly by Aristotle. The second is the ideal of Christianity and
has been defended by Christians throughout the ages.

### To be Moral is to be Rational

"To be moral" means "to be rational." This seems at first glance to be
perfectly clear and a definition easy to apply in the sense that we can by
its use classify people as moral or immoral. But new difficulties arise as
soon as we examine it more closely. If this definition is to be accepted,
must we not know the marks of a rational man? There is no use in replacing one expression by another unless we are better acquainted with
the one substituted. What is meant when someone says, "John Doe is
rational?"

A number of descriptive characteristics suggest themselves. The man
whose behavior is coherent may be considered rational because what he
says and does hang together. A rational explanation is one which follows
from basic facts or principles called "reasons" which imply what is being
explained. To be rational, then, is to act in accordance with reason, i.e., to
act consistently and in consequence of something else. The act may be
consistent with one's character, or one's beliefs, or other actions which

form a pattern with the given act. For example, we expect a thief to steal. We expect someone who believes that happiness is the greatest good to try to obtain it.

A person who has no goals nor beliefs cannot act rationally because to act rationally is to use reason in ferreting out the means for attaining the goals or in deducing the consequences of beliefs and then to act accordingly. If this is what it is to be rational, then rational action may be within the scope and ability of the most immoral as well as the most moral of persons. To be rational, in this sense, has no implication for the nature of the goals sought, or the beliefs or actions in terms of which consistency is judged. An insane person may be more rational than a sane one. There was a sense in which Hitler's acts were most rational although he was himself quite insane, for the things he did were consequences of the beliefs he held. Surely this was not what Aristotle, who tried to identify morality with rationality, meant.

Aristotle believed that there was a supreme good for man which he called *happiness*. Furthermore, he felt that since the supreme good should be centered around what was uniquely human, human happiness came through the use or exercise of what distinguished man from other animals. This distinguishing characteristic was reason. In this way, Aristotle concluded that the moral life was the contemplative life. "To be moral" is "to be rational" and this, according to Aristotle, means "to lead a contemplative life."

The expression "to be rational" is now seen to have two meanings. One of them is: "to use reason in achieving one's goals"; while the other is: "to live a life of contemplation."

The first of these is easily rejected as an expression synonymous with "to be moral" because in order to be a moral person it is just as important to aim for the right kind of goal as for the right means. So if John Doe sets out to betray his country, we would scarcely find it in ourselves to call him moral because he sets about rationally to achieve his purpose. Nor, more obviously, would it be easy to argue that a bank robber who plans his course of action with great detail is a moral bank robber.

The second is more difficult to reject, and yet it too is unsatisfactory. For one thing, it goes counter to our ordinary beliefs that the contemplative life is not identical with the moral life. Surely we would agree that a person who devotes his life to the concrete improvement of man's condition is more apt to be the moral individual than the student who spends his life in his "ivory tower." The student is not immoral (although he may be) simply because he studies. The point is that to be moral seems to involve, as we have repeatedly seen, action in the face of difficulties, temptations, and alternatives. No person who withdraws into inactivity, whether for self-protection or for contemplation, can be said to be moral.

Of course, for Aristotle, these considerations would have been beside the point. He did feel, with all the Greek love of the intellect, that only the search for knowledge was worthy of man's highest energies and, hence, only he who sought this knowledge could be moral, i.e., perfectly a human being. So, for the Greek, the do-er could not be moral although he could be virtuous. Virtues, for Aristotle, made possible action which made the contemplative life feasible. We need not pursue Aristotle's doctrine further, but there needs to be underlined a point which Aristotle, along with other moralists, assumes throughout. Morality is concerned with being what one is in essence, a rational animal for Aristotle; a happiness seeking creature for Mill; a child of God for Paley; and so on. We must keep this in mind for it will offer a guiding thread a bit later. Meanwhile we will consider the second alternative definition of "to be moral"; that is "to be like Christ".

## To Be Moral is to be Christ like

If being moral implies being perfectly a man, then Christians would, and do, claim that "to be moral" means "to be like Christ", for Christ was perfectly a man. But the very theology basic to this would make it impossible for ordinary mortals to be moral, for Christ could be perfectly a man precisely because he was God. This is, in itself, no real objection to identifying the two expressions but it would simply and strikingly underline the difficulty of moral action and, in a startling fashion, reveal the ideal nature of the moral man. To say that the moral man is an ideal is to say that one has a standard for comparison, and, therefore, even though unattainable, its description may serve to give real meaning to the expression "to be moral".

Having said this, it must still be admitted that to say that "to be moral" means "to be like Christ" is no more to tell us what it is to be moral than to say that "to be a mathematician" means "to be like Dedekind" tells us what it is to be a mathematician. What is offered is an example, and not a definition at all. If being moral consisted in imitation, this might be quite satisfactory, but the difficulty is that even Christ did many things that did not involve questions of morality. So Christ went into the wilderness – does this mean that the moral person to be such must also go into the wilderness? Christ performed miracles – does this mean that to

be moral one needs to do likewise? The "imitatio Christi" which signifies Christ's moral character seems to involve only certain acts and not
others. So to be moral is to do as Christ did when He washed the feet of
His disciples. Or, as He commanded, to forgive those who trespass
against us, might be the sort of thing in which we need to imitate Christ
in order to be moral. As a consequence, the expression "to be moral"
cannot be said to mean "to be like Christ". But whatever it is to be moral
will be achieved if one does imitate Christ in those matters that concern
human relations, and not even all these. We need a principle for the
selection of those acts of Christ that define the moral life and which we
need to imitate if we are to be moral. To offer such a principle would
be to give a definition other than to "to imitate Christ."

Evidently, even if one could indicate precisely those things that were
to be imitated, the mere imitation of Christ is also insufficient as a definition. The hypocrite can also imitate Christ's actions, and often does. In
so far as John Doe and Richard Roe both endeavor to imitate Christ,
there is on the surface no difference between them. Yet Richard Roe
may do so and be a hypocrite; while John Doe may do so out of love for
Jesus. If one objects that the hypocrite does not imitate Christ since
Christ's motive was pure, he will have hit the nail on the head. It is not
merely the action but the motive and intention as well that count.

## Marks of a Moral Person

Our reasons for rejecting each proposed definition of "to be moral"
provide us with certain evident conclusions. Chief among these is that no
person can be called moral simply because of what he does or simply
because of his intention and will. This is to say that the moral person
is distinguished from the immoral one both by the reasons he has for his
actions and by his actions. He must not merely act in a specific way when
the occasion arises but he must have a specific type of reason for doing so.
Jesus will serve as an exemplar. Jesus not merely practiced the virtues.
He did so out of love for man. But His love was not merely passive, rather it displayed itself actively in what He did. Apart from the theology, the
Cross was final evidence that Christ was the most moral of persons for
what He did was done regardless of the pain and suffering that were its
inevitable consequence. Christ did not swerve from His love for mankind that was intrinsic to all He did, even though He knew the price He
would need to pay. To use modern jargon, Christ, as moral, was selfless –
He did not count the consequences to Himself. Moreover, Christ was
moral not because He condemned evil-doing; He prevented it and tried

to bring the sinner to modify his ways. Most certainly what Christ did, or a moral person does, is a consequence of a moral principle, but to be moral one needs to act that way not because the action is a logical consequence of a moral principle but because of the love within. This, I believe, is what Kant was after when he rejected calculation as in any sense related to the intrinsic nature of the moral act. Here, too, lies the difference between the mere hedonist and the moral person, between the man of guile and hypocrisy and the man of love and morality. The greatest of all virtues is charity, not in the sense of giving alms but in the sense of loving care and kindness. Even, for that matter, the man of good will may be immoral if his good will derives not from love but from self-interest.

We can, I think, sum up now. If we want to decide whetheroor not John Doe is moral, we need to do the following things.

First, we observe the consequences of his acts. Do they tend to bring about the happiness of those who will be affected? If they do not, then we must decide whether the unhappiness is premeditated or beyond his control. If the former, the person is not moral.

Secondly, if his actions do tend to maximize happiness, what is the motive? If the actor seeks self-aggrandizement, he is not moral. If his motive is the welfare of the other person, then we must inquire concerning his motive for desiring that welfare.

Thirdly, we must ask whether the act is in accord with a moral principle. If it is not, the person may be amoral, if not immoral. If it is, then we need to inquite again concerning the intrinsic motivation.

Fourthly and finally, we need to ask whether the act done is done out of love for mankind or some lesser reason. Only if the act is a consequence of a moral law, tending to bring about the maximum possible happiness because of a love for mankind, can the person who so acts be called moral.

*Summary*

We began the investigation of judgments about the morality of persons by drawing a distinction between being moral and being virtuous. The latter was defined in terms of virtues; the former was related to moral principles. But we discovered that to be moral could not be simply to act in accord with moral principles because intention, motives, and consequences at least needed to be included in one's evaluation of a person. In addition, the obedience to a moral principle had to be free obedience and not one that resulted from any sort of compulsion. The attempt to define a moral person as one having a good will failed when it was shown that "to be moral" and "to have a good will" were not logically equivalent. Finally, brief consideration was given to two historical definitions – the Greek, to be moral is to be rational; and the Christian – to be moral is to be like Christ.

BIBLIOGRAPHY

Aristotle, *The Nichomachean Ethics.*
Bradley, F. H., "My Station and Its Duties" in *Ethical Studies.* (New York: The Liberal arts Press, 1951), pp. 98–147.
Dewey, John, James H. Tufts, *Ethics,* Rev. Ed. (New York: Henry Holt and Co., 1932), pp. 304-314; also Chapter XV, pp. 315-344.
Kant, I., *Fundamental Principles of the Metaphysics of Morals.* (New York: Liberal Arts Press, 1949).
Pratt, J. B., *Reason in the Act of Living* (New York: Macmillan Co., 1949), Chapter XXII, pp. 242-257.
Ross, W. D., The Right and the Good (Oxford; Clarendon Press, 1930), Chapter VII, pp. 155-175.
Tsanoff, R. A., *Ethics,* Rev. Ed. (New York: Harpers & Bros., 1955), Chapter VIII, pp. 143-162.

# CHAPTER XVI

# JUSTIFYING MORAL PRINCIPLES

Moral decisions are founded upon moral principles. For the most part, these principles are taken to be authoritative and no challenge to that authority is raised. But what is the source, if there is any, from which the authority of the moral principle flows? If one believes that one ought to obey God's will, then to demonstrate that to be honest is to act in accord with the divine will is to show why one ought to be honest, even if one isn't. The justification of an act is the principle which implies that the act be done. But how can we justify the principle itself?

## Justification and Deduction

The acts in our examples were justified by showing that they were either a consequence of or compatible with some moral principle. The acts were, in short, demanded if the principle was accepted. In this respect, the procedure of justifying an act was analogous to a logical derivation of a conclusion from premises. An analytic, or logical, relationship was presumed to exist between the moral principle to which the appeal is made and the act. If, so the justification ran, all people ought to obey God's will, and this is God's will, then everyone ought to do this act.

This kind of justification is reminiscent of what is done in geometry. In geometry, if one wishes to prove, for example, that the sum of the angles of a triangle is $180°$, he must show that this is a logical consequence of the axioms. "Justification" in this context means "derivation from axioms." In arguments where alternative premises are possible, it is inevitable that someone ask, "Why accept one premise (moral principle) rather than some other?"

## Moral Disagreement and Logical Issues

In a sense it is too bad that our disagreements, moral or otherwise, are not merely logical; that is, conserned with whether or not a statement can be deduced from some accepted premises. If such were the nature of moral disagreements, all we would need to do would be to consult a logician and most of the moral disagreements we have so far discussed in this book would be easily solved. Better still, we could construct a logical machine that would be able to solve disagreements for us. Most of the disagreements are concerned either with questions of fact, e.g., whether a given act is or is not conducive to happiness, or, and these are the most difficult, with the selection and acceptance of the moral principle needed. Neither of these types of disagreement is amenable to solution by purely deductive techniques. Let us illustrate a situation in which there is moral disagreement. Suppose John Doe and Richard Roe are discussing the case of a doctor who put to death a patient suffering from an advanced stage of cancer. They are considering whether or not the doctor's act was moral.

John Doe: "I think that Doctor A was a most admirable person. He must have known that the act would arouse sharp criticism, yet acting on the principle that one ought to do what will maximize happiness, he did what a merciless God kept postponing. A very moral person, that doctor."

Richard Roe: "Even if you could show that the death of his patient did maximize happiness, in the sense that it reduced the suffering of the patient, and relieved all the patient's friends and relatives of the pain of watching him die so dreadfully, surely the patient's happiness has not been increased. Perhaps he would have been happier to stay alive and suffer rather than be deprived of the suffering by death. After all, life is sacred, and one ought not to lay hands upon sacred objects."

John: "Perhaps so. Yet consider how much unhappiness was caused by the patient. To lessen that burden is surely moral."

Richard: "Let me be clear about one thing. You believe the doctor's act was moral. And you try to support the morality of the act by an appeal to the principle that one ought to maximize happiness. Is that right?"

John: "Yes. It seems to me that simple."

Richard: "But tell me, what makes this principle a source of authority? Why, in other words, do you feel that this principle is the standard in terms of which to judge acts? Why, in still other words, should I concern myself with such a selfish thing as happiness?"

The type of question that Richard directs against John is what concerns us now. In every case in which one appeals to a moral principle, what gives the moral principle its authority over his acts? Richard is really asking John to justify not his judgment of the doctor's act, but the principle he uses to judge the act.

When we are challenged, as John Doe was by Richard Roe, what are we being asked to do? Whether or not we can do what we are being asked to do is another question that will concern us in subsequent chapters. If someone who is studying geometry is asked to justify the Pythagorean theorem, he knows he is being asked to start with the axioms of geometry and provide a series of statements such that each statement follows from either an axiom or some other proved theorem until, step by step, he arrives at the theorem. Now the student may not be able to satisfy the request because of his lack of ingenuity or his ineptitude in geometric processes. But he does know what is expected of him. Before one proceeds to justify a moral principle, e.g., the theological principle, he must know whether it is possible to do so and then if he himself can justify it.

### Justification of Axioms

The axioms of a geometric system are the principles, so to speak, in terms of which the theorems are justified in a logical sense. One cannot accept the axioms and refuse to accept the theorems, although it is quite possible to refuse, in a manner of speaking, to "live by" the axioms. This happens, for example, when a contemporary physicist refuses to use Euclidean geometry in his description of what goes on in the physical realm. He finds some other geometry "superior." There are, therefore, two distinct usages of "justify," when one speaks of justifying a theorem. The first is logical justification, i.e., to derive the theorem from a set of axioms; the second is empirical, i.e., a statement is justified when its use leads to the solution of problems not logically involved in that statement.

Axioms, or principles, being the basis of a geometry cannot be derived from other axioms. Therefore, their justification cannot be logical in that sense. But the empirical justification of a theorem depends upon the empirical justification of the axioms, since the theorem is analytically involved in the axioms. So, for example, whoever wants to justify some one of the theorems of geometry empirically may need to justify the axioms of geometry empirically. To justify Euclidean geometry usually means to show that the world is constructed according to Euclidean principles.

### Justification of a Principle is About the Principle

People are usually frightened by mathematical considerations no matter how illuminating, so let us turn from geometry back to moral principles. How can one justify the use of a moral principle? Evidently this question is ambiguous because it may refer to the psychological factors that induce us to be, say, hedonists, or formalists, or to the reasons why the moral principle should be used no matter how we feel about it. In both cases, we are asked to give reasons in support of the principle as a standard. If John Doe were to reply to Richard Roe that he used the hedonistic principle because his wife was a hedonist, most of us would smile and consider John quite a wag but very few of us would take that reply to be a good reason, if a reason at all, for living by the hedonistic principle. Much the same sort of thing can be said about the other principles. To one who says, "I accept God's commandments because my father was a God-fearing man," the reply can always be that this is no reason to accept God's commandments as such since this is only an emotional matter at best. To justify a moral principle, then, involves giving reasons, to be sure, but those reasons must say something about the principle as such and not about the person who uses that principle.

### Need for Non-Moral Considerations

What we have said leads us to ask, "What sorts of reasons will count as justifications?" Let it be clear that we are asking John Doe for reasons in support of his basic moral principle and not any lesser maxim. Maxims can be, and are, justified by an appeal to the moral principle. So, for example, if one is challenged to justify the maxim "Be honest!," he could reply that to be honest will bring the greatest happiness and this is what one ought to seek. Or he might say that being honest is to express one's personality and this is the thing that all moral men seek to do. These two examples suggest a generalization. The justification of a moral principle cannot be accomplished by appeal to some other moral principle. To attempt a justification in terms of some other moral principle is not to face up to the problem, which is to justify the basic principle to which the appeal is made *in the last analysis*. Obviously, if one says that honesty brings happiness and we ought to seek happiness, then it can be asked, "Why ought one to seek happiness?" We need, then, to search for reasons that are nonmoral in nature. In other words, something nonmoral must give rise to the moral, if the moral principle is to be justified.

### Justifying Factual Statements

There are a number of ways in which nonmoral statements may be justified. Perhaps it will help to examine some briefly. Suppose the problem is to justify the factual assertion: "The cost of living has reached an all-time high." What, in fact, can be done? In this case the answer is obvious enough. To justify such an assertion, today's living costs are enumerated and compared with those of other years. Today's living costs are then seen to be higher than all other years. Or if "cost of living" is defined as an average of the cost of some twenty (say) basic items, then the average for this year is compared with that of past years. In factual statements of this sort, "to justify" means to present evidence that the facts are as stated, i.e., that the factual statements are true.

Let us consider how we would justify the statement: "The cost of living today should be higher than it ever has been." Does the introduction of "should" make any difference in the way one justifies the statement? Anyone trying to justify this statement would probably point out that it costs more to produce the things that go to make up the cost of living, and since it costs more to produce these things than ever before, it should cost more to buy them than ever before, since what an object sells for is a function of what it costs to produce that object. The statement, "The cost of living should be higher," can in consequence be viewed as a prediction of what one expects to find when the cost of living is calculated, and it is then justified by offering evidence to show that the state of affairs will be as stated. Or else the situation is conceivably this. The cost of living is known to be higher today and the fact that it is higher is justified, i.e., shown to be as it ought to be, by stating the reasons that bring it about that the state of affairs is as it is. Evidently, the justification of the statement depends upon its meaning but reduces in both cases to evidence in the form of facts.

## Justification by Description

Some important features of the problem will be made evident if we make the statement negative. Suppose we want to justify the statement: "The cost of living today should not be so high." An economist might attempt a justification in the following fashion. "The costs of production are not very high. Even with a reasonable mark-up, the cost of basic commodities are not so great that the consumer should be charged so much." The economist asserts that if we accept the rules of economics, the cost of living implied by these rules is less than that which we actually find to be the case. Someone who is not an economist may argue quite differently. He may, indeed, insist that the statement is justified because when the cost of living is so high, people are deprived of happiness, or at least life is more burdensome, and this is morally wrong. In other words, a noneconomist may justify the "should" by reference to a moral principle. His appeal is to the existing state of affairs which, he tries to show, indicates the statement true because the state of affairs is contrary to what a certain moral principle demands it ought to be. Moreover the moral principle to which he appeals is viewed as a "law."

The preceding paragraph shows us that "should" statements can be justified in two ways. In one case we may appeal to rules as we did to the rules of economics which are in point of fact descriptive either (a) of the state of an economy or (b) of the ways in which economic behavior is carried on. In either case, be it noted, the economic appeal is to the nature of something whether it be the economic system as such or the economic behavior. He who appeals to the economic system says, "Our economic system being what it is, the cost of living should not be so high." He who appeals to economic behavior says, "The rules of economic behavior being what they are such high prices should not be the case." The second type of justification appeals to something desirable, which in the strongest case, would be an ultimate goal. No appeal to a subjective like or dislike is ever an acceptable justification.

If one tries to justify the statement, "The cost of living should not be so high," by appeal to a moral principle, he assumes the moral principle itself to be somehow descriptive of a state of affairs, i.e., that it is the case that the moral principle should rule behavior. So one may attempt to justify a moral principle on the grounds that happiness, or self-expression, or social welfare, or doing God's will, and so on, are as a matter of fact desirable. Statements about the desirability of happiness, etc. are no longer to be taken as merely expressions of moral principles but as empirical statements about what is the case in exactly the same sense as the rules of economics purport to tell us the structure of the economic system. In brief, moral principles such as "One ought to do God's will" are taken to be statements of fact.

The following example illustrates another method of justification. Suppose someone is condemned to death for a crime and the judge is called upon to justify his decision. He would argue in this fashion.

"All the available evidence points to the prisoner as the culprit. The law demands that people who commit crimes of this sort be put to death. I have no other alternative but to obey the law in this case."

If the judge were told that the law was unjust, or cruel, or did not do what it was intended to do, he would reply, "You may be right, but this is the law."

In other words, the *legal* justification of a legal decision is that the decision is a consequence of the law. To show that the law applies to the case in question, the judge may appeal to the specific acts of the law-making body. If one objects to the decision on the grounds that capital punishment is contrary to moral principles, he has changed the problem. Whether the law which implies the decision is also in accord with moral principles is not relevant to the question whether the judge's decision is in accord with the law. If laws are to be justified by moral principles, then an appeal to the act of the legislature will be irrelevant.

However, those who advocate that capital punishment be abolished often appeal to the "sacredness of human life." For them this is the ulti-mate court of appeal. But the statement: "Human life is sacred" is *not* a moral principle but rather appears to be a statement of fact. The state-ment does not say human life ought to be sacred, but that it is sacred. Obviously, however, this purported statement of fact leads to the moral principle "One ought not to take another's life," and this to the rejection of capital punishment.

An obstinate insistence that reasons be advanced to support the con-tention that human life is sacred can be met in two ways. Either it could be proposed that human life is sacred precisely because it is human life, or that its sacredness is a consequence of the divine origin of all life. The former could be supported by an appeal to the very nature of human life, the latter by one to the very nature of God. In both cases one is con-fronted with an empirical task: either one needs to examine the nature of human life or the nature of God.

### "To Justify" means "To Show What Is The Case"

These examples all indicate that to justify is, in the last analysis, to show that what is asserted simply states what is the case. When someone is asked to justify some statement, he is being requested, so to speak, to present evidence that will demonstrate that the state of affairs is as as-serted. This is very general but we can make it more concrete by return-ing to the conversation between John Doe and Richard Roe. John Doe had appealed to the hedonistic moral principle (it could have been any other) and Richard Roe had asked him to justify that principle's role as a moral standard. John Doe could now say, "Look here, Richard, don't be obtuse. You know that people seek happiness."

Richard Roe replies, "That may be so but what I ask is why they ought to do so and why their doing so is to be accepted as a standard."

"I don't mean to say that the mere fact that they do seek happiness is sufficient to make of it a moral standard. Obviously people seek money, yet I would not say they ought to do so. What I am asserting is that people are so constituted that, if left alone, they will seek happiness. To seek happiness is a consequence of their human nature."

"Wouldn't it be better if men were differently constituted?"

"No, indeed," and here we have the root of the matter for John Doe, "Fortunately men are so constituted that they recognize that happiness is intrinsically valuable. So they seek it. The fact that they do seek happiness in the universal way they do, is evidence of the intrinsic value of happiness."

### The Factual Basis of Moral Justification

This, then, is the foundation upon which John Doe's justification of his appeal to hedonism rests. Happiness is such that it is intrinsically valuable. It is not *judged* to be valuable, it is *seen* to be valuable. Being intrinsically valuable, it is binding upon men to seek it. To disagree that it is intrinsically valuable would not be moral disagreement but a factual one about the nature of happiness. The statement that happiness is valuable appears to be factual and, if it is, the moral apparently does derive from the factual.

Let us ask how Richard could show that the hedonistic principle could not be justified. If to justify the principle we need to show that happiness is intrinsically valuable, or that men are so constituted that they recognize it to be intrinsically valuable, then to show the principle not justifiable it would be necessary to demonstrate that happiness is not intrinsically valuable or that men are not so constituted that they can recognize it as such. That men do not seek happiness by nature, that they cannot recognize its intrinsic value, would mean that the hedenistic principle is not justifiable. This seems to make sense, for to say one ought to seek as a final end what is not intrinsically valuable is utter nonsense. In addition, to say that happiness is intrinsically valuable but that no person can possibly recognize it as such is to utter a sentence completely useless in a moral context.

The various methods of justification that have been examined all have in common that they ultimately appeal to some actual or presumed state of affairs. Moral principles too are justified, then, by an appeal to (a) the intrinsic value of the end to be sought and (b) the state of affairs.

### Human Nature

The ultimate source of the authority of moral principles has been attributed to many things. The easiest approach to the discovery of such a

source has been by appealing to the structure of man. Historical systems
of ethics have approached the problem in precisely this way. Aristotle,
for example, explicitly states the object of his Nicomachean Ethics to be
to discover what is valuable in itself, the "summum bonum." The highest good for man, according to Aristotle, must be related to that characteristic of man that makes him truly a man and not an animal. Man, says
Aristotle, is by nature rational and hence the exercise of reason is the
highest good. On the other hand, the Stoics and Epicureans as well as
Hobbes, Bentham, and in the contemporary world, Schlick, said men
seek by nature to achieve happiness. The appeal to what man is has constituted a common type of justification both for moral principles as well
as their denial. An immoral act is often justified by some remark such as
"Well, people are selfish," or "What can you expect of people?" Karl
Marx too saw happiness as the ultimate good but defined human nature
as well as happiness in terms of the "material modes of production." In
other words, Marx justified morality in terms of the existing structure of
society. Hedonists may agree that happiness is the highest good, yet
disagree completely on the definition of happiness because of their
divergent views of what man is.

### Nature of World

Realizing that man may change, at least in his modes of thinking,
has led some to refer the authority of the moral principle to the structure of the world. Kant, for example, believing for one reason or another
in a cosmos, natural as well as moral, rather than a chaos and, hence, in
a moral order of law analogous to the natural order sought his justification of moral principles in the very law-abiding character of the world.
Hence, he identified the good with the good will, and this he defined as
a will that acted out of respect for the moral law. Taking the nature of
the moral law to be analogous to the physical law, Kant derived the universality, apodeicticity, and categorical characteristics of the moral law.
The moral law is, for Kant, justified by its ontological implications. He
tried to show, so to speak, that the obligatory character of the moral
law is built into the very nature of the cosmos.

### God

Apart from philosophers, the vast majority of ordinary people would,
I believe, justify their moral principles not so much in terms of man or
the world as of God. God commands and His authority as the Supreme
lawgiver is sufficient warranty for the value-character of things as well

as the obligation to act in accordance with moral principles. To say of a moral principle that it is God's command is to justify that principle in a fashion quite different from justification by appeals to the world or human nature. When one appeals to the nature of human nature as a justification of moral principles, one asserts that the moral principle expresses something about human nature and cannot be altered without an alteration of human nature. To act contrary to a moral principle is to act contrary to one's nature. But God as the ground of the justification of moral principles cannot be held subject to them. He creates and can destroy moral principles and his nature remains the same. However, God being what He is never "repeals" a moral principle since these are expressions of His nature. In essence, a moral principle is justified by God's very nature, and the authority the moral principle possesses is there by virtue of God's authority.

Quite obviously the person who denies that God exists would never accept such a justification, while the believer would find no other justification satisfactory. Those who deny that God's nature is the source of the authority of moral principles must find the source of the authority of the moral principle elsewhere, be it in man, or the state, or the world, or in the moral principle itself. Their task is more difficult than that of the person who seeks to show that God does indeed impart values to things and types of behavior.

### Ultimate Good

Sometimes the moral principle is justified not by an appeal to a source of value but to an ultimate good. Moral principles are then said to have their authority in the fact that they enable us to attain this ultimate good. Many things have been called ultimately good and only a few will be mentioned. Happiness of one sort or another is almost universally said to be good even when it is not considered an ultimate good. Knowledge has been proclaimed by many as the ultimate good. Self-realization as well as self-expression have had their advocates. Yes, and freedom too has been put above all other things as the most valuable and the highest good. And, of course, salvation and the attainment of the City of God must be included in the list. Accordingly, moral principles are justified by being shown to be fruitful in advancing the attainment of the highest good. A justification based on a higher good demands evidence that what is proposed as a highest good really is so. This evidence would be either the nature of man, of God, of the world, or of the good itself. In every case the evidence would be factual.

*Justification of Moral Principle*

We are now in a position to describe what we are expected to do when called upon to justify a moral principle. The problem of justification has two parts. One is to establish that the goal of the moral principle is at least a good, and is such that it is the good (or highest good) needed to be sought in the moral situation in question.

Now how can one proceed to justify a moral principle? A number of steps suggested by the discussion in this chapter can be taken. In the first place, one could try to show that the good in question is intrinsically such. This would, no doubt, be very difficult. The very fact that people disagree that happiness, etc., are intrinsically and ultimately good evidences the great difficulty of proving happiness ultimately good. Everything ever offered as an ultimate good has been rejected as such by worthy people, even though there is wide-spread agreement on what is or is not good.

Secondly, an effort could be made to show that the very nature of man, God, or the universe implies this good as a necessary characteristic of its structure, i.e., that the moral principle is a theorem from something else more fundamental. Such an endeavor would quite obviously necessitate a description of human psychology, or biology, or of the world, or of God. This would involve encyclopedic knowledge and may be beyond our ability. If anthropology did indicate one or another of the goods to be necessary conditions for human existence, or if theology did demonstrate clearly that God's nature implies the good, or if it could be shown that the universe cannot be conceived without moral principles, then we would, to all intents and purposes, have a justification of the moral principle in question. If, for example, it is claimed that happiness is the highest good, then that statement would be justified if it could be shown either (a) that the nature of man is such that nothing is as good as happiness, or (b) the cosmos is such that this is so, or (c) God is such that this is so, or (d) God commands us to seek happiness above all else. The first of these alternatives could be supported by showing, for example, that everyone does seek happiness while there is nothing else that everyone seeks. This would not prove the point since everyone may seek happiness because all people are sinners and seek something less than the highest good. But it would be a kind of empirical evidence in favor of happiness. None of these procedures outlined above deductively or inductively would however "prove" a highest good to be such. They merely aid in recognizing it to be what is claimed.

The second part of the justification of a particular moral principle, namely, to show the context relevant to the moral principle, is more an attempt to show that it is proper to use that moral principle in the given context. There is reason to believe that what moral principle one invokes is a function of the situation in which the moral problem occurs. To try to apply one and only one moral principle in all cases often leads to grossly immoral behavior. There are occasions when, to take an analogy, even justice must be tempered with mercy. Strict adherence to the dictates of justice can lead to the most terrible decisions. To seek happiness above all else in every kind of situation has led men to commit untold as well as well-described crimes. These crimes were often the consequences of a rigid, unswerving attempt to force every situation into a single pattern. A person with an "idee-fixe" is almost worse off than a blind man. To justify a moral principle, at least in the context of making decisions, involves that one be prepared to show that the conditions of the problem demand this rather than another moral principle.

It is unfortunate, but again there are no fixed rules for justification. One must know the problem, examine its aspects, consider the consequences of using one or another moral principle, compare the case with others of similar nature and then decide in the light of one's best knowledge and judgment.

*Summary*

In this chapter, we tried to discover how to justify a moral principle. First we described ways of justification of statements in general and considered: a) theorems, b) axioms, c) empirical statements, d) "should statements," and e) moral statements. In each case it was concluded the justification ultimately rested on an appeal to something factual. Moral principles are justified, therefore, by showing a) that the end it describes as ultimate is actually so and b) that the world is such that the end is to be sought. However, we noted, no ultimate end has been universally accepted as such, and there is no universal agreement about the nature of the world, man, or God. The justification of moral principles, therefore, cannot be demonstrated in any simple fashion.

### BIBLIOGRAPHY

Edel, A., *Ethical Judgment,* Glencoe, Ill: Free Press, 1955.
Edwards, Paul, *Logic of Moral Discourse,* Glenoe, Ill: Free Press, 1955, Chapter VI, pp. 123-127.
Feigl, Herbert, "Validation and Vindication", in W. Sellars and John Hospers, eds. *Readings in Ethical Theory,* New York: Appleton, Century-Crofts, 1952, pp. 667-681.

Hare, R. M., *Language of Morals,* Oxford: Clarendon Press, 1952, Chapter IV, pp. 56-78.

Laird, John, *Study in Moral Theory,* London: Allen & Unwin, 1926, Chapter II, pp. 12-40.

Prior, A. N., *Logic and the Basis of Ethics,* Oxford: Clarendon Press, 1949.

Stace, W. T., *The Concept of Morals,* New York: Macmillan Co., 1937.

Toulmin, Stephen, *Reason in Ethics,* Cambridge: University Press, 1950.

Weiss, P., "The Nature and Forms of Natural Law," *Journal of Philosophy,* LIII, No. 23 (November 8, 1956), 713-721.

# CHAPTER XVII

# NATURE OF MORAL STATEMENTS

## Types of Statements

This chapter will explain briefly the various types of statements and then indicate how moral statements can be plausibly interpreted as one or another type of statement. It should be quite evident that the deliberations we are about to undertake are very important. The intelligent person most assuredly is curious about his moral utterances. He not only wants to know how to make moral decisions, but he desires to understand the significance of the statements he uses in arriving at these decisions. Those who happen to be content simply with the ability to use moral principles to make moral judgments perhaps will find this chapter less interesting. Nevertheless, the analysis will unquestionably have its relevance to moral situations. Knowing the nature of a moral statement is important, not so much in the making of a moral decision in a direct fashion as in comprehending what is happening when two people utter incompatible moral statments, especially when these express moral principles or moral judgments. For the necessary steps in solving disagreements are indicated more clearly if we know whether a moral statement is a statement of fact, an emotive expression, or something else.

Our understanding will be helped if we try to list and analyze some of the types of statements found in ordinary communication. Suppose Richard Roe says, "There was a terrible wreck down the street." To which John says, "Come, come, you are fooling." If Richard said, "I am not," John would most likely say, "What makes you say so?" Now Richard has asserted that something has happend. A statement asserting what has happened is called a "factual statement" and the reasons that must be given in support of Richard's statement should also be factual statements. Richard might refer to the sound of screeching brakes followed by a crash that he had heard. But he could not offer his feeling of depression as a sound reason for the truth of his assertion. On the other hand, suppose he had said, "I like black olives," and John had replied, "I don't believe you." Richard could not have replied, "Indeed I do. Black olives are black and weigh an ounce or less." The physical properties of the olives would not in ordinary circumstances be taken as reasons for liking olives. The physical properties of olives are expressed in factual statements.

Of course, the expression "I like olives" may be a simple statement of fact. In that case we would use a period at the end of the statement, and Richard's avowal would be sufficient evidence in most cases that he does indeed like olives. But when we put an exclamation point, "I like olives!," this denotes that Richard is giving vent to an expression of his emotion. The statement, "I like olives!" with an exclamation mark, is called an "emotive statement."

If one says: "One ought to be honest," the reply to a demand for reasons must be factual statements, if this is a factual statement. Usually, however, "One ought to be honest" is considered a value statement. It is, however, also possible to say: "One ought to be honest!" and intend merely to express one's feelings about honesty. This, too, would be an emotive statement. Finally, "One ought to be honest" may merely be another way of saying: "Be honest!" which is an hortatory statement.

How shall we interpret moral principles; as factual, emotive, or some other kind of statement?

### Definitions, Value Judgments, and Facts

This type of problem may surprise someone who meets it for the first time. Doesn't everyone know what he is saying and what constitutes a reason in support of it? As a matter of fact, many people do not. Sometimes someone makes a statement which he takes to be a matter of fact, yet is really the expression of an emotion or of a bias. For example, the Marxist asserts that every capitalist nation is "war-mongering," and since the United States is capitalist, he will argue, it too must be anxious to incite wars. Now, no evidence of any sort will convince the Marxist that the United States desires peace. If he had asserted a factual statement about the United States, then presumably facts of one kind or another could refute the statement or support it. But no matter what evidence is proposed, the Marxist can always so interpret it as to support his statement or else explain it away. In the same way, anyone who hates John Doe very intensely will never accept any evidence that tends to go counter to his opinion that John Doe is a detestable creature, for his emotions simply refuse to allow him to accept evidence that disagrees with his emotion. He believes he is making a factual statement when he is simply camouflaging his emotion of hatred in factual terms. We cannot always infer from the syntax of the sentence what it intends to say. In some situations, no one is fooled by the mask. When a departing guest says to his hostess, "I had a most wonderful evening," no one takes the guest to be necessarily stating a fact. He may have had a most boring time; but this is a conventional utterance that expresses nothing more at times than a polite "Thank you and good night."

## Factual Statements

The factual statement is the most familiar of all types. For the present discussion the two terms "empirical" and "factual" are used interchangeably. An empirical statement is one like; "The sun is shining," "The paper is white," "Bill can add figures faster than Jim," "The stick in the water is really straight," "The earliest Gospel was written forty years after the death of Jesus," "John approves of honesty," or finally, "John thinks one ought to be moral."

All these examples of factual statements have two interrelated characteristics. They all assert that something is or is not the case and, hence, they are all either true or false even if at the moment we do not know which. Secondly, facts make a difference where there is a disagreement about the truth or falsity of the statement in question. So if someone denied that John approved of honesty, he would cite some situations in which John acted in such a way that it appeared he didn't approve of honesty. If it was claimed that Bill could not add more rapidly than Jim, the matter could be tested by timing their speed of addition.

It will help us in our later discussion to note that the statements, "John is a criminal" and "John is a perjurer" are also empirical statements since facts do make a difference if their truth or falsity is at issue. To show that John is a perjurer would involve presenting evidence of cases where John swore to tell the truth and deliberately lied. This could be be very difficult to do. However, only facts could presumably establish the truth or falsity of the statement.

Factual statements, then, are statements which can be meaningfully said to be true (or false) and, conversely, any statement which can be said to be true or false is factual. To determine whether or not a statement is factual, we need to inquire whether it is the sort of statement of which it can be said that it is true or false. To show that it cannot be true or false would be to show the statement not a factual one.

*Definitional Statements*

There are statements that have the appearance of being factual but are really not. Consider the following one. "Democracies are forms of government where every citizen has a vote." The interesting thing is that this statement looks like one that could be said to be true or false. Yet if one asks what sort of evidence would show it to be true, he is brought up sharply. If this were an empirical statement, one would point to existing democracies and show that their citizens all have votes. But the contrary is done. If some existing form of government, say that of the United States, is formed which does give every citizen a vote, that government would be called a democracy and if it did not do so it would be said not to be a democracy. In fact, however, if, as in the United States, certain persons are excluded from suffrage in some places, we refuse to deny that the United States is a democracy. We prefer to call the United States an "imperfect democracy." Since actual facts seem to make only little difference, the statement in question is not truly factual; rather it appears to have the nature of a definition. We define something and then use the definition as a criterion. So we define "democracy" and use it as a criterion or as a classificatory term.

If someone denies that democracies do allow everyone to vote, he is proposing the following alternatives. He is rejecting the definition and tacitly replacing the given definition by another. Or else he is saying that on the generally accepted enumeration of democracies he doesn't find the given criterion satisfied. To each of these objections the person who defines "democracy" as indicated would, in all likelihood, reply. "Yes, but this is what I mean by a democracy. Your examples make no difference; existing so called democracies are simply not democracies." In brief, the sentence is a definition of what is meant by "democracy" and cannot, therefore, be said to be true or false. One may not accept the definition, but if he does it will be because of something other than facts, such as, for example, his desire to apply the term "democracy" to some nations and to refuse to apply it to some other nations.

*Persuasive Statements*

There is a third type of statement that also has the appearance of being factual. Suppose a war breaks out. There will be a call to enlist, to aid the war effort in every way possible. Everywhere people will begin to read and hear statements such as: "Americans always do their duty. Join the military forces!"

The statement, "Americans always do their duty," is quite evidently false. Americans do not always do their duty. The existence of traitors, of criminals, and of turncoats shows that. The patriotic American, however, stirred by the call to arms would never be convinced that the statement is false. He would, for example, insist that anyone who did not do his duty under such circumstances could not possibly be an American. Yet "doing his duty" is not part of the definition of "being an American." Even the most rabid patriot would agree that Communists may also do their duty. The second statement, "Join the military forces!" indicates the true nature of the first. Sentences like the first are usually either explicitly or implicitly followed by requests or commands to do something. Even if the first sentence happens to be literally true (or false) yet that fact will be irrelevant to the total situation. Most advertising is of this nature. The function of the statements is persuasion. They seek to win the hearer to some action or to get him to commit himself to do or believe something.

*Expressive Statements*

There is a fourth type of sentence that must be noted. This may at some times appear factual and at other times not. We refer to sentences that express the emotional responses of persons who use such expressions. Such expressions are most familiar to us in the form of exclamations such as: "Lovely!," or "Oh!" (expressed in tones of horror or ecstasy, or disgust, etc.), or "Pooh!," or "Hurrah!," or "Hiss-ss." Sometimes these expressions take the form of statements which may be true or false, yet have as their chief function the expression of an emotion. Consider this situation. The country is at war and its arms are successful everywhere. John Doe finds himself among neutrals and the discussion centers around the great victories of his country's forces. He feels himself quite proud and says, "I am an American." Now, everyone knows he is. As a bit of information, the comment was entirely superfluous. But no one points that out for the utterance is recognized for what it is, not a statement of fact but an expression of John Doe's emotion. Indeed, any request for a birth certificate to prove that Joe Doe was an American would be considered absurd.

Sometimes the situation is much more subtle than this. For example, when D. D. Eisenhower first ran for the presidencey, there was a direct attempt made to arouse favorable emotional attitudes towards him. His political proponents pointed to his smile, to his personality, to his achievements as a military leader and even to his wife, whom people began to call "Mamie." Anyone who questioned Mr. Eisenhower's qualifications for the office, quickly discovered that the ardent Eisenhower supporter rejected any criticisms whatsoever. In the last analysis many statements in support of Eisenhower's election were simply equivalent to the slogan, "I like Ike", an expression of emotion.

Quite often the emotive intent of what looks like a factual statement is revealed by the use of "colored" terms. For example, in the following sets of statements:

(a )    She is an elderly spinster.
(a')    She is an old maid.
(b )    He is a citizen of the Soviet Union.
(b')    He is a Red.

"Red" is a biassed term carrying connotations which "citizen of the Soviet Union" does not. So also "old maid" tends to be a derogatory synonym for "elderly spinster." Both a' and b' not only convey some factual information, but in most usages also express an emotional attitude.

### Commands and Rules

The last two types of statements we shall discuss are somewhat different in nature. They express commands or rules of behavior. Commands usually have the form of imperative sentences, for example, as "Close the door!," or "Don't smoke here!," and so on. The sign: "Please don't smoke here," is intended both as a command and as a rule of behavior. It means "Don't smoke here" and it also signifies that people do not smoke here. Rules of behavior that are not commands except quite indirectly are: "The fork is used with the left hand," or "When making an introduction always present a younger person to an older," or "Letters are begun with the expression 'Dear —,' or "In court, one always rises when the judge enters." Now all of these could have been expressed as "should" statements. So, for example, "One should use the fork with the left hand," or "One should start a letter..." and so on. This would disguise the rule of behavior in the form of an obligation sentence, whereas as first stated it sounds like a factual statement. Actually it is neither since no question of fact nor any obligation is involved. If one is told that the fork is held in the left hand, one might ask, "Is this the custom?' but not "Is it true?" Nor, in general, would the statement be taken as a command, but rather as a rule of behavior. What is stated is the way in which people behave if they follow the rules. Commands are often camouflaged in other ways. So the employer may say to his employee, "You won't make the same mistake again, will you?," and what he intends to say is, "Don't make the same mistake again!"

### Moral Principles as Factual Statements

Discussions of this sort have an intrinsic interest. There is today a keen awareness of semantical problems. But the classification of types of statements has a direct relevance to any discussion of the nature of moral statements. Each type of statement has, especially in recent years, been defended as the implicit prototype of the moral statement. Consequently, a consideration of the various proposals can throw light on the nature of moral decisions.

Quite possibly the average ordinary person who says, "John is a moral person," or "One ought to do one's duty," or "The act was right," or "Happiness is good," believes he is saying something factual whether it be about John, duty, acts, or happiness. Such sentences are taken to be statements of fact and, hence, are conceived to be true or false. To say, "John is moral" or "Happiness is good" is to utter something for which evidence presumably can be presented and this evidence should consist of facts. To be sure, predicates like "good", "moral," "right," etc. are not the same sort of predicates as are "yellow," "hard," "tall," and so on. But they do resemble these latter terms in so far as they are predicates. Since, however, they are predicates of another sort, the kind of facts which need no be offered to support them may need to be different from those offered as evidence for such statements as "John is five feet tall," or "John's eyes are blue."

Those who believe that moral statements really are statements of fact in which moral predicates are affirmed of some subject and that these moral predicates denote moral attributes that can be "observed" are usually called "objectivists." To them moral qualities are objective and, so to speak, are either in the object or in a realm of their own.

### Pseudo-factual Statements – Definitions

Since we have already seen that what looks like a factual sttaement grammatically need not be so in meaning, it will come as no surprise that moral statement have been claimed to be only *apparently* factual. How can such a claim be made plausible? Perhaps an analogy from mathematics may be of help. Let us examine the following sentence: "In Euclidean geometry, a straight line is the shortest distance between two points." If someone asks: "Is it not false that a straight line is the shortest distance between two points?" what sort of evidence could be possibly proposed that would show a straight line not to be the shortest distance between two points? Any line that was not the shortest distance between two points would not be accepted as a straight line! This is to say that nothing would be called a straight line unless it was the shortest distance between two points, and, as a result, no evidence could conceivably turn up to indicate that the straight line was not the shortest distance between two points. In brief, the statement that a straight line was not the shortest distance between two points could not be proved precisely because being the shortest distance between two points was what defined a line as a straight line. What is proposed as a statement of fact turns out to be a definition. The statement should read: "Straight line" means "the shortest distance between two points." As a consequence, if anything is a straight line, it is the shortest distance between two points, and if it is the shortest distance between two points it is a straight line. Moreover, if it is not a straight line it is not the shortest distance and if it is not the shortest distence it is not a straight line. A definition of this sort is never true or false; it is either accepted or rejected, useful or useless.

Let us apply these ideas to the statement: "Self-realization is good," or "Happiness is good." What could possibly convince anyone who held one or the other of these to be false? Is not the statement "Happiness is good," simply a definition? Or, at least, is not "good" a part of the definition of happiness? "Happiness" means "good," or includes "good" by definition. If "happiness" means "good" or includes "good," then there could be no evidence that would convince the person who accepts the definition that they are not the same. He would respond to an example purporting to show that there is an instance where happiness is not good, with the remark, "But this is not really happiness, because if it were you would see it was good or included good."

*Moral Statements as Persuasive*

Another type of non-factual interpretation of moral statements is suggested by the way moral statements are used. Whenever two people are engaged in moral deliberations, the chances are that there is a course of action at stake. The analysis of the moral situation indicated clearly that there was one factor essential to all such situations – action. Someone wanted to decide what to do or what should have been done. The moral principle was, indeed, a guide to a decision about what to do. All our examples of such situations involved a choice among acts. And not only did the moral principle say what ought to be done but the moral person was defined in terms of what a person did do.

All of this is quite imporant and it is easy to see this element of action as the real core of all moral situations. Starting from this premise, namely that moral situations involve a decision to act, moral statements are taken to be persuasive in nature despite their factual appearances. To say "John Doe is moral" is to persuade or attempt to persuade someone to act toward John Doe in a certain way; for example, to praise him or to give him a job. To say "Killing is wrong" is to utter a statement derogatory to the act of killing, so that people will be induced not to kill. To say "Happiness is good" is to try to persuade people to act in ways that will make for happiness. All moral situations are then said to be ones in which persuasion is taking place.

Words like "good," "evil," "moral," "wrong," etc. have no real meaning on this view. They are simply "trigger" words used to set off response patterns of a certain sort. They are, so to speak, simply stimulus words which, when used in conjunction with other words, set off pro- or con-behavior patterns. This, say the adherents of such an interpretation, explains why some people do not do what these terms are supposed to cause them to do. They are psychologically orientated in a contrary fashion. And when two people disagree on the rightness of an act, they are really only disagreeing on what to do in these conditions. Evidently there is no question at all of truth or falsity. Statements which persuade or attempt to do so, may quite clearly, incidentally, say what is true or false, but often they do not. As one famous cigarette slogan has it, for example, "Smoke X – Live Modern." What, indeed, is true or false about this? The slogan tries to persuade the listener to smoke this brand of cigarettes. So "Be honest – don't cheat on an examination" is the same sort of thing. It simply tries to persuade people not to cheat. The expression "be honest" is then nothing but a sort of soothing sound which is to induce in the listener a favorable attitude. It can perhaps be likened to the whistle of a man for his dog, or the coo-ing sounds made by women to babies.

## Moral Statements are Expressions of Approval

Closely related to the view that moral statments are persuasive is the view that they are nothing but expressions of our own approval or disapproval. As expressions of approval or disapproval, they do not tell us anything about the person, act, or end being judged, but they do reveal something about the one who expresses approval or disapproval. The evidence for this interpretation is based usually on two sets of considerations. In the first place moral statements are said to be incapable of *empirical* refutation or support. The lack of empirical evidence, however, is not due to the presence of a definition. The lack of empirical evidence is the result of the fact that moral predicates are not factual terms at all. What empirical evidence shows that happiness is or is not good? That people enjoy happiness shows that happiness is enjoyed and not that it is good. Likewise, when one says, "To express one's self is to be moral," or "To do one's duty is moral," there is apparently no empirically observable characteristic called "moral." In fact, "moral" is not an adjective in the sense that "tall" or "blue" is and hence cannot be empirically indicated by showing a characteristic that corresponds to it. To urge that doing one's duty leads to a smooth-running society, is not to show anything about the moral character of that principle but simply what its consequences are. Hence, no empirical considerations can affect moral statements and, as a consequence, they cannot be factual.

The second set of considerations amounts to this. If moral statements are not factual, notice when they are used. Consider these two statements:

"Honesty is virtuous."
"I approve of honesty."

Or these two:

"Killing is evil."
"I don't like killing."

Whenever the first of these is said to be true (or is uttered), the second will also be said to be true (or would be uttered if need be). Conversely, whenever "I approve of honesty" can be said to be true, the same circumstances will lead the speaker to say the first is also. The same thing will be the case for the falsity of the one or the other. Hence, the two statements in each set are logically equivalent. But the second expresses approval or disapproval. It would appear that moral statements are always equivalent to expressive ones. When, therefore, one says: "Honesty is a virtue," one is merely saying, "Honesty – hurrah!" or if one says, "One ought to do one's duty," he is really saying, "I approve of doing one's duty."

## Approval and Commands

The attempt to reduce moral statements to emotive expressions is surely a fascinating one but it has, as do all these interpretations, difficulties into which we need not enter. No matter how appealing such a view is, there is one important thing it fails to explain. In an earlier chapter, we saw that moral principles and moral statements in general are easily converted into the form of commands. Moreover, a command, or for that matter a directive, is also not the sort of sentence that is true or false. It seems plausible, therefore, to propose that moral statements are either commands or directives. In general, commands as well as directives are propounded in order to get something done. In this respect they are like the rules of chess, or poker, or any other game. This means that if someone wants to play a particular game, there will be a set of rules that need to be used as guides for action. Whoever does not follow the rules is excluded from the game. Furthermore, a person may challenge a given interpretation of the rules, i.e., question whether according to the rules one or another move is permitted. But given the game, no other set of rules can be viewed as in any sense appropriate to *this* game. If a different game is to be played, then other rules will be followed. So those who want to play the democratic game will obey such rules as: "One ought to be allowed free expression," or "One ought to protect the rights of *all* persons regardness of race, color or creed." If we view forms of government as games, then one cannot say these are better or worse rules than, for example, those of an absolute dictatorship, because if one plays the game, i.e., lives under an absolute dictatorship, then he follows the rules of an absolute dictatorship. To interpret moral statements as rules of behavior accords closely with the fact that moral statements imply commands. If, however, moral statements are viewed as merely emotive expressions, then this feature is reduced to nonsense.

Another form of the reduction of moral statements to commands is the following one. Given a society, then for it to run smoothly there will be a set of rules (morals, mores, laws) which must be obeyed. In another society, another set of rules will prevail. Moral statements are then simply the rules to follow in a given society if that society is to (say) run smoothly, or if you want to live in that society without conflict with others. This, however, is subject to the same criticism that rules are not *moral* commands.

## Interpretation of Moral Statements

Now that the major interpretations of moral statements have been enumerated, what is their nature? This question does, indeed, make a fundamental assumption, namely, that a moral statement has a unique nature. The very variety of possible interpretations seems to belie this and calls for some explanation as to how such a diversity is possible. In a sense the solution is obvious. Different persons take moral statements to be what they want them to be. So for one person a moral statement is an assertion about matters of fact. To say, "One ought to do God's will" or "Killing is evil" is to indicate something factual either about the nature of God's will or of killing. To another, a moral statement is simply a definition or an analytic expression. To still others, it is a rule of action, a persuasive statement, or an expression of approval, or some other emotion.

Yet it is not likely that a person will arbitrarily assert one or another of these interpretations. The significant thing is that whoever selects one or another interpretation defends that selection by pointing to things about moral statements or the situation in which they are used that support his interpretation. When people assert that killing is evil, or that happiness is good, or that John is moral, they often do intend such remarks to be not merely commendatory but expressive of their emotions and attitudes. Surely, it is desirable also that people do have emotional attachments to virtues and dislikes of evil doing. Again, a social relativist can really mean that moral statements are rules for social behavior. He may be wrong, but he is pointing to the fact that no society is possible unless there are moral rules and people do make moral statements whose significance is other than than that of a personal, or purely personal, emotional reaction. Of course, purely arbitrary personal likes or dislikes as well as mere definitions apart from something being defined, provide no basis for moral behavior in the sense of behavior based upon universal, obligatory principles. Nor do they make sense of moral disagreements and arguments. But of this more in the next chapter.

The point is that it is necessary to distinguish two problems: (1) What does the person who utters a moral statement believe he is doing, stating a fact or a definition, or expressing himself emotionally, and so on? (2) Given a moral statement, what does it purport to say regardless of how the one who utters it uses it? This second question assumes that the moral statement is what it is and that people can and do use it correctly or incorrectly. It makes a distinction between the meaning and the use of moral statements. Moral statements may be used to incite action, express emotions, or communicate knowledge. They may mean to express what is the case.

## Values us Facts

In this chapter, we have not intended to solve the problem of the nature of a moral statement so much as to indicate what the problem is and the possible alternative solutions. In a sense, the discussion was much more logic than ethics. Yet, the importance of the interrelation of the logical and the ethical should be obvious. The most significant distinction is that between value-statements and fact-statements, because the problem of evidence depends for its adequate solution on that distinction. But value-statements themselves can be either subjective expressions of preferences or objective assertions about value-facts. In any case, the type of evidence in support of a statement depends upon what type of statement is at issue. Evidence in support of preferences may or may not be acceptable when offered in support of facts. But value predicates are, in any case, different from physical predicates, and, therefore, the method of verifying value-statements can be expected to be different from that used to verify fact-statements.

Another major distinction is between factual and non-factual statements, with value-statements tending to be classified as non-factual. This is the core of the entire discussion of the nature of value statements. Is it a factual statement or one of the types of non-factual statements? We conclude the chapter with the suggestion that the way people tend to defend their moral judgments and decisions, indicates that for the most part they incline to the view that moral statements are a species of factual statement.

Much of what has been said in this chapter will come to have greater clarity when we discuss the nature of moral disagreements.

## BIBLIOGRAPHY

Ayer, A. J., *Language, Truth and Logic,* New York: Oxford University Press, 1936, Chapter VI.

Ewing, A. C., *Ethics,* London: English Universities Press, 1953, Chapter VII, pp. 115-144.

Hare, R. M., *The Language of Morals,* Oxford: Clarendon Press, 1952, Chapter II, pp. 17-32.

Kaplan, A., "Are Moral Judgmens Assertions?" *Philosophical Review,* 1942.

Nowell-Smith, P. H., *Ethics,* Baltimore, Md.,: Penguin Books, 1956, Chapters V and VI, pp. 61-95.

Prichard, H. A., "Does Moral Philosophy Rest on a Mistake?" *Mind,* 21, 1912.

Stevenson, C. L., "The Emotive Meaning of Ethical Terms," *Mind,* 46, 1937.

# CHAPTER XVIII

# MORAL DISAGREEMENTS
# AND THEIR RESOLUTION

*The Difficulty of Resolving Moral Disagreement*

Considering the amount of moral discussion that goes on almost interminably, it might appear that making moral decisions ought not to be too difficult and that moral disagreements should be easily resolvable. Yet it is terribly clear that just the opposite is the case. Making moral decisions remains an extraordinarily difficult task at times and moral controversies rage on without anyone being able to offer a solution. Is it or is it not immoral to segregate Negroes? One would think this a simple question, easily answered. Yet unless one wants to "poison the wells" in the discussion there are honest people on both sides of the issue. Is one who believes war immoral making a moral decision that "holds water" or is he simply deluded? Again, there are people who believe war always immoral and some who do not. These are perhaps large issues, but the same basic disagreement and controversy rages between persons over lesser problems and often in one's own soul.

In a sense, this is the difficulty of making moral decisions, our very lives are "engaged" and almost everything we do or say is implicated. It takes much effort to keep from making a decision in terms of our own selfish interests rather than the demands of morality. Why should it be so very difficult to make a moral decision, and why is it so much more complicated a matter to resolve moral disagreements than, say, disagreements about what physical ailment is troubling a person?

*Sources of Disagreement*

In order to clarify the discussion, two kinds of disagreements other than moral will be explained. The first of these is a disagreement between two stock market speculators about the future behavior of a given stock, and the second a legal disagreement over the guilt or innocence of a person accused of breach of contract.

Consider two speculators whom we will call "A.B." and "C.D."

They are discussing the behavior of "Tin Can Preferred." A.B. feels that the stock will rise, C.D. that it will fall. The disagreement is simple and each one knows precisely what to look for to see whether he is, or rather was, correct. If the price of Tin Can goes up, then C.D. will be compelled to admit he was wrong; on the contrary, if it falls, then A.B. will have been wrong. But even though they both know how to determine who will have been correct, at the present moment they want to know, or guess, what will happen. A.B. supports his contention that the stock will rise because he is aware that the Tin Can company is about to declare a dividend. C.D. replies that, although that is true, a new product has just come on the market which will bring about a reduction in sales of tin cans and the stock will fall. A.B. had been unaware of this before C.D. mentioned it. However, after some thought, C.D. remarks that the new product may have a contrary effect. It may stimulate sales of tin cans since a new product will bring the attention of people to the existence and availability of tin cans. Now we don't need to go any further because the main points are before us.

Both speculators have in common certain principles and facts. They both know what it means to say, "Tin Cans preferred will rise." They both know that the behavior of stocks is affected by certain kinds of conditions. They may disagree, however, on whether the conditions making for a rise (or fall) are present. Each knows what conditions affect the stock market because they are acquainted with the principles of economics as they relate to the stock market. They may know specific facts or they may disagree concerning these facts. And, finally, they may know the same facts but disagree concerning the impact of these facts on the market. If the principles in terms of which they carry on their deliberations were to change, then C.D. and A.B. would never arrive at concerted action. This last point is quite evident in the present state of confusion that exists in the minds of economists over the so-called "creeping inflation." There seems to be some evidence that a change in the economic principles governing inflation is taking, or has taken, place in recent years. As a consequence, although economists have most facts in common, they are at a loss as to what to do. Here there is a basic disagreement concerning the principles involved.

Let us consider another example, the case of a presumed breach of contract. Such a situation is more complex. The law provides that contracts ought not to be broken and also describes the means and modes of obtaining enforcement of the contract or redress for its violation. In a case of breach of contract there is no question but that the principles of contract law are to be applied. There is no disagreement over this. Where the performance of a contract might result in undue hardship, the courts can put it aside, at least temporarily. However, we are not interested simply in the legal problem as such. Disagreements can and do arise concerning the application of the definition to the situation in question. So an attorney may try to show that there was no contract in the first place. In short, he may insist that his client never did enter into a contract and, therefore, could not break one. Such a disagreement would center on the question: "Is this the sort of situation in which the principles of contracts are at all involved?" This disagreement can, theoretically at least, be decided by considering whether the conditions defining a contract were present. These conditions are described in the laws and in previous cases, the precedents. This may not be an easy thing to do, especially since it is possible that the precedents may conflict, but, at least, the mode of procedure is definite.

### Questions of Principle and of Fact

In legal processes there are two major problems, the determination of the law in question, and the determination of the facts. Usually the court decides questions of law after hearing argument, while questions of fact are left to the judgment of the jury. Obviously disagreements can be about legal questions or factual ones. Lawyers can and do disagree about what the law is in a given case; juries disagree about what happened. Having heard the decision of the judge stating what the law is in such matters, the jury decides what the facts are and applies the law to them. In a breach of contract suit, neither the judge, the jury nor the attorneys question the definition of "contract" as such. This is a matter for the legislative bodies. No jurists, for example, can say outright, "The law says a contract involves condition A, but I don't think so. Hence in deciding this case let's forget it." He may, indeed, modify the definition by deriving certain consequences from it, but at least he must save the appearnce of going along with the law.

Finally, it is possible that both sides will agree that a contract was made, but disagree concerning its performance. For example, one person may claim that another had contracted to paint his house but had not done so, while the other may agree that he had contracted to do the work but within six months and that time had not yet elapsed. Usually such a disagreement could be resolved by an examination of the facts. If the contract was written, then the date of performance was in all likelihood, as well as the date of the agreement, in it. If not, then, perhaps, there were witnesses who heard the conditions, or other factors could be introduced to show that the contractor could not have agreed to perform in less than six months.

## Moral Disagreements

We are, I believe, ready to move on to a consideration of moral disagreements. First, we shall consider the case where two people disagree about what is or is not moral to do even though they both accept the same moral principles. Such a situation can be illustrated in the following fashion. Let us modify the conditions describing the problem of returning the gun to its owner who meanwhile has developed homicidal tendencies. We shall assume that John and Richard disagree about returning the gun, John believing it should and Richard it should not be returned, but that both accept the formalistic principle – "One ought to do one's duty."

John believes that the gun must be returned because it is one's duty to keep his promise, while Richard insists that it cannot be one's duty to provide a potential killer with a deadly weapon. To this, John replies that what the owner does with his property is no concern of his. His duty is clear and in pursuance of that duty he cannot consider the consequences of his act. Richard agrees that one ought to do his duty regardless of consequences but, he continues, it cannot possibly be one's duty to return the gun under these conditions. Richard feels that if duty compelled one to act in such fashion under conditions of this sort, there would be chaos and this is a clear indication that it cannot be John's duty to return the gun.

In this example, the disagreement concerns the application of an accepted principle. Does this situation reveal itself as one in which the principle of duty applies?

The source of disagreement may be elsewhere. Consider the case of cheating on an examination. Someone might argue in the following fashion. "If you cheat, you will pass the examination and increase everyone's happiness even if your conscience does trouble you." Another might reply that the morality of cheating cannot be decided on the basis of the resultant happiness or unhappiness. These have nothing to do with morality. The real question is either what principle is to be used or what is the moral principle? One may agree that hedonism is a moral principle, yet disagree that this is the principle to use. Or one may refuse to accept hedonism as a moral principle at all and pronounce it irrelevant to moral decisions. If one insists that the hedonist principle cannot be considered a moral principle at all, but that some other principle, e.g., the theological principle, is the true moral principle, the disagreement is much more ultimate. The principle as such is rejected and another proposed. The first kind of disagreement may be called a *legalistic* one; the second is more truly *moralistic*.

### Sources of Moralistic Disagreement – Facts

Quite clearly, the nature of a moralistic disagreement is a function of the nature of the moral principle. If moral principles are taken to be descriptive – as factual, then the disagreement may be factual in a mumber of ways. A survival principle, for example, may be rejected on the grounds that in point of fact self-preservation is not obligatory. Or it may be denied that it is a fact that one ought to do God's will, or help preserve society, or express one's self. The egoist may reject all altruistic action by insisting the facts are that one ought to be selfish.

The disagreement remains factual, however, if it concerns the presumed factual nature of the principle itself. One may reject the claim that a moral principle is factual by insisting that moral principles are simply instinctive reactions or something of that sort.

On the other hand, if moral principles are emotive in nature, then moralistic disagreements are simply antagonistic emotional responses. There is then no cognitive disagreement at all.

Another type of factual disagreement is illustrated in the following fashion: suppose someone said, "Look here! This simply isn't the sort of world in which you ought to do your duty," or to the universal hedonist; "People are simply not made in such a way that they ought to seek the happiness of others." Such disagreements have their root in quite different views about the structure of reality or of man. To some degree this is the sort of disagreement that exists between (say) a Marxist and a Christian. The former believes he needs to remake the economic structure of the world in order to create a world of universal brotherhood, while the latter sees universal brotherhood as part of the moral structure of the universe as created by God and men as failing to act accordingly. Such disagreements are also factual, but they concern the foundations of the moral principle.

### Disagreements over Authority of Principle

The disputants may be agreed that moral principles do, indeed, express something about the nature of reality, be it about the spiritual order, the human order, or the social order, but do not agree that the principle under debate has authority and is, therefore, binding. This is illustrated by what happened when Hitler came into power in Germany and wrote an Aryan code of "laws." There was much debate by jurists outside of Germany over the question whether these really were laws to which Germans were bound, or whether they did not so depart from the nature of a law as no longer to be properly so-called. For those who agreed that law has a "nature" the problem was to determine whether Aryan laws possessed the defining characteristic of law. For those who defined law simply as a rule of behavior established by an authorized group of citizens with sanctions for its enforcement, then "Aryan laws" are laws.

## Pseudo-Disagreement

As we have already suggested, if moral principles are simply expressions of one's approval or one's emotions, then there is no real disagreement. A disagreement involves at least two people who are at odds over what is the case. If John says, "One ought to seek happiness" and merely means "I like to be happy," while Richard denies that one ought to seek happiness, and means that he likes something else better, there can be no real dispute. John likes what he likes and Richard what he likes, and they can like completely different things or even each like what the other dislikes, and there can be no disagreement in the sense we are using the term here. There may be a real disagreement, however, if it concerns the correctness of liking something or, in general, the correctness of an attitude. In this case the type of disagreement is real and either one of fact or of principle. But when people simply differ in their likes, they do not disagree objectively. And even where specific acts are concerned, people may appear to disagree but actually don't. If John says, "Killing is evil," or "To cheat in this examination is wrong," and means that he doesn't like killing or cheating, then he need not be in disagreement with Richard who may like to cheat or even kill on occasion.

It is only when John tries to convince Richard he ought not to like killing because of the evil consequences it brings about that they begin to disagree, for Richard may urge that the beneficial consequences outweigh the evil ones. In such an argument, there is no longer merely a difference of what is liked but an interpretation of moral predicates in terms of consequences. Both now agree that certain consequences may be preferable and the real issue in moral judgments is this preference. This being so, the real disagreement is not a moral one but, we might say, a scientific one, because what they disagree about are the results of the act.

### Disagreements Over Who is or Who is Not Moral

The final type of disagreement we shall discuss occurs when someone is to be called "moral." For example, suppose two persons, A and B, are discussing the character of Henry Ford. A believes that Henry Ford had been a most moral person, while B denies this and maintains that Henry Ford was, if not actually immoral, then at least not a moral person. Now A may conceivably try to convince B that Henry Ford was moral by citing Mr. Ford's good works. It is possible that if A cited a sufficient number of good works, B might change his opinion. On the other hand, B might counter by recalling evil deeds that Mr. Ford may have committed (assuming there were such) or he might argue that Mr. Ford obtained his money fraudulently or by vicious methods, and, therefore, could not be considered moral at all. If B could prove a sufficient number of evil deeds or presented convincing evidence of Mr. Ford's methods, he might get A to change his mind. But both of these possibilities assume that A and B have agreed, at least tacitly, to call Mr. Ford "moral," or to denounce him as "immoral" on the grounds of what he did in the past or how he obtained the means to do "good works."

### Disagreements over Evaluation of Facts

Let us assume, however, that A and B both are thoroughly familiar with Mr. Ford's life story. They both know all his deeds and misdeeds, yet they still disagree about Mr. Ford's moral character. This sort of situation occurs quite frequently when historical figures are under criticism and even more frequently in literature. What kinds of disagreements are now involved? For one thing, A and B may place different weights on different deeds. A, for example, may consider the donation of sufficient funds to build a hospital and equip it properly of greater significance in judging Mr. Ford's character than the way Mr. Ford acquired his wealth. B, contrariwise, may feel that the construction of a hospital by Mr. Ford, was only giving back to people the money that rightly belonged to them anyway and, therefore, not an important factor in judging Mr. Ford. But an evaluation of Mr. Ford in such terms judges Mr. Ford on the basis of the consequences of his actions, or the type of thing he did.

There is still another angle to this. B may be quite willing to concede that giving money to construct and equip a hospital is praiseworthy. It is the sort of thing a moral person with money would do. Still, B may point out, the political "big-wig" can do the same thing to get himself nominated to the Senate. Even immoral persons can do praiseworthy deeds. If urged to explain himself, B might insist that it isn't what he does that makes a man moral, it's why he does it that counts. This returns the discussion once again to the role of motives.

### Disagreement over Relation of Motives to Morals

A and B may now be disagreeing either about (1) whether motive plays a part in being moral, or (2) what Mr. Ford's motive was. They are accordingly either in disagreement on what is the definition of "moral" or on the nature of Mr. Ford's motive for doing what he did. If they are at odds over the definition of "moral," they may be arguing a purely linguistic question because they may be trying to decide whether either in the dictionary or in common usage the word "moral" is so defined as to include "motive." If this is what they are arguing, then there is no real moral disagreement in the usual sense of the term, and the issue can easily be resolved by an appeal to a dictionary or to common usage. However, the argument may be about what it is to be moral and this is, as we have seen, an almost irresolvable one.

But when two people disagree on the role of motives in the evaluation of someone as moral, they are at odds over an issue that cannot be settled by appealing to a dictionary. They want to know whether to be moral does or does not involve proper motives in its very nature and whether or not Mr. Ford had these proper kinds of motives in acting as he did.

The disagreement is again purely factual. Whether or not Mr. Ford has the motive attributed to him by B is not in itself a moral problem. Nevertheless, the answer to the scientific question: "Did Henry Ford have a given motive?" will help decide the moral question: "Is Henry Ford moral?"

### Techniques to Resolve Moral Disagreements

Perhaps we have distinguished a sufficient number of kinds of disagreements that arise in moral issues. What techniques can be used to resolve them? Loosely speaking, this question seems quite unambiguous. But it isn't. What are we trying to do when we seek to resolve moral disagreements? We may be seeking agreement or we may be trying to decide what is the truth of the matter. The former is not necessarily equivalent to the latter. A person may agree that Henry Ford is moral, in the sense that Mr. Ford acts as if he really was, because, for example, he may feel that no good can come of disputing the matter. Yet at the same time the person may know, in his heart, that Ford is immoral. People do at times feign agreement even when inwardly they still demur. For example, after a heated contest to decide which candidate will be the best in the sense of most likely to win, a particular person is "unanimously nominated." Surely his opponents still may not believe he is actually the best man, yet they agree with the majority for the sake of "party unity" in the coming elections. In this fashion, too, many people come to accept quite immoral behavior in the interests of social harmony or their own social advancement. It should be evident that to resolve disagreements of this sort one needs to use threats, cajoling, bribes, force, flattery, appeals to sentiments, (such as self-interest, patriotism, pity, love, etc.) punishment, and other such things. When these methods are effective, they do resolve moral disagreements because there is no divergence of opinion apparent. Any community in which someone wants to protest against some accepted mode of behavior offers plenty of evidence of the effectiveness of such methods.

## Use of Force

One can argue reasonably that there is no real agreement where force is used despite the absence of overt objection. Perhaps not. But if such a contention is advanced, it is because "resolving moral disagreements" is taken to mean that one or the other advocate is brought to recognize the situation for what it is. This, of course, assumes that moral statements say what is or is not the case. If moral statements were not factual there would be nothing wrong in using the techniques which have been described. For example, if A says, "Killing is evil" and B says "Killing is good" and all they have done is express their approval and disapproval, then they can reach agreement if either A learns to approve of killing or B to disapprove. Now, if A can get B to disapprove by threatening to kill him if he continued to approve, then the approbative disagreement will have been resolved. It is interesting that in general there is emotional disapproval of the use of such methods of getting agreement on moral issues. If moral statements are expressions of approval or disapproval, the existence of this emotional rejection of such methods signifies that we consider these methods immoral. In general, we feel that rational persuasion is much more appropriate. An opponent is to be shown by reason and rationally convinced that he is in error by bringing him to an awareness of this error.

## Rational Solution of Moral Disagreement

Two assumptions are made when we try to resolve moral disagreements by the use of reason. One is that if the disputants could eliminate their biasses, they would be more apt to see the "truth" of the situation. The second is that if all the facts were known, the resolution would come easily. These two assumptions define two conditions for the rational solution of moral disagreements – (1) Be unbiassed, and (2) Be as informed as possible. Since a disputant is most often biassed, it is usually taken for granted that he cannot resolve the disagreement without the aid of someone not involved in the conflict. Of course, if the person not involved in the conflict is also indifferent to the issues being debated, he may be of little help. It may very well be that one is engaged in a dispute precisely because he knows the correct evaluation. Since "to be biassed" means to give more weight than is due to certain factors which favor oneself, concern need not be accompanied by bias. Surely a judge who is indifferent to the outcome of a suit would not be a good judge. He would be unbiassed, but only because he gave no weight to anything. His concern must be with the "correct" solution of the legal dispute; that is, with seeing that the dispute is settled in accordance with the law and legal principles.

## Appeal to an Ideal Observer

The two conditions for rational solutions of moral disagreements suggest that moral disputes can be settled by some ideal observer, or by God. An ideal observer or God could be unbiassed and well-informed. An ideal observer could be some bystander who is acquainted with the facts of the controversy, is not personally involved in the dispute, and is concerned with the issues. His decision would presumably be "rational." God being omniscient and ordinarily conceived as being on the side of morality would perhaps be the best of all judges. In legal disputes the thesis of a third person leads quite easily to the jury system.

The difficulty with this sort of resolution of moral disagreements is evident in the following example. Let us imagine that a doctor is trying to decide whether he ought to lie to a sick patient about the imminence of death. This is a moral decision he needs to make and the disagreement exists in his own mind. So he calls together a group of citizens consisting of a theologian, a lawyer, and a lay person and asks them to decide the issue. Not merely are factual problems involved such as whether or not they know all the facts, and whether or not they are unbiassed, but a much more serious question arises. Assume they agree on a course and so advise the physician who decides to follow their advice. The point is that the physician is no longer making a moral decision since it is no longer *his* choice. He merely submits. Nor can it be argued that he had chosen to follow their advice rather than not to do so. His decision to follow their advice may be one of convenience, in which case he is certainly not making a moral decision. It may be that he raises the question, "Is it right for me morally to follow their advice?" in which case he is confronted with another moral debate which, indeed, he may solve for himself, or he may decide to ask other bystanders. The upshot of these remarks seems to be that someone who appeals to a bystander or ideal observer may, perhaps, do the moral thing but his act is not a moral act. What he does may, indeed, be right, yet not because he is moral. The disagreement would be resolved but at the cost of one's character as a moral agent. Nor is this difficulty avoided by defining a resolution of a moral dispute as one which involves submission of the disagreement to an ideal observer, since the same outcome results. The disagreement is removed, but the disputants have surrendered their prerogatives as moral agents. However, for the purposes of social harmony this may be the lesser of two evils.

If God is the "bystander," such an undesirable consequence need not result. Anyone who takes God as the "judge" in a moral dispute would do so because for him God is the norm for moral behavior, and to ask "What is God's will?" and then to act accordingly, is to do so in the light of a moral principle. It is not that the agent simply does what God wills; rather he chooses that act which God wills, even though it is possible for him to choose another. God is not conceived as choosing for the agent, but, rather, as indicating what he ought to choose.

The problem is altered if instead of trying to decide what ought to be done, one wanted to judge whether (say) John Doe is moral. In this case the decision is not in itself a moral one but concerns another's morality. The question becomes "Would a bystander, (or the ideal observer, or God) judge John Doe to be moral?" If the ideal observer or God possessed the qualities necessary for being an ideal observer, he could answer the question more adequately than the one who raises it. But the possibility of alternate criteria, or even definitions, of what it is to be moral may influence the judgment of the ideal observer. Presumably, God knows what it is to be "moral" and would, therefore, not be affected by this possibility. The bystander, ideal observer, or God could be adequate for the resolution of such a disagreement.

*Casuistry as a Method*

There exists another method of resolving moral disagreements that has close affinity with both inductive logic and the legal method of case-study (precedents). Both moral discussions and legal ones are carried on by reference to cases (the lawyer calls them precedents). This method of solving moral debates is called "casuistry," and proceeds by means of analogy. In order to decide whether or not to lie, situations similar to the one under consideration are recalled or constructed and an attempt is made to see whether or not it was moral to lie in these other cases. If it was and if the present case is like the others, then, it is argued, what was done in the previous case should be done in this one. The following example of someone opposed to the use of violence and arguing in defense of his belief can be taken as an illustration. His opponent is likely to use an argument that goes: "Suppose a murderer was trying to kill your wife; would you use force to prevent it if it was the only way of saving her?" Presumably this argument implies that if you would use violence under such conditions, you cannot refuse to use it in other cases. Actually, this is a bad inference since the question is not what the non-violence advocate would do in crisis situations but what he thinks it is right or moral to do. But even though the search for cases often involves this sort of invalid inference, yet it can be used to show inconsistency with principles and hence to indicate what ought to be done.

Such a technique for resolving moral disagreements may demonstrate the inconsistency of a proposed decision with either other instances or the avowed moral principle. If two people disagree, or if someone is puzzled about the morality of an act, then they or he may come to a decision after an examination of a variety of situations (cases). Such a procedure may involve all the risks usually run by empirical investigations such as the selection of special cases, or an insufficient number of different instances, and so on. At bottom, I believe this method is valid only if one agrees that the case is somehow in itself illustrative.

*Resolution of Moral Disagreements*

We can now bring this discussion to a close and we will try to formulate some principles of procedure for the solution of moral disagreements. Notice first that much of the discussion has been in terms of bringing about agreement and not of finding the truth of the matter. Presumably if the truth could be demonstrated, there would be agreement, but there could be agreement even if what is agreed upon is completely false. A people, or at least great numbers of them, could agree it was quite moral to exterminate Jews or to segregate Negroes, even though precisely the opposite may be true. Truth, however, either of fact or of value does not guarantee agreement. For example, there are people who insist that Negroes should be segregated because of biological inferiority, and when they are told there is practically no scientific evidence of natural inferiority will reply that that made no difference. The following suggestions aim to bring about agreement rather than to arrive at the correct solution of the moral disagreement. Quite loosely speaking, however, and for the most part, where there is agreement there is more apt to be truth, even though the exceptions to this are disturbingly numerous.

In order to make the comments concrete we will use the example of euthanasia. Can two people who disagree on the morality of putting to death someone suffering from an incurable disease, resolve their disagreement? Clearly from the discussion, they first need to decide what the disagreement is all about. They need to ask whether they accept some common moral principle but disagree upon its application to the particular problem. If this is the root of their disagreement, then agreement could come either by more adequate consideration of the case at issue, or by accepting some other person as an authority. Where the disagreement is the result of the diversity of opinion about how the principle is to be applied, and the disputants cannot agree either by further consideration of the case or upon an acceptable authority, there is a strong suspicion that the disagreement is chiefly emotional.

The agreement on the moral principle to be used may be there, but the disagreement may concern whether or not the present application of euthanasia will lead to the desired consequences (say, the greatest degree of happiness). This is an empirical matter and agreement could be reached by a consideration of other instances and their consequences.

The disagreement in the case of euthanasia may be on facts. For example, someone might say that if he were sure the disease were incurable, he would believe euthanasia moral. Whether the disease is incurable is a factual matter and its decision can only be left to research scientists. However, it needs to be noted that for some, no matter what the evidence for or against a cure, the possibility of one is always hoped for.

The final kind of disagreement is the one in which the point at issue is the moral principle itself. Shall we invoke the hedonistic principle, or that of the sanctity of life, or the principle that asserts that God alone gives and should take life? A disagreement over such an issue is often simply irresolvable. What we can do is to explicate cases, and to try to see what evidence can be invoked in favor of one rather than another of the disputed principles. We shall consider the problem of euthanasia in some detail in Chapter XX.

Unsatisfactory as this final discussion is, it remains true that no set of rules can be given which will automatically resolve moral debates, precisely because moral issues cannot be resolved by any mechanical means. To be able to set up a "decalogue" for the solution of moral debates is to undermine the morality of the act. To be lawabiding is not yet to be moral.

BIBLIOGRAPHY

Aiken, Henry D., "Moral Reasoning," *Ethics,* 64 (1953), 24-37.
Ewing, A. C., *Ethics,* London: English Universities Press, 1953, pp. 115-144.
Falk, W. T., "Moral Perplexity," *Ethics,* 66 (1955-56), 123-131.
Firth, R., "Ethical Absolutism and the Ideal Observer," *Philosophy and Phenomenological Research,* XII (1952), 317-345.
Mandelbaum, M., *The Phenomenology of Moral Experience,* Glencoe, Illinois, 1955, pp. 183-309.
Rice, P. B., *On the Knowledge of Good and Evil,* New York: Random House, 1955, pp. 247-270.
Russell, B., *Human Society in Ethics and Politics,* New York: Simon and Schuster, 1955, 82-91, 128-134.
Stevenson, C. L., *Ethics and Language,* New Haven: Yale University Press, 1945.
Vivas, E., *Moral Life and Ethical Life,* Chicago: University of Chicago Press, 1950, 185-249.

# CHAPTER XIX

# FREEDOM AND RESPONSIBILITY

### Compulsion and Responsibility

There are certain special problems that need to be considered before we are done. These concern the making of moral decisions in a most intimate fashion and illuminate what is involved in such decisions. One of the most seductive and difficult of these problems occurs when a person accused of an infraction of a moral principle tries to defend himself or excuse his action by an appeal, "I couldn't help it. I wasn't responsible for what happened." This is the cry of Oedipus when it was revealed that he had killed his father and married his mother. Oedipus' plea was that he could not be held responsible because he committed the crimes in ignorance of the facts. Such is the defense of the person who pleads "temporary insanity." He didn't know what he was doing and was impelled to do what he did by uncontrollable impulses and emotions.

Whether or not people are responsible for what they do is a significant question in moral considerations because all moral judgments assume responsibility. Without responsibility moral pudgments lose their significance. Everything that has so far been said bears out this contention. One who makes a moral decision does so because he is, indeed, responsible for what he does. If he were not responsible he could not act in a moral fashion.

### Ambiguity of "Responsible"

Yet there is a possible ambiguity because surely one could say of an irresponsible person that he is immoral precisely because he acts irresponsibly. Even so, the person who is responsible for his irresponsibility is usually judged adversely while he who is so constituted that he is irresponsible by nature becomes an object of pity rather than condemnation. We pity rather than condemn because we feel that one who is by nature irresponsible does what he does without any true alternatives. He cannot help himself, since it is not in his power to do otherwise. In that sense the act is not truly *his,* and, therefore, he cannot be held responsible for it. Common everyday speech has many expressions denoting a lack of responsibility. People speak, for example, of acts done "under compulsion." There are evidently two meanings of "irresponsibility." One of these is usually indicated by using the word "irresponsible," the other by the expression "not responsible." Infants, for example, are irresponsible in a sense different from a sane person who acts irresponsibly.

### Responsibility and Choice

The statement "John was compelled to lie because he would have been shot if he hadn't. He was, therefore, not responsible for the lie but he was responsible for its consequences," makes sense only if the word "responsible" is ambiguous. Speaking generally for the moment, John cannot be morally reprehensible (culpable?) because he lied in these circumstances, yet he did cause the consequences that resulted from the lie. Suppose Mary and Jean were discussing whether John, having lied, was moral. Mary asserts that since John lied he was immoral, Jean that he was at least not immoral. Mary bases herself on the belief that John is responsible for his acts even under threats. He was confronted with a choice between lying and telling the truth and the threat to his life was but one factor he needed to consider. He chose to lie and is responsible for his decision. He is immoral. Jean's rebuttal is supported by her belief that a person cannot be held responsible for doing what he was compelled to do and under the given conditions John reacted instinctively. He was going to preserve his life because this is a law of nature. He couldn't help but lie under these conditions.

Mary is asserting that John made a free choice and was responsible; Jean that, at least in this case, his act was determined in the sense of compelled. Two questions need to be asked both of Mary and of Jean. What is meant by saying that John is free (or determined) and hence responsible? What kind of evidence would show that John is free (or compelled)?

First a word of warning. It is tempting to say, as we have, that one cannot be responsible unless one is free. But this, if so, would be the case only under a specific meaning of "responsible." So one can say, "The explosion was responsible for the death of three people," and it would be nonsense to assert that this meant the explosion was free. In the same way a person causally determined to act as he does may be said to be responsible for the consequences of his act. But here "be responsible for" would mean "causes."

## Meaning of "John is Free"

When Mary says that John is free, she apparently is saying that John somehow or other of himself, even if not by himself, acted in the way he did. Jean on the other hand seems to be asserting that given the conditions $A_1$, $A_2$, ..., $A_n$, John's act was as much a necessary consequence of those conditions as any theorem in geometry is of its axioms. The lie, in other words, is uttered by John much as if he were a robot or any I.B.M. machine. On the other hand, Mary seems to be saying that either no *chain* of conditions necessitating the lie exists, or that given the conditions $A_i$ ($i = 1, \ldots n$) John could still have told the truth; John's lie was not something so inextricably tied to the conditions that he had no true alternative. Even though these conditions did exist at the moment of action, still John had the ability to lie or not to lie. The issue may now be sharpened in the following fashion. Given the conditions, Mary asserts the lie is not "entrained"; Jean asserts it is. The dispute is not about the existence of the conditions but about the relation of the conditions to John's act. Is the act simply a link in a chain, or is it not? If it is not, than John may be responsible for it and consequently be called immoral.

This complicates the problem. Suppose John says, "I lied because I felt compelled to do so out of respect for the moral principle that one ought to preserve one's life." In short, John tells us that his act was one he was compelled to do precisely because among the antecedent conditions was recognition of his obligation to be moral. He concedes that if he were to be moral, he had no alternative but to obey the moral principle to which he adhered and lie. This shows explicitly that the ordinary way of conceiving this problem must be incorrect. Surely, to be compelled to act morally by the moral principle is not the same as to be compelled to kill by an intense emotion. To be compelled by the laws of arithmetic to say "$3 + 2 = 5$" is not the same as to be compelled by a hypnotist to say "$3 + 2 = 5$." The question is not whether John is compelled or not compelled to act as he does, but what it is that compels him and the circumstances which give rise to this compulsion. To be compelled to act righteously by reason of one's acceptance of moral principles is more closely related to morality than to be compelled to act righteously at the point of a gun.

*Proving "John is free"*

There is another difficulty in reducing this question of responsibility to "entrainment." Neither Jean nor Mary could possibly demonstrate their assertion beyond cavil. Jean could never complete the chain and Mary could never show the chain could not be completed sometime. To prove John was compelled to lie, it would be necessary to give a complete detailed picture of the past history of the universe and indicate all the links in the complete chain leading to the given act. This is not merely an obvious impossibility but to assert that a complete picture of the past history of the universe would present such a complete chain is to beg the question. It is possible that a complete picture could still be full of gaps. The practical embarassment is that if responsibility is to be defined in terms of such a chain, one never could be sure that John is or is not responsible. Perhaps then another approach by way of a consideration of what the word "responsible" means may be possible.

*Usages of "Responsible"*

If we revert to linguistic usages, we remark that "responsible" is an adjective and a cognate form "responsibility" is its noun. So, for example, people say, "The president of the Bank is a very responsible person," or "His responsibilities weighed heavily on him." Even though in many cases the subjects of the sentences in which the word "responsible" occurs are persons, we do at times have as subject events or things. For example, the farmer may say, "The hot weather was responsible for the crop failure," or the lifeguard may say, "The heavy rains were responsible for the drownings." In such contexts the word "responsible" means simply "caused." Sentences of this type can, therefore, be translated without loss of meaning in this way.

> "The hot weather caused the crop failure."
> "The heavy rains caused people to drown."

Where "is responsible for" means "causes," we have cases of no concern to us. Our problem lies in those usages where more is meant and we cannot without radical change of meaning translate the term "responsible for" into "causes." The sentence "The president of the Bank is a very responsible man" loses its meaning if we take "responsible" to mean "cause."

Similarly to say "John is responsible for the explosion" is not quite to say "John caused the explosion." To be responsible for the explosion may involve some sort of causal connection between John and the explosion but there are other connotations. What else the statement implies is evident when we describe the circumstances in which we would say "John is responsible for the explosion." For example, if John is an engineer and blasts rock we would not think of saying he is responsible for the explosion. It is only when something goes wrong, when the explosion (say) takes place when it should not, or when someone gets hurt as a result of the explosion that the question of responsibility arises. Responsibility for the explosion in a situation of this sort connotes blame. In the same way we ordinarily would not say of a bank president that he is a responsible person. It is when some question arises such as whether the president of the bank can be trusted, or whether the bank is in good hands, that the character of the bank president comes into question. Responsibility here connotes trust.

### Responsibility and Blame

It is interesting in this connection to observe how closely related the question of responsibility is to that of blame. If John had dashed into a burning building to save a beautiful girl, we would feel it strange to say "John is responsible for saving her life." We would be much more apt to say "John saved the girl's life," or "She owes her life to John." John could be held responsible for the girl's life but not for saving it. Even when we speak of a person's responsibilities "weighing heavily upon him," we seem to be saying that he is concerned over all the things he needs to do which if he didn't do would make him culpable. A responsible person is one who does the things he is obligated to do and, hence, can be expected to be unblamed. "To be responsible" connotes that there is an act which it is obligatory for the person to perform if circumstances should demand it. Moreover his failure to perform the act would subject him to criticism and censure, while his performance of the act is ordinarily taken as a matter of course and an indication of good character.

The concept of responsibility is extremely important in legal matters where its implications are recognized more clearly. When two persons are involved in an automobile accident it is of basic importance to establish responsibility. In most general terms, a person who drives a car is under obligation to do certain things. For example, he mustn't drive over the speed limit; he must give advance warning of his intention to turn, and so on. These actions are demanded of him by the statutes of the community. Now if he did not do one or more of these things and as a consequence the accident resulted, then the court holds him responsible, blames him in other words. He is compelled, in consequence, to pay damages, which means to repair the harm he did. The legal responsibility is there when there is a legal duty to act in a certain way and this is not done.

## Responsibility and Duty

So far then we see that the idea of responsibility involves the existence of something that ought to be done or refrained from (a duty) and the implication that if the duty is not performed, blame and accountability result. This shows that "responsible" is usually followed explicitly or implicitly by two prepositions, "for" and "to." One is responsible for an act, or for failing to act, or for a person's behavior and so on. Since the failure to act or do the duty involves blame or punishment, the responsibility is also "to" someone or something. The automobile driver is responsible *for* driving carefully but he is responsible *to* the courts or to society. The bank president is responsible *for* the conduct of the bank and *to* his depositors or the community. The person (or thing) to whom the agent is responsible is usually the source of condemnation and/or punishment that results when the responsibility is not met. In brief, the word "responsibility" also carries along the connotations of "response-ability" and since one responds to and the response is for a goal, what is responded to and what the response is for need to be clearly indicated. A person may have a responsibility to himself since he may have duties to himself and be blamed by himself if he does not perform them. Self-condemnation is a well-recognized phenomenon in our modern society.

Let us now apply these considerations to the problem of moral responsibility. To be morally responsible means that there exists a moral duty which a person is obligated to perform and which if he fails to perform will entail moral condemnation at least. To whom or what one is morally responsible will evidently depend on the particular moralist. To the hedonist, the moral responsibility lies in doing what brings happiness and is to oneself or to "mankind." To the theological moralist, the responsibility is to God and for doing God's will. The source of moral condemnation (and perhaps punishment) for the hedonist is man or society and for the theological moralist, God. Moral responsibility exists, therefore, only where there are moral duties, i.e., what ought to be done morally. Any moral theory that abolishes moral duties also abolishes moral responsibility just as, as Hobbes showed, if there are no legal duties, there can be no legal responsibility. Parenthetically, since, if there are no moral principles there are no moral duties, moral responsibility is possible only where there are moral principles.

Whether one believes the universe to be a purely mechanical system or not, this much will be agreed upon. Before anyone can be said to have responsibilities or to be responsible, or to be condemned for doing some·thing or other, he must be able to do something other than it is his duty to do, i.e., something contrary to his duty. No ordinary person would say that an I.B.M. machine has responsibilities, or is morally delinquent when it adds incorrectly, or has a duty to calculate correctly. Moral responsibility can exist only *if* it is in the agent's power to do something other than moral principles dictate. In a purely mechanical world, the actor is not an agent and hence cannot be morally responsible. His act may be what the moral principle dictates, but he could not have done otherwise. The act of a moral agent is his act in a sense quite different from what is meant when we say of a machine that it is *its* act. We usually do not speak of a machine's actions, but of the way it operates.

*Freedom* vs. *Determinism*

Obviously, the discussion has reverted to a consideration of a variation of the "freedom vs. determinism" controversy which belongs to another area of investigation. Freedom usually signifies the ability to will, or act, or refrain from willing or doing; while determinism means that what a person does is not within his power to alter. As we have said, this problem is fundamental to moral decisions, but is not within our scope to consider. The solution of the problem depends upon the possibility of giving a complete description of the world from its beginning to the moment in question such that the moment in question is seen "entrained" by the past. Those who deny freedom insist such a complete description is possible and would demonstrate determinism; those who affirm freedom insist that a complete description is impossible, but even if it could be given would not demonstrate determinism. The determinist argues in this fashion: "If we could get a *complete* description of reality, we might be able to see that every act is unavoidable." The argument in support of this conditional is usually in the form of an inductive argument that runs like this: "History shows that, more and more, we have been able to fill in the description of so-called free acts. Hence, it is reasonable to suppose, we shall be able to complete the picture."

To these two arguments the person who believes in freedom could reply: "Perhaps so; *if* we could get a *complete* picture we might be able to see the act was simply one link in an unbroken chain of events each of which is completely entrained by its predecessors and no other chains are or were possible. But then we might discover that the chain does not and cannot have every link entrained completely by its predecessors. Furthermore, you use the idea of "complete" in a special sense. Why cannot a complete picture still have gaps? Perhaps after all details are given, there are still holes in the picture simply because there are no more details there.

"As for the inductive argument, true we give better and better pictures, but never has a complete picture been given. Cannot we say, therefore, that probably it never will?"

For our purposes we will leave this debate as it stands. Intuitively we feel that quite often we do have it in our power to do or avoid doing things. This feeling, as well as the existence of internal moral struggles and inter-personal debates, we can take as sufficient evidence to permit us to assume that responsibility is not a delusion but a fact. In any case, to pursue the problem further would necessitate excursions into ontology and natural science too extensive to be possible within the compass of a few pages. A person who is confronted with the task of making a moral decision, or judging another or his act, does proceed as if it is in one's power to do or avoid the act, and that it is possible for there to be circumstances in which one's deeds are unavoidable.

There are, then, two facets to the phrase "in his power to do or avoid." For example, if we want to know whether it is in a given person's power to commit robbery, we must know 1) that he could do the act, i.e., that he had, say, a gun, was physically able to oppose his victim, was courageous enough to face the possible consequences of his act, and so on; 2) that he could do otherwise, i.e., that he could change his mind, could refuse to go through with the act, and so on. So also to have it in one's power to be charitable, one must be able to afford charity, to have someone to whom he could be charitable, and so on; also to have it in one's power to be charitable involves that one could be uncharitable, i.e., refuse (say) to give alms to the poor, want to see the needy suffer, and so on. An act which a person can do but doesn't, a thought which he can think but doesn't are within his power. The person who is able to tell the truth and cannot avoid doing so, or the person who is able to will good but is psychologically incapable of avoiding willing the good, are neither of them doing what lies in his power.

A person who commits murder sometimes pleads that he was not responsible because although he could and did murder the victim, he could not have done otherwise. He claims that he was driven to the act by a mental disease or a terrible emotional strain that made him unable to control his acts. In the same way someone who rescues children from very hazardous situations may be capable of rescuing them, but if he is driven to such acts by an uncontrollable impulse resulting from some traumatic experience in his past so that he couldn't do otherwise, he too is doing something not within his power to avoid. His *act* may be praiseworthy, but he is not responsible and therefore not to be called moral or, for that matter, brave.

### "Could Have Done Otherwise"

The frequent use of the phrase "could have done otherwise" makes it advisable to comment on it. We say of a wealthy man who has given a dollar to a worthy cause that he could have done otherwise for he could have given ten dollars or none at all, just as easily. Or we say of a man who has cheated on an examination he could have done otherwise and been honest. Or we say of a man who has just divorced his wife that he could have done otherwise and tried to patch up their differences; or that things could have been otherwise if only he had not been so absorbed in his business. In every case the person involved had a choice of doing one thing rather than another. Both were in his power to do, and conditions were such that it was up to him to choose the one or other act. If, however, conditions were such, either because of the sort of person one is or the sort of circumstances one is in, that he is compelled either psychologically or physically to do what he does, then we can not say he could do otherwise. This boils down to the fact that the phrase "could have done otherwise" does not merely imply a set of logical alternatives, but a set of factual ones as well. Logically speaking, there always are things that could have been otherwise. In the case of the divorce, there are the things that could be done; divorce, or temporary separation, or calling in a marriage counselor, but the two people concerned may have driven themselves into such psychological conditions that no other possibility was left but divorce.

Furthermore, it is essential that the person could have done otherwise *in the conditions present*. If conditions were different, then surely he might very well have done otherwise. The ability to do otherwise must be present in the present circumstances before it could be said of the person that he could have done otherwise and, therefore, was responsible for his act.

What has been said so far indicates what needs to be considered in deciding what is in a given person's power to do or avoid. Three classes of conditions affect one's power to act, psychological, physiological, and circumstantial. It is uncontestable that a person suffering from compulsions or manic psychoses of various sorts is doing things not in his power to avoid. Similarly great emotional stresses such as overwhelming fears, anxieties, and passions of various sorts also drive a person to do what is not in his power to refrain from doing. A will written while the maker is under great emotional stress may be overturned by the court precisely because the court decides the maker was doing something not in his power to avoid. A promise made under threat of death is not considered binding because the promisser could not have done otherwise. Although breaking a promise is wrong, and one who promises is responsible for the performance of the promise, where there is compulsion there is no promise.

The third type of conditions is illustrated by the following example. A person who kills an unarmed enemy in the heat of battle cannot be held responsible (culpable?) for the death of his enemy. He does not have it in his power to alter the circumstances in which he finds himself at the moment. Again, we can learn something from the law. A person who kills someone when his car is wrecked because the steering wheel suddenly broke cannot be held responsible for the other's death, unless it could be shown that the wheel had been cracked and the owner had failed to have it repaired. If the car owner had been negligent, he could be held responsible (culpable?) because had he not neglected to repair the car, the wreck could have been avoided.

All attempts to define what a person had or did not have it in his power to do at the time he acted are extremely intriguing but tremendously complicated. Much legal debate has sought to clarify these issues in connection with legal responsibility. The general issues are quite similar to those in moral responsibility except that since the law is usually fairly explicit concerning what is or it not the duty of a person, it is somewhat easier to decide in specific cases than in moral problems.

*Summary*

We can sum up before we turn to a statement of rules for deciding moral responsibility. Moral responsibility exists if there is

1) a moral principle which defines
2) a moral duty to do or refrain from doing something (i.e., an obligation) which
3) is within the power of the person to do (can do) and
4) is such that the person can do otherwise.

Furthermore, there must be

> 5) some source of authority to whom the person is responsible and
>
> 6) is the source of punishment or blame, reward or praise for responsible actions.

We can see now what one who pleads that he is not responsible for his deed can mean. First we notice that he is not saying his act was irresponsible, for this has a different meaning. To be irresponsible is to act without any consideration of the responsibilities involved. Not to be responsible signifies that the conditions of responsibility are acknowledged but one or more of them do not apply. A person who has responsibilities may yet be an irresponsible individual.

To take another example: If John claims he is not morally responsible for the act of marital infidelity, he is trying to claim that one or more of the following conditions are present.

1) No moral principle is involved. This is untrue but could be urged by those who regard sexual relations as purely a physical act, and reject the view that marriage imposes restrictions as well as privileges.

2) The moral principle involved does not define an obligation to refrain from acts of marital infidelity. This can be advocated by some forms of hedonism which might insist that such acts are more conducive to greater happiness than restraint and fidelity. Some forms of State-ism (e.g., Nazi-ism) may claim, indeed, that the obligation to provide children for the State is a higher one than that of marital fidelity and, hence, marital fidelity is not a responsibility if no children have resulted from the marriage.

3) Marital fidelity is not in a person's power and hence infidelity cannot be avoided. This is supported by pointing to the strength of man's sexual drives and an attempt to prove that when so driven a person simply cannot control his actions. In other words, it is claimed that one is not responsible for an act of infidelity because of the intensity of the passion.

4) The act of infidelity is not prohibited by anyone or anyone with authority. To show this in the case of marital infidelity would be difficult, if not impossible. True, in modern American society it appears that neither the wife nor the husband may object to infidelity, especially their own, but the State still does, and for religious persons God does. A person is not released from his responsibility because the one to whom he may owe the duty does not object to its violation, because there may

be many sources of authority to whom the person is responsible. To take another example, everyone is responsible that his actions not injure another, and this remains even if you agree to be killed. In a democracy at least, you cannot surrender your right to your life and, hence, cannot release a person from his duty not to kill you.

5)    There is no one who will punish, blame, reward, or praise an act of marital infidelity. This too seems impossible to demonstrate in this case. Even if the husband or wife does not do so, society, or the state, or God will.

It needs to be said that the moral responsibility derives from the presence of moral principles and not conversely. The moral principle defines the responsibility. So where a moral responsibility exists, it may be used as a criterion for the involvement of moral principles .

Another matter of interest is the importance of Condition 4. One may, indeed, refuse to accept a responsibility precisely on the grounds that the source of authority is not recognized, i.e., that one is not responsible to this presumed authority. For example, one may refuse to accept the responsibility of supporting a war effort on the grounds that one's responsibility is first to God, and not to the State.

Finally, we need to be aware of the fact that in many cases, if not most, when someone claims that he wasn't responsible for what happened, he is really urging that it was not within his power to do the act and could not have done otherwise than he did. This means that responsility is denied or rejected on the grounds of the absence of freedom to choose and do what is chosen. This, I think, could be made plausible only if the person were shown to be sane and ordinary people would agree that a sane person, under the given circumstances, could have chosen to do something else.

BIBLIOGRAPHY

Campbell, C. A., "Is Freedom a Pseudo-Problem", *Mind*, 1951.
Edwards, Jonathan, *Freedom of the Will*, New Haven, Yale University Press, 1957.
Ewing, A. C., *Ethics*, London, English Universities Press, 1953, Chapter VIII, pp. 144-181.
Garvin, L., A *Modern Introduction to Ethics*, Boston: Houghton-Mifflin Co., Chapters III and IV, pp. 59-102.
Lamont, W. D., *Principles of Moral Judgment*, Oxford: Clarendon Press, 1946, Chapter VIII, pp. 194-219.
Nowell-Smith, P. H., *Ethics, Penguin Books*, 1954, Chapters XIX and XX, pp. 278-315.

Ross, W. D., *Foundations of Ethics,* Oxford: Clarendon Press, 1939, Chapter X, pp. 208-252.

Schlick, M., *Problems of Ethics,* New York: Prentice-Hall, 1939, Chapter VII, pp. 143-159.

Stevenson, C. L., "Ethical Judgment and Avoidability," *Mind,* 47, 1938.

Stout, A. K., "Free Will and Responsibility," *Proceedings of the Aristotelian Society,* 37, 1936-37.

# CHAPTER XX

# AN EXAMPLE OF MAKING
# MORAL DECISIONS: EUTHANASIA

In this chapter we shall analyze a particular moral issue in order to illustrate in some detail the kind of considerations involved in arriving at a moral decision. However the discussion will not be conclusive and the reader will not be able to say: "Euthanasia is moral" or "Euthanasia is immoral because the book on *Making Moral Decisions* says so." From all that has gone before it is apparent that the statement, "Euthanasia is moral (or immoral) because the book says so," is not a moral statement. Nor, indeed, is one making a moral decision when he accepts or rejects the statement, "Euthanasia is moral," on such grounds. This chapter should be viewed, therefore, as an illustration of method and not a final judgment about euthanasia. A moral decision is not based on someone else's deliberations.

We shall discuss the problem of the morality of euthanasia for the following reasons. First, it is a problem that is of concern to people and involves very deep-seated fears and anxieties. Secondly, many honest people sincerely disagree on the morality of euthanasia. The consequences are that the issue is live and the considerations are many and diverse. Finally, disagreement over the morality of euthanasia does not seem to arouse intense hostility as it does in other problems. Extraneous considerations are, in consequence, not so easily introduced.

There are two things that people fear greatly, death and pain. Either, separately, can often be faced with courage but the thought of a lingering painful death brings terror to the hearts of most humans. Even those with faith in the significance of pain and death in a divine scheme are upset by the thought of a painful death. Yet no one can escape death and few, if any, fail to experience pain some time in their lives. Science and civilization have devoted tremendous time, energy, and material to prolong life and reduce pain in an effort to make life last as long as possible and to reduce pain to a minimum. At the same time, man has increased his techniques for killing by methods ranging all the way from drugs that put one to eternal sleep gently to atomic bombs.

One thing is clear, if one wants simply to avoid pain above everything else, then death is apparently the way to do it. When one is dead, one no longer feels pain. People have committed suicide rather than live in continual pain. People have killed their loved ones in an effort to "put them out of their misery." Doctors have put patients to death to relieve them of their pain. The most distressing situation of all is to see a loved one suffering with no hope of a cure or even a permanent (until death) alleviation of the pain. In such a context, men have raised the question of a painless death deliberately induced. To this act has been given the name "euthanasia."

Webster's Unabridged Dictionary defines "euthanasia" as:

"Act or practice of painlessly putting to death persons suffering from incurable and distressing disease."

The moral problem consists in whether it is moral to put to death painlessly a person suffering from an incurable and distressing disease. The question is whether a moral person ought to do this sort of thing, and not whether it is the right thing to do to alleviate pain and distress. Death will relieve the pain, and in this sense is right, but we are interested in the moral question and not merely the instrumental one.

## Meaning of "Euthanasia"

At the risk of seeming to labor the obvious, let us list the conditions enumerated in the definition in order to avoid any misunderstanding of the problem. The death must be painless. This is out of consideration for the patient, but if additional pain were involved the problem would become more complicated. The person must be shown to be suffering from an "incurable and distressing" disease. If it is either not incurable or not distressing, then the problem is changed. These two conditions must be present before one can begin to consider the morality of euthanasia. Since euthanasia tries to reduce pain, any increase in pain would contradict the avowed purpose of euthanasia. If the disease were not incurable, then euthanasia would be an act of murder. Whether the disease is incurable and distressing appear to be factual questions; but they may not be so wholly. It would appear that the possibility of curing a disease should be one that could easily be decided by doctors. But this, doctors being human, seems not always to be the case. Diseases pronounced incurable have become curable; and diseases one doctor cannot cure because he is unable to diagnose them may be curable by another who can. But even apart from such instances there are those who insist that no disease is incurable and, therefore, that as long as one is alive there is hope of a cure. This may or may not be so! The hope of a possible cure is taken as evidence that the disease can be cured. Evidently, to one who believes a cure is possible always, euthanasia is like murder.

All of this indicates quite clearly that it may be extremely difficult, if not impossible, to meet the definition of "incurable" so that a decision to kill based on the presumed incurable nature of the disease may be completely misguided. Such difficulties are not in themselves to be taken as an indication of the immorality of euthanasia. If euthanasia is moral, then the fact that one cannot say of a particular disease that it is incurable would not alter the morality of euthanasia. One must take risks in this insecure world of ours. Moreover, if "euthanasia" is defined in the way it was, then there is a chance that the conditions cannot be met, so that in a practical situation it may be impossible to decide whether the killing was euthanasia. Here too one can deal only with probabilities. A doctor who is treating an ailment must select a medicine even if he is not certain what the ailment is.

"Incurable" is, moreover, ambiguous. Does it mean "cannot be cured" or "cannot be cured now?" If the latter, then, perhaps, it could be tomorrow; and if not tomorrow, then perhaps the next day. However, this temporal difficulty can be eliminated by adding some specific conditions. For example, "incurable" means that at the present state of knowledge about the disease there is no way of curing it known to anyone and, furthermore, it does not appear likely that a cure will be found even if the patient were allowed to die in the ordinary course of events. These comments concern the definition of "euthanasia" and not yet its morality. But one cannot help noting how tragic it would be if the definition were satisfied and two weeks later a fortunate experiment revealed a cure.

The second condition, that the disease be distressing, is less difficult to define. Disease is, indeed, always more or less distressing to those who love the patient. A child with a cold can be quite distressing to its parents. To neurotics a slight stomach upset can involve an emotional reaction. The fear attached to the word "cancer" is terribly distressing to one who is told he suffers from a tumor even though it is quite curable. Of course, what the definition has in view is the distress accompanying such a disease as cancer in its terminal phase where hope is virtually gone, the patient in great pain, and the whole thing is an emotional and economic drain on all friends and relatives.

Many circumstantial questions still plague us, but we can formulate the moral question in the following way.

## The Moral Issue

Is it moral to put to death someone suffering from a disease for which there is now no known cure, and for which there probably will be no cure in the foreseeable future, and in which the patient is in great pain causing emotional and economic distress to himself and his loved ones?

In this form of the question, there are no restrictions on who is to do the killing. So a father might put to death his child; or a lover his beloved; or a neighbor his friend, and so on. Perhaps we should leave the problem as it is rather than try to define who may or may not kill under these conditions, because if the act is moral, it ought to be so for anyone. We do not want to confuse the morality of euthanasia with the necessary conditions for meeting a specific problem. So it may be necessary for a panel composed of at least some doctors to grant permission for euthanasia, and certainly we would need the opinions of medical authorities on the medical question of possible cures. But these factors would not make euthanasia moral, nor even, perhaps, be relevant to the moral question.

Nor do we want to make the moral decision simply a corollary to a legal one. Quite obviously, if murder is an act of killing that is wilful and premeditated, euthanasia would fit the definition because much thought and preparation are needed to arrive at the decision to put to death some ill person. As a consequence, if it was concluded generally that euthanasia was moral, it would be necessary either 1) to modify the definition of murder, or 2) to restrict the definition so as to make euthanasia an exception, or 3) to legalize euthanasia by a special act so as to protect the one who performs it from the penalties of murder. Arguments, therefore, that euthanasia is immoral because it is murder which is illegal really beg the question. It may well be that the definition of murder is too wide, as I have said. In that case, we would need to distinguish between murder and euthanasia. If the distinction is a valid one, then not even the fact that murder is both illegal and immoral would be relevant to the morality of euthanasia except perhaps in some analogical fashion. At the moment, euthanasia is illegal precisely because it is viewed as murder, even though the sentence imposed upon someone who commits it is at times not very heavy. Public opinion tends to excuse such acts, if not to condone them.

## Economic and Moral Justification

We need to make one other distinction, that between the economic justification of euthanasia and its moral justification. It is sometimes argued that euthanasia is justified because a person dying from, say, incurable cancer who lingers on week after week needing medical attention and, perhaps, hospitalization is a severe economic drain on the meager resources of his family. It is then argued that just as in some primitive societies infants were exposed and the aged put to death for economic reasons so the unproductive no longer capable of becoming productive should also be removed. Whether or not this is right on economic grounds is not our concern. What does matter is that ordinary people in our civilization feel this to be entirely incompatible with moral principles, and, hence, the economic tolls involved are not considered a justification of the morality of euthanasia. What is good for economic reasons is not necessarily good for moral reasons, even if the advocates of economic expansion may wish it were so.

We can now turn to our problem and first ask what ends are being sought by euthanasia. Presumably the chief goals are the amelioration of the pain of the patient as well as the anxiety and distress of his relatives. Euthanasia, then, must be considered a means to achieving these ends. Two questions need answers. Are the ends good? Is the act right? We recall that an end was good when 1) it was approved, 2) it was desirable, 3) it was better for it to be than not be and, 4) it was worth having for its own sake. The act is morally right on the other hand if 1) it is conducive to the end; 2) it is the act that would be done by a moral person acting on the basis of moral principles to achieve a good end under appropriate conditions.

### Are Ends Good?

It is obvious that the amelioration of pain is almost universally approved. This does not mean that it is always desirable to lessen pain. Pain is considered by most people something to be avoided if possible. Yet it is not always desirable to avoid pain. Two examples occur in support of this, perhaps strange, remark. The remark that it is not always desirable to avoid pain is strange because most people would initially, at least, say that it is always desirable to avoid pain. The reason is that pain is known by all to be unpleasant. But there are times when pain serves a purpose and it is not desirable to avoid it. For example, Christian theology teaches that Christ, as God, came to redeem man by becoming man and suffering all the ills of humans. As a result, Christ had to suffer the pain of the cross. Although, in general, the alleviation of Christ's pain was something to be approved, it was not desirable precisely because if Christ had not suffered pain as humans do, the purpose of His coming would not have been possible of successful attainment. Christ could atone for the sins of man only by suffering as a man. And although it would have been better that the pain could have been ameliorated than suffered in all its intensity, yet this amelioration is not worth having simply for its own sake. In Christian dogma, it was of course better that Christ suffer than that his mission fail. Indeed, Christ, although desiring that He not be made to suffer, yet realized the necessity of the suffering.

The second example is from a more human sphere. Some psychoanalysts claim that a woman who does not suffer the pains that come in giving birth is psychologically injured. Althought, then, painless childbirth is to be approved, it is not desirable especially if the pain is artifically alleviated. In fact, even some obstetricians who do not accept the psychoanalytic theory maintain that pain serves a purpose in the process since it causes the woman to "press down" and aid the passage. In either case, the alleviation of the pain is not worth having for its own sake but only if it would not do any harm to the mother.

### Alleviation of Pain not Intrinsic Good

Enough has been said to show that the alleviation of pain is not always good. In our modern society where pain can be reduced so very easily in most cases, there is a tendency to accept the alleviation of pain as an end in itself, intrinsically good. But even apart from any theological doctrine which views pain as necessary for atonement, it has a function as a sort of alarm. We could not survive very long if we lost our capacity to feel pain.

Perhaps, though, the point is not sharp enough. Granted that the alleviation of pain is not an intrinsic good, is it good in the kind of case we are considering, that is, of a person dying of a disease that is painful with no hope of recovery? One is strongly tempted to say, "Of course it is!," but let us consider. Suppose the patient has a life expectancy of two years, or one year, or six months and is in full possession of his faculties. Is the alleviation of his pain necessarily good? It might be indeed! We should, however, at least recognize that there are those who maintain that the alleviation of the pain is going counter to the will of God. If these people are correct, then we would need to admit that there were conditions under which it would not be good. But short of some doctrine such as this, in general, most ordinary people would probably feel the alleviation of pain approvable and desirable. Moreover, if the pain serves no purpose but to make the patient miserable, most people would feel that it is better for the alleviation to take place. If the patient, however, was one who considered the pain to be God's punishment, it might be better for the pain not to be alleviated. We may consider such a patient psychologically abnormal, but if his peace of mind depends upon the pain (not too excessive, of course) then to alleviate the pain is not good in itself.

The upshot of the discussion seems quite clear. There are cases in which the alleviation of pain is very much to be desired, is approved and is worth having for its own sake, just as there are cases where it is not.

### Is the Act Right?

Let us assume that we have a case where the alleviation of the pain is good and yet possible *only* by putting the patient to death. Would this make euthanasia right? If an act is right whenever it achieves the goal intended, then euthanasia would be right in such cases. This would be true simply by definition. But we have seen that for an act to be morally right much more than the fact that it leads to the desired goal needs to be considered. For example, it is necessary to ask, "Would this be what a moral person would do?" A consideration of the consequences of an act of euthanasia will help throw light on the answer to this question. Not that the consequences would stamp the act as right or wrong, but they do reveal the nature of the act so that one can "see" its rightness or wrongness more clearly. We need to consider the consequences to the patient, to the doctor, to other persons, and to society at large.

### Consequences of Euthanasia

Let us record the obvious. To the patient the consequence of prime importance is his death. This is said neither to appear solemn nor pedantic but to preface certain remarks. Either the patient is conscious of his impending death or not. If he is, then either he has agreed to be put to death or he has not. If he has, in the face of pain and distress, agreed to be put to death, then there is a definite sense in which he is committing suicide. One may or may not think suicide is moral, but the possibility that he might be committing suicide needs consideration. Moreover, a person in great pain cannot always be held responsible for all his decisions. He might quite well agree to euthanasia under the stress of the pain. If the patient is conscious but does not agree to this euthanasia, the act is immoral no matter what sort of committee agreed it should be done. To take a man's life under these circumstances surely is not moral.

If the patient has reached a stage in which he is unable to know what he is doing, then his consent cannot be obtained and to put him to death would clearly be doing violence to his person.

But even if consent to euthanasia could be obtained, the morality is not yet demonstrated. It may not be the case that consent makes euthanasia moral. There is the more basic question whether one has the right to destroy his life. If life is God-given, then, perhaps, only God has the right to take it. For those who have such beliefs, clearly, one cannot consent to have his life taken. At least, there is the possibility that euthanasia may involve either violence to the sick person or an undercutting of the principle of the sanctity of life.

As far as the doctor is concerned there are some perfectly obvious and relatively inconsequential consequences when he puts to death one of his incurable patients. The doctor is relieved of the burden of a patient for whom he can do but little. He may also be freed from the emotional disturbance that must be felt when someone is in pain and approaching death. There are more pertinent considerations. Doctors do have it in their power to kill their patient. But doctors are presumably dedicated to the preservation and prolongation of life. If euthanasia is a moral act, then this would mean that cases occur when a doctor may take it into his own hands to kill a patient. And this would go counter to the basic goals of a doctor. The doctor, in a sense, becomes a sort of superior being with the power of life and death. Now this may be quite proper, but we need to recognize that it would be one consequence of allowing doctors to practice euthanasia. What such power would do to the character of the doctor is quite difficult to say, but it is not impossible to imagine that it could corrupt doctors in the most insidious fashions.

One wonders also what happens to the emotions of a person who deliberately kills for whatever reasons. Can a doctor, who, despite our contemporary attitudes, is but a human being, resist the callousness that develops as he kills patient after patient? One may put to death one or even two patients suffering from an incurable disease without too much strain on one's character. But to continue in this sort of procedure could have decidedly bad intellectual and moral consequences. This alone may not make the act immoral because it may be better, all in all, to take such risks. Nevertheless, we need to be aware of these facets of the situation. We may need to weigh the alleviation of pain and distress against the corroding effect of such euthanasia, if there is one. This is not to mention the possible effect on the efforts of doctors to cure their patients. Killing incurable patients is, in one sense, an easy way out. A doctor who does it even under appropriate conditions may find it easier to call a baffling case incurable than to continue to fight to the last ditch for a recovery.

As for the consequences to the friends and relatives of the patient, some are quite obvious. They will no longer be called upon to stand helplessly by watching their loved one suffer. They will no longer have their own lives so radically disturbed. And they will be able to go about their daily lives without the constant anxiety and worry. Finally, they will no longer need to worry about the tremendous expenditure of money involved. Yet one must admit that none of these consequences in themselves, or collectively, mean anything. Only if one appeals to certain kinds of principles does it make any difference whether or not the disease is costly. This is logically evident if one asks questions like these. If euthanasia is immoral, what bearing does the cost of the disease have upon that fact? If euthanasia is moral, what bearing does the fact that the disease is not costly have? The irrelevance of the economic factor is also indicated when it is realized that if euthanasia is moral, it would be so regardless of whether or not those bearing the cost were so wealthy they easily absorbed the expenses. In similar fashion, we could ask this. Suppose the patient had no relatives or friends, would that make euthanasia immoral? These remarks indicate that the consideration of consequences to friends and relatives may from some points of view be irrelevant in evaluating the act. But again, the consequences, if any, need to be noted.

*Euthanasia and Moral Principles*

Would a moral person who has considered the consequences, approve of, if not himself perform, euthanasia? To answer this question it is necessary to consider the relation of euthanasia to the moral principles that may be invoked. It should be quite evident that any of the principles involving the Self of the patient either would make the problem meaningless or else imply that euthanasia is immoral. The patient's Self can hardly express itself or develop its potentialities when the body in which it resides is dead (assuming we don't live after death). However, since the patient, by hypothesis, is in a state in which his Self cannot express itself anyway, self-principles may seem irrelevant to the problem. There is one point that does need consideration and has been mentioned. If euthanasia implies an unwarranted act of violence to a Self, then there would be definite reasons why a moral person would refuse to assist in the destruction of the Self no matter how advanced the disease and painful the condition.

It is sometimes said that since euthanasia delivers a suffering person from his torment, it is an act of mercy. Logically this assumes that every act that releases a person from suffering is an act of mercy. This is not so, for if it were, then murders committed against people in pain would be acts of mercy. However, it is rarely an act of mercy to the person involved if his deliverance is achieved by destroying him, even though we misuse the word to speak of a "merciful death" when we mean a painless one or a less painful one. When, for example, it is said, "God in His mercy released the poor soul from pain," we must not forget that this means that the suffering soul goes into a state of blessedness. It would hardly be meaningful to say that God "mercifully" released the person from his pain and sent him to eternal damnation. In the human sphere we would hardly call a person "merciful" or his act one of "mercy" if it released from one misery only to bring about another. Death may be merciful only in the sense of release from suffering, but if immortality is not assumed, it may not be mercy at all but condemnation.

To those who appeal to theological principles, the problem has other complications. If it is God's will that the person suffer, to take the least complicated form, then euthanasia is evidently going counter to God's will. This, it is apparent, introduces the whole problem of suffering and its relation to God. In more complicated form, if the suffering is a prelude, and a necessary one, to salvation, then to alleviate suffering is to obstruct the divine plan for the salvation of the patient's soul. In another form, which was also mentioned earlier, life is sacred and it is only God's prerogative to give or take away. Men who of their own will endeavor, for whatever reasons, to take life assume God's prerogative. This is one of the sins of humankind, the attempt to become God or, at least, to act as if they were God. Of course, one can also urge that if it is God's will that this patient be released from his misery, then clearly euthanasia would be the means God uses to achieve that goal. The problem then resolves itself into the determination of God's will in a particular care.

We have already seen that the principle of the sanctity of life is inextricably part of our problem. Whether life be considered sacred because it is God's gift, or because of itself, if life is so considered, then it must be maintained at all costs. In general, this is the attitude of doctors who struggle to keep the patient alive and as comfortable as possible for as long a time as lies within his ability. This, quite evidently, places the mere prolongation of life as a value and an ultimate good above all else. Hence anything, on this basis, which shortens life cannot be moral.

The difficulties involved in using the principle of duty are always great in practical situations where the question is at issue. From the nature of the medical profession we know that it is a doctor's duty to do his best to cure his patients. We know that if he allows monetary considerations to dictate the degree of his care, then he is failing in his duty as a doctor. But is it a doctor's duty to his patient in the sort of condition we are assuming to take the patient's life painlessly? This, of course, is the very question at issue. The answer is not at all obvious and could be reduced to one or the other principle. If it is God's will, then it is the doctor's duty. Or, if it is an act of mercy, it is his duty. And so on. But is it God's will, or is it an act of mercy? Or is it contrary to the principle of the sanctity of life and, therefore, it is the doctor's duty to preserve his patient?

We now accost two principles that seem quite clear in their answers. Too clear, in fact. Consider first the societal principle: "One ought to do what is best for society." There can be little doubt or debate that a person so much of a drain upon the time of the doctor, medical facilities, money, and emotional energies of so many people is detrimental to society. In fact, his very condition makes him a complete social liability. He not only uses up resources but does so without creating any new goods. In the interest of society, if it is evident that his usefulness is gone never to be regained, the patient should be killed. Yet, the very statement of the argument from the societal utility point of view seems quite callous and disturbing. It is based on the view that a human being is but a means to the preservation and the benefit of society. We are reminded that infanticide as well as the exposure of the aged are both justifiable on those grounds. It somehow seems very wrong to subordinate human life to society.

The second principle is that of hedonism in its various forms be it egoistic or altruistic. If we take egoistic hedonism first, we need to ponder this. If the happiness to be computed is that of the patient, the calculation becomes impossible. We are apt to take the diminution of pain as intrinsically valuable. From this point of view its weight in the calculation becomes greater than any other factors. There is no real calculation involved as a consequence. But whose pain is to be lessened? Quite obviously that of the patient. But then he will be dead, and in a sense when dead to speak of "diminution of pain" is meaningless. We need to notice that the assumption is made that death is better than staying alive with the pain and despair of an incurable disease. This is not, however, the egoistic principle of hedonism but rather a principle about the nature of life and living.

In the case of universalistic hedonism, in many instances it is easy to assume that the greatest happiness for the greatest number of people would in many cases be best served by euthanasia. But, as I indicated earlier, this is not necessarily so. It may be that the emotional repercussions of killing the patient may involve much greater unhappiness than simply allowing the patient to die as a result of the ordinary course of the disease. There are, quite often, factors too difficult to evaluate when a hedonistic calculus is invoked. If, however, one could quite reasonably infer that by far the greatest happiness for the greatest number is served by euthanasia, the altruistic hedonist would need to approve euthanasia and call it moral.

### Euthanasia as Praiseworthy but Immoral

It is necessary to say that an act may be praiseworthy even though immoral. Its praiseworthiness may come from some of the consequences it induces; its immorality from the fact that it goes counter to a moral principle.

No matter what moral principle we invoke, there are apparently circumstances in which a particular act of euthanasia may be praiseworthy. Speaking rather generally, I don't believe many people would condemn a doctor or even an ordinary person for alleviating the terrible suffering of an incurably ill person. At the most, they might reprimand and perhaps even mildly punish such an act but not because euthanasia is completely wrong but because at the moment it is illegal and one doesn't yet feel safe in making it an approved course of action. Nevertheless, it may still remain immoral because it goes counter to the principle of the sanctity of life, or it involves violence against the person, or is counter to some other moral principle. Under some principles, on the other hand, euthanasia may be completely moral following as a consequence of its conduciveness to the highest good expressed in the principle.

In the final analysis then whether euthanasia is or is not moral is a question of what moral principle will turn out to be the true moral principle.

# CHAPTER XXI

# MAN, MORALS AND THE STATE

Men live in states. This quite obvious, trite, and seemingly trivial remark has weighty implications for our discussion. Men make their moral decisions within the confines of state organizations. The state, in other words, is one locus of such decisions. Living in a state in which one tries to make moral decisions, a person finds himself confronted with conditions, demands, and situations which have direct bearing on his decisions yet are of a different kind from the circumstances we have so far been compelled to take into account.

## Is State a Moral Agent?

Our discussion can be introduced in the following way. During the last war, the people of the world recoiled in horror at the atrocities visited by the Germans upon people in concentration camps and upon civilian populations conquered during the fighting. As a result, the victorious nations created the Nüremburg trials to decide the question of guilt for these atrocities. The defense argued that all these terrible acts were done in the name of the State and could only be attributed to the State. The individual soldier, or commander, who carried out his orders was simply performing his duty to the State. However, since the State was not a moral agent, it could not be held morally responsible. Therefore, no one could be held responsible for these atrocities. The counter arguments took two forms. The first was that the acts of the State are acts of those running the State, i.e., the leaders. The second was that even if the acts of the State were not those of a moral agent, nevertheless, those who carried out the orders of the State were moral agents and, as such, could have refused to commit the atrocities. (There were other arguments such as the question whether some of the acts did not violate the principles of war. These do not concern us.)

These are, quite evidently, the kind of arguments that can go on indefinitely and make life interesting. Yet it is equally apparent, or should be, that their resolution depends upon questions of meaning. Before the question "Is the State a moral agent?" can be answered, the question "What is the State?" or "What does the word 'State' mean?" must be answered. Is the State, in other words, the kind of thing of which it is meaningful to assert that it is a moral agent? What makes the answer to this question important is this. If the State is a moral agent, then the following statements become meaningful: "Germany was immoral in violating the neutrality of Belgium in 1914," or "The U.S. was immoral in using the atomic bomb on Nagasaki." If the State is not a moral agent, then these statements become meaningless expressions much like saying, "The potato was immoral because it did not grow larger." From a more practical point of view also, the answer to the question "What is the State?" determines the way in which one would justify a national decision. If the State is not a moral agent, then moral considerations are meaningless or irrelevant.

### Is "Moral" a Proper Predicate for Names of States?

Consider now these two statements:

    a.   John Doe is moral.
    b.   The United States is moral.

These look very much alike in structure. They describe a subject term, "John Doe," or "The U.S.," and predicate the word "moral" of this term. If we know the person John Doe named in the first sentence, we can either agree or disagree with the statement. After our considerations in Chapter XV, we know, in general, what we are saying about John Doe. We are affirming that John Doe acts (i.e., chooses what he does) in accord with a moral law and his choice is decided by the fact that his act will tend to maximize human happiness and is chosen out of love. This means that John Doe can choose his act in accord with moral principles, have motives, and anticipate consequences. If we want to challenge his morality, we might try by adroit questioning to find out from John Doe what his real motive was, or we might watch to see how he behaved. In brief, we can test the statement by observing John Doe directly or by talking with those who can observe him. Having the ability to do the things that entitle him to be called a moral agent is precisely what gives us the right to say, "John Doe is a person." Only the names of persons can be the subjects of predicates like "moral," for only persons can have the attribute called "moral." Names of persons are ordinarily called "proper" names and where instead of proper names we use expressions that define one and only one person (i.e., act as proper names do) we call these "definite descriptions." For example, the expression "the present president of the U.S. ('present' meaning August 1964)" is a definite description.

We need not concern ourselves with logical questions about proper names or definite descriptions, but we can formulate the problem in this fashion. In the sentence "The U.S. is moral," is the expression "The United States" a proper name of the same kind as "President John. F. Kennedy," or "Jackie Coogan," or, is it, perhaps, a definite description like "the boxing champion of 1960?" Certainly it acts as if it were one or the other of these in the sentence. But "John Doe" refers to a person who can be indicated and whose nature is such that he can do these things. "United States" does not indicate a person like John Doe even if it may indicate a person of a different kind.

Suppose we take a sentence like this: "The United States chooses war rather than submission to tyranny," and describe the kind of situation in which such a statement may be made. A series of events has taken place. The President and his cabinet with the approval of the Congress has decided to undertake a war. Under the American form of government the President cannot set in motion the wheels of war; only Congress can declare war. But Congress is surely not the United States; nor do Congress and the President make up the United States. Yet what actually takes place when the decision is made is an agreement by at least the majority of Congress to embark upon this venture. True, nobody wants war, but for one reason or another Congressmen choose it. The upshot of these comments seems to be that the sentence apparently means something like the following:

"The elected representatives of the people choose to commit the people to war rather than accept certain other states of affairs."

### Names of States and Distributive Nouns

It appears to me that all sentences in which the expression "The United States" occurs can be analyzed in the following way. For example, suppose we analyze the sentence: "The United States is a member of the U.N." Here too the case seems to be this. The United Nations is an assembly of the representatives of groups of people known as nations. The appropriate agency or official of the people sends a person to represent the people. These representatives deliberate and make decisions. "To be a member of the U.N.," then, means that representatives of the people participate in the actions and deliberations of this assembly. At the present time, Adlai Stevenson represents the American people in the U.N. If these analyses are correct then the expression "The United States" may be syntactically a proper name but semantically it does not refer to the same kind of person as "Adlai Stevenson" does. The United States does not make choices, those who deliberate do and these are persons. Expressions of the form "the State chooses" are elliptical expressions which upon expansion become, "The leaders (or representatives of the people) choose."

Since statements about the choices of nations can be translated into equivalent statements about the choices of persons, it follows both that nations are not the sort of things that make choices and that the word "nation" refers somehow to persons. If nations are not the sort of things that make choices, then to say "Germany chooses to invade Belgium" is meaningless. If "nations" refers to persons, then the statement tells us something about German people. In either case "nation" does not refer to a moral agent as does "John Doe." Whatever a nation is, or whatever the word "nation" may mean, a nation cannot be called moral or immoral nor its acts contrary to moral principles. The things a nation does are what people do in its name, so to speak. This assumes that there is such a thing as a nation. If we say, on the other hand, that a nation is simply an aggregate of people living under a comon set of laws and rulers, then our analysis indicates that expressions like "The United States is moral" are actually statements about its rulers. "Germany was immoral in violating the neutrality of Belgium" then tells us that the rulers of Germany did not keep their promise not to invade Belgium.

## Justifications of National Decisions

This leads to the problem of the justification of national decisions. Recently Great Britain and France decided to invade Egypt, and did so. Immediately the American people protested since they felt this was not the right thing to do. How could the invasion be justified? Evidently, from what we have said, the decision to invade was one made by those who conducted the affairs of their nations. The justification given by the leaders in Great Britain and France was that the invasion was made in the national interest. Egypt had seized the Suez Canal and this threatened the security of the people of England and France. The invasion of Egypt was made, therefore, to assure safe passage through the Canal. The Prime Minister of Britain and the Premier of France, if pressed, would in all likelihood urge that it was their duty as leaders of their people to look after the welfare of those whom they had been selected to serve.

The decision, as all such decisions, of the leaders could then be attacked in two ways. First, from a purely utilitarian angle, it might be shown that the decision was a wrong one, because it did not serve the best interests of the people. Secondly, it might be urged that it was not the duty of the leaders to protect the interests of the people. Both of these put national interests at the top of the things that need to be considered and assume that where national interests are concerned there are no questions of morality. But if the decisions are, as we have tried to show, made by persons, leaders of the people, then it is possible to say that the decision to invade was decidedly immoral. A moral person would not order an invasion because invasions not merely violate the rights of other people but also use force upon a weaker nation to get concessions they had a right to withhold.

### National Interests and Moral Questions

If national interests are placed above all moral considerations, then any decision made by a national leader is to be judged in terms of national interests. National leaders would be confronted only with the question whether a given act or decision did serve national interests. However, if the leaders remain moral agents, and the nation is the collection of people, national interests do not transcend moral issues. National interests then become subordinated to moral principles. If national interests are paramount, then a promise not to invade is really not a promise at all. It is a declaration that at the moment invasion is contrary to national interests and will be avoided as long as it continues to be so. If moral principles transcend national interests, the promise is binding even at the expense of national interests.

But, that moral principles do transcend pure "political realism" can be shown as follows. The political realist not only takes national interests as of paramount importance, he proclaims that they ought to be placed before all other matters. In brief, he makes a moral principle of his political maxim. Moral considerations simply cannot be avoided.

Quite clearly there are other very puzzling problems that arise. Is a promise binding upon a new national leader if made by his predecessor? Is a promise binding if to keep it would lead to the defeat of the nation's military forces? Fortunately, we are not concerned with politics but with considerations about them, and we can avoid such questions in this book.

As interesting and important as are these problems, most people who worry about such matters are concerned with the relationship of the individual making decisions on moral grounds to the laws of the State in which he lives. Let us consider the following situation. Suppose Hans is a German citizen at the time Hitler ruled. Hans was ordered by law to help capture Jews who were to be put to death for being Jews. Morally Hans knows this is wrong, yet he feels that, as a citizen, he is obliged to obey the law. What should Hans do? This was the situation in which many Germans were placed when Hitler came into power. Or let us describe a possible situation in the United States. Suppose the majority of Americans *voted,* freely and democratically, that all Negroes were to be segregated in the slum areas of cities and provided with "equal but separate" schools. Since this is the will of the majority, it becomes the law of the land. Suppose Joe Blow was one of the minority who voted against the measure and he was ordered to help round up the Negroes, what should he do? Obey the law, or be moral?

## Good Citizen and Moral Man

There are two matters that need consideration. There is the question of the relation between being a good citizen and being a moral person on the one hand, and the relation between moral principles and legal principles on the other. Let us first ask: "What is meant by the term 'good citizen'?" This seems to be a relatively simple question to answer. When someone says, "John is a good citizen," he may mean that John is a person who not only obeys the laws but expends his efforts in doing his civic duty. But there are persons who obey the laws but are not good citizens. So a person who never gets into trouble with the law but doesn't vote, for example, would not in general be called a good citizen. People who participate in public affairs for the benefit of the society are good citizens. The complex nature of the problem is revealed when someone who is a candidate for the title of "good citizen" is confronted with a law which he knows is wrong and which would involve an immoral act if it were obeyed. We are tempted to say that if a person is a good citizen, he is expected to obey a law which he considers bad while seeking to change it. This would be fine except for the hypothesis that the law enjoins an immoral act. When this happens, then if we mean by a good citizen one who obeys the law, the good citizen must be immoral. The converse is quite possible also. In Hitler Germany it was illegal to aid a Jew trying to escape the gas chambers while it was immoral not to do so. So one has a choice between being a good citizen but an immoral one, or being a moral person but a bad citizen.

The fact that to be a good citizen and to be a moral person ace not the same thing, demands that one decide upon some order of importance. Should laws be subordinate to moral principles, or moral principles to laws? We cannot put them on the same plane since they quite clearly dictate different actions at times. Which takes precedence when morals and laws conflict depends upon how we conceive the nature of law. If laws are expressions of moral principles, as some would maintain, then theoretically where there is a clash between the law and a moral principle, either the law is not "really" a law or else it is an inadequate expression of the moral principle. If, for example, the law says, "Jews should be exterminated," and the moral principle says, "Thou shalt love thy neighbor as thyself," then the law is not a law at all. If the law, however, is simply a rule of behavior which makes social living possible, then its dictates may be either paramount or subordinate to those of moral principles. If the moral principle is thought to be absolute and apodeictic, then rules of behavior must conform to it. If moral principles are justified in terms of social survival, then if the rule of behavior (law) aids social survival, it must be put above the moral principle which may be a disintegrating force, at times making for the destruction of social solidarity. If moral principles are justified in terms of God's will, then the law is secondary.

If laws are taken to be part of the "furniture" of the world in which we live, then there is need to make a distinction between laws as expressions of legislative bodies and that which they seek to express. The former we can call "written laws," the latter "natural laws" ("laws of nature" is taken in the sense that these are laws expressing the character of nature as a whole. These are not physical laws or scientific laws). In this case the written law must be a more or less accurate expression of the natural law, and, therefore, if there is a clash between the written law and moral principles it is because the written law does not adequately express the natural law. In this way, natural law could be viewed as on the same level as moral principles, if these are themselves taken to be natural laws.

*Criticisms of Laws*

Some light can be thrown on the relation between laws and morals if we examine the kinds of criticism one may level at a law. Consider the segregation laws in Southern states. These laws have been attacked with increasing vigor in late years. Segregation laws enforce certain modes of behavior on Negroes. So, they may compel Negroes to travel on public conveyances in special seats only, or they prohibit Negroes from using certain schools, or they do not allow Negroes to use the same public recreation facilities, and so on. The objections to such laws have taken the following forms:

a)  They are economically unsound.
b)  They violate certain constitutional rights.
c)  They are immoral causing people to mistreat others, and humiliate people of darker skin.
d)  They violate religious principles such as the universal brotherhood of men before God.
e)  They aid the Communists in their struggle against democracies.

That segregation laws are economically unsound alone would be no strong argument against them for people might be quite willing to pay the price. There is no serious moral conflict between the legal obligation to segregate Negroes and the economic unsoundness of the practice, since there is no moral obligation to economic soundness. At best, the appeal to the economic consequences of segregation laws is one to selfish interests and those in favor of such laws can then easily hail an economic loss as a sacrifice.

## Constitution and Moral Principles

That segregation laws violate the constitutional rights of persons has two faces. If the Constitution is simply an agreement to live by the rules laid down in it, then a clash between these laws and the Constitution could be solved by changing the Constitution. After all, on such a view the Constitution is a kind of rule book according to which the "game" of living together is played. If the people want to have segregation rules, then their constitution will include them. What, however, makes an appeal to the Negroes' constitutional rights much more appealing is that the rights of persons guaranteed in the Constitution are considered moral rights transcending existing laws. The Constitution is taken to be an expression of some such moral obligation as: "One ought to respect persons," or "Persons ought to be treated as ends-in-themselves." Even segregationists at times tacitly agree to this. For example, the segregationist may urge that the Negro be given his rights as a person even though segregated. This is a long way from the days when segregationists tried to show Negroes were not persons at all.

At least that much progress has been made. For one who takes the Constitution to be based upon moral principles, where the law is definitely in violation of these principles, the choice is completely clear.

Arguments against segregation laws on the grounds that they enjoin immoral acts are unambiguous with respect to our problem. If one argues that segregation laws are to be abolished because they violate moral principles, then the argument is valid only if it places moral principles above laws. All laws must either be neutral with respect to moral principles or conform to them. If laws are neither neutral nor conform to moral principles, they are to be rejected. Placing moral principles above laws implies much more. A State, or legislative body, has no authority to create laws which compel immoral acts because moral principles are not created by men nor are they in any sense arbitrary or relative. The moral principle is above the law which must conform to it. It is interesting that segregationists do from time to time insist they are interested in the welfare of the Negro. This is a tacit admission of a moral obligation toward the Negro.

## Laws and Religious Principles

The appeal to religious principles, like the appeal to moral principles, recognizes something above the law which cannot be contradicted by the law. The form of the argument against segregation on religious grounds is similar to the argument on moral grounds. But the reason for the superiority of the religious principle is God. The segregationist quite often accepts the same religious principles, but tries to show that God intended the Negro to be segregated. In any case, the supremacy of moral principles and God's will over mere man-made laws is recognized by both segregationist and integrationist.

## Morals Above Laws

The overwhelming evidence tends to indicate that laws are quite often criticized in terms of their compatibility with moral principles. If moral principles are standards for judging laws, then where there is a clash, moral principles take precedence over laws. The moral man is the good citizen whenever the laws of the state conform to or are neutral with respect to moral laws. He is not a good citizen if they do not, in the sense that he refuses to obey laws that enforce immoral acts. The good citizen is not necessarily moral for a number of reasons. First, as a good citizen he may commit immoral acts because the law commands him to do so. Secondly, he may do the same thing the moral man does, not because of the moral principle involved but rather because the law commands him so to act. Good citizens cannot be made moral merely by seeing to it that the laws enjoin moral acts, i.e., acts which a moral person would do.

One thing is quite clear. A good State will, among other things, pass laws which avoid the creation of problems for moral persons. This is to say that the good state, among other things, will make moral decisions easier rather than more difficult. The moral thing to do must not be made an illegal act, nor must a legally directed act be one that a moral person would refuse to do. The moral person does not need laws in making moral decisions, but the laws may be necessary to protect him while he acts in accordance with moral principles.

## Individual and State

The relation of the individual to the State is not confined to problems of conflict between laws and moral principles. There is also the problem of the responsibility of the individual for the acts of the State.

Let us analyze this problem in terms of Hans who lived in the Nazi State. Was Hans morally responsible for the acts of the Nazi State? The expression "acts of the Nazi State" needs clarification. What, for example, would an "act of the Nazi State" be? Such things as the invasion of Poland, the destruction of Lidice, the cremation of Jews, are ordinarily called acts of the Nazi State. If, however, we describe what took place in each of these cases we find, as was indicated before, that the "Nazi State" as such becomes a sort of phantom and is replaced by decisions, orders, and performances of individuals. The invasion of Poland was the march of German soldiers into the territory of Poland as a consequence of orders given them by their leaders who chose this course of action for very specific reasons. A similar analysis can be made for each of the other examples. Apparently, therefore, the term "act of the State" can be replaced by a description of the acts of individuals. If Hitler had not ordered the invasion for whatever reasons, and if his generals and all their subordinates down to the lowest private had not obeyed, there would have been no "act of the State."

If this is correct, then the question becomes two questions, 1) "Was the individual German morally responsible for obeying the orders of the leaders of the Nazi State?" and 2) "Was he morally responsible for the deeds of the leaders of the Nazi State?" We have seen earlier in this chapter that laws and directives of political leaders were subordinate to moral principles. If this is the case, then the orders of the leaders of the

Nazi State were also to be judged in the light of moral principles. Since what they commanded was morally wrong, Hans, by obeying their orders, was committing a wrong act. To the extent that Hans chose to obey the orders, he was morally responsible for his act. The crux of the matter resolves itself into the question: "Was the individual German, Hans, living under the Hitler regime a moral agent, i.e., free to choose his act?" Obviously, if he failed to do as ordered, either by law or by the Nazi Party, he would have been a "bad citizen."

It is easy to make sweeping judgments that oversimplify issues. People can be so conditioned to fear the law that they cannot choose but to conform, no matter how cruel or absurd the law is. But if all people were so constituted there would be no criminals. The very existence of crime indicates that people can and do choose to violate the law. Treason, revolt, and civil wars are possible only because people do choose to disobey the law. It seems plausible, therefore, that many, if not all, individual Germans who, for example, participated in cremations could have refused to be a party to such acts. The penalty would have been severe, but great moral decisions at times make such demands. Hans conceivably could have become a martyr or an anti-Nazi. He could have been one of those who chooses to pay the penalty rather than act immorally. The praise that is heaped upon those individuals who sacrifice themselves for freedom, or defy the immoral commands of a tyrant, is evidence that ordinary people do assume that some at least can choose.

Hans was able to choose his act and, to that extent, is morally responsible for acting as he did.

### Citizen and Acts of His Ruler

The second question is much more difficult. In a dictatorship where the ruler assumes power by force and retains it, it is difficult to see what, if anything, a citizen can do except refuse to obey the dictator. In a democracy, or any form of government where rulers are elected, there is a sense in which the citizen shares the moral responsibility for the acts of his ruler. In any State where a ruler can assume power only with the consent of the people, the people would seem to be at least indirectly responsible for the acts of the ruler. Finally, if the ruler acts with the consent, explicit or implicit, of the people, they share the responsibility also. Where the ruler would have done otherwise had he had public opposition, those who failed to provide the opposition, being able to do so, are to that extent at least responsible for what happens. Hitler came to power because people like Hans supported him. Hans, therefore, shares the moral responsibility for the acts of Hitler.

These considerations should not be taken to be complete and de-finitive. They are merely indicative of the complexity of the human situation and the obligation to be moral. The political situation in which men find themselves imposes a set of baffling conditions which make moral decisions even more difficult than they would be. Man may be a political animal. He always lives within a social and political system, and in this he must act. Not merely are his personal decisions influenced by these conditions, but he at times finds it necessary to make moral decisions precisely because of the conditions. He not only needs to decide whether or not to keep a promise, but at times the promise becomes a contract and his decision is then conditioned by the fact that he may be compelled under penalty to fulfill his contract (keep his pro-mise) even though he recognizes the evil consequences that may flow from doing so. Men may recognize that killing is evil and try to live up to this principle; but, then, the State goes to war and they are compelled to kill by order of the political authorities. The whole question of so-called "private" versus "public" morality arises to plague us. This question, however, vanishes if moral principles are seen to be above the state, and public morality a pseudonym for "political realism." This is not to eradicate the distinction between moral principles and political ones.

## BIBLIOGRAPHY

Ewing, A. C., *The Individual, the State and World Government*, New York: Mac-millan Co., 1947, Chapter IV, pp. 174-225.

McKeon, R., "International Relations and Morality" in *Moral Principles in Action*, ed. R. M. Anshen, New York; Harper and Bros., 1952, Chapter 16, pp. 343-328.

Tsanoff, R. A., *Ethics*, rev. ed., New York: Harper & Bros. 1955, Chapters 16 and 17, pp. 325-375.

Weldon, T. D., *State and Morals*, London: John Murray, 1946, Chapter 5, pp. 221-287.

Wright, Quincy, "Moral Standards in Government and Politics," *Ethics*, LXIV, April 1954, No. 3, pp. 157-169.

# CHAPTER XXII

# TEMPTATION AND STRUGGLE – CONCLUSION

In this final chapter, I want to take a look around and see the relationship between human living and moral decisions. It should be evident that making moral decisions is a terribly difficult thing, and in our era, not always fashionable. We have become so indoctrinated with the so-called "behavioral sciences" and "psycho-analytical" concepts that we tend to consider moral problems disguises, moral concepts meaningless, and moral decisions rationalizations of what we would do anyway. There appears to be a trend to equate "immorality" with "disease" and "morality" with "self-enhancement." The most amazing thing about all this is that men tend to make of themselves simply aggregates of material particles whose behavior is the result of "drives," "impulses," "chemical imbalances," or "childhood frustrations." Under such influences, words like "responsibility," "human dignity," and "freedom" lose all significance. In fact, the whole problem of making moral decisions loses not only its importance but its very import. This simply cannot be correct because human living is a direct contradiction of such a view. Men do make moral decisions and they do, at times at least, act as moral agents.

Ever since the beginning of recorded human history, the voices of prophets have been heard calling men to morality and condemning evildoing. Indeed, it is quite true that "If we say that we have no sin, we deceive ourselves, and the truth is not in us." Sin and immorality are not synonymous, but they are closely related, and we are called to penitence and pray, "Wash me thoroughly from my wickedness, and cleanse me from my sin." Down through the ages, these voices that speak out against immorality and sin are heard in our theological treatises, in our pamphlets, in our newspapers, and in our great works of literature, drama, and poetry alike. The struggle to do those things that ought to be done, and to avoid the things that ought not to be done, is a bitterly severe one. It is not too much to say that it is also part of the very nature of human life. Man would not be man were he not constantly tempted to do evil and constantly struggling to do good. Temptation and stuggle make up so much of human living that without a recognition of their tragic and resplendent moment, one is utterly incompetent to envisage what human life is about.

It is part of the glory of being human and part of the tragedy of living a human life that man is capable of being tempted to do evil and can struggle against that temptation. See what a picture it gives us of man! In a world in which the forces of evil seem at times overwhelming and often are, men face their enemies with courage as well as fear, with dignity as well as craveness, to confront these and to set their force against them. Man is a puny creature in physical size and strength, yet he is a mighty one too as he defies the forces that go counter to his far-reaching vision and almost divine aspirations. Knowing the inevitability of death, he dares to hope that death can be overcome too.

What I take to be most curious, as well as singular, is not the temptation but the struggle. Temptation is a common enough phenomenon not only among men but also animals. The animal is tempted away from its young ones by the scent of food. The man is tempted by sexual invitation to stray from his family. People are tempted to commit evil and even to betray God by the hope of pleasure or other reward. Yes, a Faust could be tempted to sell his very soul for the hope of happiness. But the struggle – that is quite another thing.

Struggle against temptation means the awareness of a dichotomy in the world – good versus evil. The anguish of soul that such struggle involves is the token of the knowledge that morality is better than immorality. The willingness to destroy one's very physical existence in this struggle manifests a transcendance of the physical world and an admission of the superiority of the moral. Hamlet knows the evil he does and the penalty he will pay. To be beyond good and evil is to lose one's being as a human and become either God or the Devil. But even this is to say too much. God does struggle against the Devil, even though God is beyond temptation, and the Devil does struggle against God, even though he has no hope of ultimate victory.

One of the great mysteries of the Adam and Eve story in the Old Testament is the introduction into the Garden of the serpent and the consequent seduction of Eve who in turn tempts Adam with the fruit of the forbidden tree. Yet, I believe, my theme is supported by this interpretation of that incident. The presence of the serpent signifies the existence of evil in the world right from the start. Any world being less than God must have evil in it. But even more, the serpent is temptation. Adam and Eve are, somehow, not yet human before the fall. Living in a world without sin, having no real moral decisions to make, they seem unreal even if potentially they are human, for the ability to do evil is already present. When the serpent tempts Eve, he argues with her. He gives her reasons for choosing to do what is forbidden. Eve then chooses to eat. She makes her own moral decision, and by doing so she becomes the first woman-human. Until Eve knew good and evil, she could not be human and not being human could not die. As for Adam, we are told he ate being given the fruit by Eve, whereupon he knew good from evil and was subject to death.

It is interesting to note that the serpent lied in two respects when he tempted Eve. First, he told her that if she ate, "Ye shall not surely die" and then that, "Ye shall be as Gods, knowing good and evil." In a sense, these are generalized versions of all temptations. Adam and Eve became subject to death as soon as they knew the difference between good and evil because not being Gods, they would at times succumb to evil and "the wages of sin is death." Moreover, knowing good and evil, they became *as* Gods, but again not Gods. They became as Gods because the Gods, or God, know good and evil, but they were not Gods so again the knowledge of good an evil leads to the choice of evil. Human history begins with the fall because of evil. From then on men struggle to do good. They are, indeed, human, all too human, for they find the doing of good terribly arduous.

If we do away with the ideas of temptation and struggle, the result is a world vastly different from what it appears to be. Even the word "human" comes to signify something else. Men are, then, bits of chemical substances whose actions are the resultant of physio-chemical forces to some of which are given such names as "drives," "needs," "desires," and so on. The word "choice" signifies at best an act for which there is at the moment no complete description. Moral decisions are neither moral nor decisions. Emotions are but the effects of chemico- physical disequilibria. Men are human, only as this signifies a species of animal. In all other respects "human" signifies nothing at all. It is not that such a conception makes a mockery of human existence, it is rather that it makes it exceedingly puzzling. It replaces a mysterious, but enlightening, bifurcation by a pseudo-evident, but completely baffling, monism. It eliminates "God" and "the Devil" but solves nothing by doing so, for it cannot explain why "God" and "the Devil" in the first place.

The struggle to become and be moral has been and is in terms of what is not. Man has been able to oppose himself to what is and call upon what is not to direct his activities and to be a standard for his actions and his self. This, in itself, is a most extraordinary phenomenon, – this contrast with what is. Man is a part of the world in which he lives, yet over against it at the same time. He rejects what is and tries to bring into being what is not. But that which he tries to make actual is in no sense and never has been part of the actual. Men have always cheated, raped, lied, killed, and destroyed. This has been necessary, or so it was claimed, to live. Yet despite the ubiquity of these immoralities, men have rejected them in terms of something not merely termed "better" but actually better, more noble, and more divine. They developed words like "hope," "charity," "honesty," "loving kindness," "generosity" to talk about what could be or was desirable. The very expression "moral de-cision" is one that runs counter to what is to be expected. To decide that something ought to be done, or ought to be avoided, because of its in-trinsic nature, what sort of decision is that? Is it not a most extraordinary kind of thing?

We have seen that making moral decisions requires the doing of so many different things that some of our brethren would like to eliminate such things. Not the least we need to do is to recognize the moral prin-ciple which asserts what ought to be done even if no one does it. The baffling thing about moral principles is that we do not really know how to account for our awareness of them. Yet, quite obviously, no moral decision is possible to those who are not aware of the standard for their evaluation. Hence, we are tempted to push moral considerations aside and we make the istinctive assumption that people can be made better, i.e., more moral, by supplying them with conditions that do not call for moral decisions. Unfortunately, there can never be such conditions. Let me explain this.

As I write these pages the United States is facing a serious problem of juvenile delinquency in a rather violent form of assault and battery, even to murder. This is particularly alarming at the moment in New York City. The "juveniles" involved, incidentally, are "teen-agers," that is, youth between the ages of 15-23. Various civic groups aroused by this situation are trying to suggest possible remedies. The suggestions often recognize situations that do cry out for remedial action, but they are inadequate. Youth does need play facilities – but suppose these are obtained, will they cure the situation? I doubt it very much. There is need of family counselling to aid families in their problems. But neither is this enough. Many of the things which are associated with crime rates are the effects of the same causes and not themselves causally related to the crimes. The one point these suggested remedies overlook is this. People are no longer accustomed to making moral decisions. Youth has been taught to judge actions in terms of prestige and economic factors, not moral ones. Divorces, and consequent broken homes, result from the breakdown of moral considerations. Psychological hedonism, and not even moral hedonism, rules our decisions. Marriage becomes an excuse for pleasure and not a responsibility. It is almost a disgrace to say that rape is immoral, in the contemporary state of pseudo-knowledge. One is much more *au courant* if he says either that the rapist is a sick person, as if one cannot both be sick and immoral, or else that society is at fault. Our youth no longer thinks it wrong to use violence to attain their ends. Until we grow accustomed to engaging in moral considerations, we cannot expect immorality to decline. The startling thing is not the restlessness of youth. This is a phenomenon we expect. It is rather that it takes the form of brutality so easily. The disturbing thing is that these young people apparently enjoy beating old men and other youths even to death with no realization of the sheer immorality of the act. How deep is the infection is indicated by the facility with which they do these immoral acts, and the extent to which the immoral person becomes the exemplar for those seeking prestige.

I am reminded of something one of my students said. In beginning a course in Ethics, I have found it helpful to ask students to describe a moral problem they have recently confronted and tell how they tried to solve it. In recent years, I have found to my growing surprise that this quite simple demand caused a good deal of bewilderment among students. They apparently did not know what I was asking or could not recognize a moral problem. One sweet young thing in one class looked particularly disturbed, so I urged her to speak up. She did, with this rather startling result. I cannot quote her exactly but in effect she said she had no moral problems and could never recall having any *because* her parents were quite wealthy and she always had what she wanted. In brief, she obviously was a moral infant! Nor is she an exceptional case.

The moral degeneration of our age seems oddly enough to be the result of our increasing knowledge and our increasing wealth. It is strange indeed that as we have come to know more and more about human existence, at least on its material and physical side, we have become more and more ignorant of the spiritual side and have hastened to fake generalizations. It is even more odd that the improvement of our living conditions and standards has not lessened, but even increased, im moral behavior. The years that have passed since the thirties have revealed the true poverty of all economic interpretations of human action. Economic insecurity was, in those years, thought to be the source of aggression, prostitution, lying, murder, and the whole battery of criminal and immoral behavior. Reduce immorality by replacing insecurity with security! This was the battle cry of those years. But, at least in the United States, this has not been borne out. We live today in a condition of unparalleled well-being. We have all the food and comforts we want. We have unemployment compensation, and old-age retirement benefits. These are, indeed, all good, but not the good. They *can* help make up the good life, but they do not automatically bring it into being. Man seems to be able to ignore their benefits and do evil nevertheless. Divorce rates are high; assault and battery is widespread; and dishonesty is rampant.

Our knowledge of human behavior, or rather the use made of it, has tended to reduce the sense of responsibility. How can you hold a man responsible for cheating, if the act is the result of an anxiety created by past experience of which he is not aware? How hold someone responsible for murder, if the act is the consequence of hostility feelings generated by frustrations in his youth or early childhood? This kind of "explanation" of behavior, which confuses conditions with causes, tears the very heart out of human nature. It removes the one major difference between animals and robots on the one hand and man on the other. Only man can say, "I am free!" Only man can defy his past and create his future. But he can do these things, if he is aware of his potentialities. And if he can do these things and knows he can, he can be taught to be morally responsible. If he is told his actions are not his except in a very superficial sense, he loses that freedom by not practicing it.

To be able to say, "I am free," is to be able to accept responsibility for his acts. It means that despite frustrations, despite childhood experiences, despite anxiety feelings, despite libidinous drives, a man can choose what he will do. His choice is made in the light of his knowledge of the past and his hope for the future. He can, so to speak, confront the inevitable sequence of events and deny, defy, and negate its inevitability. He can oppose the irresistible force of tyranny, physical or psychological, with the power of a moral force which enables him to say in a most paradoxical fashion, "I can do nothing else." Man can do nothing else when he is morally bound precisely because he can do something else and choose freely not to do so. I can't help but hate my enemies, so I love them. I can't help but lie, so I tell the truth. These are paradoxical, yet humanly significant. Man loses his freedom when he says, "I can't help but love my enemies," and loves them; or when he says, "I can't help but kill you," and kills you. Sinner as well as saint are both symbols of man's freedom. To be a sinner, one must choose sin; to be a saint, one must choose holiness. Without the choice one is neither sinner nor saint but an inanimate object tossed by the forces that exist both within and without.

Yet to be able to say "I am free," is inadequate for it can lead to the arbitrary decisions of a mad-man or of a dictator who places himself above all things and persons. Freedom alone is never enough, for its demands are irresponsible and its deeds chaotic. Sartre, in "The Flies," paints the terrible picture of Orestes who remains free, and it is an awful one. For Orestes can say "Je suis libre" only because he is alone, completely and dreadfully alone, in all the cosmos. He has no ties, no relatives, no home. He has no fear, either of God or man, and no responsibility to anyone or anything. This being the case, Orestes is free – free to do anything and to dare anything. Orestes is bound by no obligation, moral laws, or even God's commands. Justly, even Jupiter is afraid of this appalling creature who, from this view, is even superior to God himself, for God having created the world and all there is in it even to the moral law is not free in that way. This type of free man is the lonely man. He is the man who is not a man, for man is what he is because of his ability to be free in the ties that bind him to his God and his fellow man, and above all to his vision of a better world. There is, in Sartre, a basic distortion of human nature even though he has seen, if darkly, that to be a man one must be able to say, "Je suis libre."

The development of this sort of free man is seen vividly in Camus' play "Caligula." Caligula is an absolute dictator, and one would believe that, as such, he is free to do and to obtain what he desires. But, Caligula is mad – he wants the moon, he wants his courtier's wife. He can get the latter, but not the former. Only in madness and death that is annihilation can freedom mean this sort of thing. Caligula is free, yet alone, and mad!

To equate human nature with the ability to say, "I am free" is to warp it because of an imbalance. Just as important is to be able to say, "I am a sinner." If man is only free in this sense, there is no temptation and the only struggle is that involved in getting what you want. Paradoxically enough, man becomes no different from animals, or perhaps not even an animal. The sense of sin, of guilt, is an essential ingredient. What other creature can say, "I have sinned?" What other existent can say, "Father, forgive me?" It is this which lies at the root of responsibility and moral decision and makes human life possible. If there is no responsibility, there can be no moral decisions, only appropriate ones. Where there are no struggles between alternatives, there can be no sense to moral discussions. To be able to say, "I am a sinner" keeps one from the awful consequences of freedom. It compels consideration, deliberation, and evaluation before acting, but in terms of moral principles and moral values.

Nietzsche describes his Superman as a "transvaluor of values," as one who, by declaring "God is dead," refuses to say, "I am a sinner." So, the Superman is free because he is not bound by God or man to consider anything but his freedom. His temptations are only those proferred by the weak to seduce his strength; his struggle is only to assert himself and to dominate. The result is the acts of a power-mad person, not a human at all. Nietzsche's Superman is, without question, "the Blonde Beast" exactly because he cannot say, "I am a sinner." As a consequence, he is to all intents and purposes "beyond good and evil." Because he is, he is no longer man, and here Nietzsche is wrong. The "Blonde Beast" is no longer man, not because he is "superman" but because he has become less than man. Morals are not the instrument of the weak to subdue the strong but an expression of human nature to which both the strong and the weak owe their human-ness. To be beyond good and evil is not to become a superman but to become divine or satanic.

The expression "I am a sinner" is a sort of paradigm for us. What it tends to express is this. To be able to say such a thing, one must know that one's actions and thoughts are removed from what they ought to be. It is to acknowledge that there is a standard in terms of which shortcomings are seen to be shortcomings. The expression occurs most easily in religious contexts for there the standard is, in a sense, most obvious – God. Theologically, "to be a sinner" is to be "estranged from God." This is to say that one does the things God prohibits and for which one is responsible to God. The recognition of sinfulness tempers the pride and irresponsibility of freedom. I am free, but I am also a sinner; I am a sinner, but I am also free. The first half of the preceding sentence keeps us from running wild; the second half from surrender to the evil about us. As a free man, I can rape, murder, lie, cheat and do what I will. As a sinner, these are freely rejected and I freely abstain from them to alleviate my sins and make atonement and "re-birth" possible. As a sinner, I feel the weight of evil, the compulsion to do the immoral. I feel despondent, for "there is no health within us." But as a free man, I know I can do what goes counter to the sin; I can seek to do good rather than evil and I am able to struggle against the evil within me.

More is involved in the notions of temptation and struggle. The expression "I am free" is a challenge to the explanations of human behavior by the behavioral sciences. I am not saying they are not valuable and they do, indeed, provide us with data about the conditions under which human choice is made. If the reduction of behavior to the terms of the behavioral sciences is complete, actually or potentially, the expression "I am free" as well as "I am sinner" are both utter nonsense. The moral agent who exclaims, "I am free" is throwing a challenge to those reductionists. He is proclaiming something like this: "Find your psychological, physiological, and other reasons. After you have said all you have to say and described all you want to describe, I still remain free. My actions are still mine to choose. I can break into the chain of events. I remain a surd in a rational world, and my behavior is ultimately absurd in your coordinate system."

The absurdity is not a true one, but only one in the coordinate system of the behavioral sciences. The freedom proclaimed is the freedom to choose according to principles no factual sciences can include. Moral principles are not and cannot be directive in factual sciences, for as we have seen moral agents must choose their acts and this is not permitted in factual sciences. In terms of these, men cannot choose; they cannot do other than they do. Actions are simply the resultant of forces pushing in certain directions. But the struggle which gives significance to freedom declares that the calculated resultant is not necessarily what takes place. "Struggle" does not mean merely contortions. It implies possibilities. Men may struggle in vain, but the "struggle" is not a term signifying nothing.

Nor is man enslaved by his adherence to moral principles. Even here there is choice, and this is the terrifying thing about man. The moral principle may tell what ought to be done, in the sense that it points out what is the sort of action that a moral person would do. But whether or not one chooses to do this act, is up to the agent. We do know what is right and wrong in a moral sense, yet we may, despite our knowledge, do the opposite. A person can will to do evil while knowing full well what he does and that he is wrong in doing it. Too often we feel that to know what is right is to do it, and we assume that a person who does evil does it because he is not really cognizant of its evil. This was the Greek view, it is not the Christian view. We need to do more than know right and wrong; we need to be able to go beyond a mere recognition of what is moral or immoral. We need to develop character that is inclined to do good when it is recognized. Respect for the moral law is not enough, it must be accompanied by the will to act out of respect for the moral law. Where moral principles come to be scorned, as perhaps "unrealistic," or "unscientific," or simply "meaningless," there can be no such character. This is, as I have indicated, the tragedy of our age. We have left moral principles to the people we no longer esteem. Our ideals are the conquering soldier, the successful speculator, the ingenious engineer, the skillful gangster, the clever politician, or the organizing industrialist. None of these are saints. In fact, our books, our plays, our television shows, all glorify the sinner. From time to time the picture of a saint is presented, but there is always a touch of scornful amusement at his predicament for he simply is ignorant, so it is said, of "life."

Here is the crux of the moral degeneration of our age. Every age has its moments of such decay. But, in past generations, these were seen as "falling away," as a failure to develop moral character. Today, any reference to developing moral character is pushed aside or misunderstood. There is a widespread feeling that to develop moral character is impossible, impractical, or automatic with occupational training and psychiatric advice. In fact, moral problems are quite often equated with emotional ones. The result is the contemporary scene.

Moral character can be developed and respect for moral principles inculcated. It involves a recognition and explication of moral principles; it involves a consideration of consequences. Responsibility can become as much a part of a person's make-up as his knowledge of the multiplication table. Practice in analyzing moral situations can be as meaningful as that of the law student in his analysis of legal situations. Above all, we must realize that men are moral agents, morally responsible for their actions, and not the puppets of nature or society. The ability to make moral decisions is the truest sign of the mature person. The ability to act in accordance with those decisions is the most significant index of the free person. The ability to struggle against temptation is the sign of the truly human being.

# INDEX